BONAVENTURE AND THE COINCIDENCE OF OPPOSITES

BONAVENTURE AND THE COINCIDENCE OF OPPOSITES

by

EWERT H. COUSINS

Introduction by
Jacques Guy Bougerol O.F.M.

Franciscan Herald Press ● 1434 W. 51st Street ● Chicago, Illinois 60609

Library of Congress Cataloging in Publication Data

Cousins, Ewert H.
  Bonaventure and the coincidence of opposites

  Includes bibliographical references and index.
  1. Bonaventura, Saint, Cardinal, 1221-1274.
I. Title.
BX4700.B68C68   230′.2′0924   77-2604
ISBN 0-8199-0580-1

NIHIL OBSTAT:
Mark Hegener O.F.M.
Censor Deputatus

BX
4700
.B68
C68

IMPRIMATUR:
Msgr. Richard A. Rosemeyer, J.C.D.
Vicar General, Archdiocese of Chicago

December 1, 1977

MADE IN THE UNITED STATES OF AMERICA

CONTENTS

To
my wife Kathryn
and our children,
Hilary, Sara and Emily,
who with me
made a Franciscan pilgrimage
to
Assisi, La Verna, Rieti, Bagnoregio
and
Jerusalem

PREFACE

It is difficult to express adequately my gratitude to the many people who have contributed to my work on Bonaventure. This work has been in progress for over fifteen years and has taken shape within several different communities of scholars in the United States, Europe and the Middle East. It has grown in the context of publishing projects, research in the United States and abroad, and national and international conferences. I hope that the following will at least acknowledge the majority of friends and colleagues without whose encouragement, inspiration, intellectual enrichment and critique this book would not have come to completion.

An initial debt of gratitude is due Robert Pollock, the great teacher of medieval philosophy at Fordham University, who opened for me the dynamic nature of Bonaventure's thought. In the early sixties Bill and Mary Louise Birmingham, then editors of Mentor-Omega Books, brought me in touch with the texts of Bonaventure by involving me in translation. Through them I came to work with the distinguished theologian Father Georges Tavard, A.A., and to profit from his extensive research in Bonaventure. At this time I met José de Vinck, the translator of some five volumes of Bonaventure's works. He not only shared with me his deep knowledge of Bonaventure, but also brought me in touch with Father Jacques Guy Bougerol O.F.M., who was then organizing several projects related to Bonaventure.

vii

In 1968 I was invited by Father Bougerol to the Colloque Saint Bonaventure at Orsay, France, and began to work with him in his capacity as chairman of the International Bonaventure Commission for the celebration of the seventh centenary of the death of Bonaventure in 1974. This launched the long friendship and collaboration which he describes so graciously in his introduction to the present book. My debt to him is enormous, both personal and professional. Work on the commission brought me in touch with Father Ignatius Brady O.F.M., the eminent authority on Franciscan sources, of the Quaracchi research center (Florence-Grottaferrata). Through the years I have consulted him on many points; he has always responded with a graciousness matched only by the high level of his professional accomplishment. Early in my work I came in contact with Father John Quinn, C.S.B., the specialist in Bonaventure at the Pontifical Institute of Mediaeval Studies, Toronto. Through the years I have been enriched both by his personal friendship and by his extraordinary technical knowledge of Bonaventure's thought. I am especially indebted to Father Jean Chatillon, of the Institut Catholique of Paris, the distinguished scholar of the twelfth century Victorines, for his encouragement at an early stage of my work and for his guidance in appreciating the Victorine influence on Bonaventure. In the case of these specialists and the others I mention in this preface, although indebted to them, I do not wish to imply that they would support wholeheartedly my interpretation of Bonaventure. For this I take full personal responsibility.

A major context for the development of this book has been the series of Conferences on Medieval Studies sponsored by the Medieval Institute of Western Michigan University. It was at one of these conferences, in 1968, that I presented my first paper on Bonaventure and the coincidence of opposites. In the succeeding years the central ideas of several of the chapters of this book were explored in papers I delivered at these conferences. I wish to express my gratitude to John Sommerfeldt and his staff for providing this excellent forum for scholars to share their research with others in the field for their critical evaluation. Recently these conferences have been rendered even more beneficial for my work by the special sessions organized by Paul Kuntz, of Emory University, and Marion Leathers Kuntz, of Georgia State University. Among the many fruitful associations that have emerged out of these medieval conferences, I would like to single out that with Grover Zinn, of Oberlin College, with whom now for many years I have shared a continued exploration of Bonaventure and the Victorines.

In the mid-sixties Father Michael Meilach O.F.M., editor of *The Cord,* showed interest in my work and published in his journal my first article on Bonaventure, and subsequently a number of other articles whose contents have been integrated into this book. I am grateful to him and to the editors of the following publications for their permission to use here material which I had previously published with them: *Franciscan Studies, Etudes franciscaines, University of Toronto Quarterly, International Philosophical Quarterly, Proceedings of the American Catholic Philosophical Association, S. Bonaventura 1274-1974, Atti del Congresso Internationale per il VII Centenario di San Bonaventura* and *Studies Honoring Ignatius Brady, Friar Minor.*

In the later phase of my work I came in contact with Father Alfonso Pompei, O.F.M. Conv., of the Seraphicum in Rome and organizer of the International Congress on Bonaventure in Rome, 1974. I have been enriched by his deep understanding of Bonaventure as well as by his personal friendship and hospitality. I wish to single out in a special way Father Zachary Hayes O.F.M., of the Catholic Theological Union in Chicago and specialist in Bonaventure's theology. Although we worked independently for years, when we met in 1974, we found a great compatibility in our interpretation of Bonaventure. As I state in my first chapter, I am especially indebted to him for my understanding of Bonaventure's theological method. Also I am grateful for his reading the manuscript of the present book and offering detailed suggestions.

As a teacher I am indebted to my students, especially to those who have written doctoral dissertations at Fordham University under my guidance on subjects related to Bonaventure: Sister Lillian Turney, C.D.P., Father John Dourley, O.M.I., Leonard Bowman, Father Regis Armstrong, O.F.M. Cap., and Kevin Keane. I owe a special debt of gratitude to Susan Potters, of Columbia University, whose dissertation research on the coincidence of opposites in Dante's *Paradiso* clarified for me many points in Bonaventure. I am also grateful for her reading the manuscript of this book and making suggestions.

It would be too complicated to express here my gratitude to those who have influenced me in the areas of contemporary thought treated in this book. Concerning Teilhard and process thought, I have done that elsewhere in the book I edited entitled *Process Theology*. However, I would like to single out the area of world religions because of its importance in shaping my interpretation of the coincidence of opposites. In this area I am especially indebted to three friends of many years: Raimundo Panikkar, of the University of California at Santa Barbara; Robley Whitson, of the United Institute; and Thomas Berry, of Fordham University. They have opened for me the vast horizon of hermeneutics that emerges when one considers the religious experience of mankind. I am grateful to another colleague of mine at Fordham University, José Pereira, for many stimulating discussions from which I derived specific categories of interpretation related to world religions. Further clarification came from John Borelli, whose dissertation at Fordham made correlations between Bonaventure and a Hindu theologian.

My Bonaventure work has involved much travel and periods of time devoted exclusively to research. I am grateful to Fordham University for granting me a Faculty Research Fellowship for the fall of 1968 and for the academic year 1972-73. On this latter occasion I also received a Fellowship from the American Council of Learned Societies which made possible my spending the year as a resident scholar, along with my family, at the Ecumenical

Institute for Advanced Theological Studies in Jerusalem. The Institute provided a most congenial community atmosphere and stimulating setting for theological research. In a very special way I am grateful to the international community of scholars there that year for the enrichment that came from sharing the results of their research and from their critical response to my work.

Further aid for travel to international meetings and conferences was provided by the American Council for Learned Societies and Fordham University. Research in Italy and France in 1970 was aided by a Faculty Research Grant from Fordham University and in France in 1971 by the American Philosophical Society.

In my travels in the United States and abroad, I have always been warmly welcomed at Franciscan houses. I would like to make special mention of Quaracchi, Grottaferrata and the Seraphicum, whose hospitality I have enjoyed on many occasions. I am also grateful for the assistance of Franciscan librarians, especially Father Romano Almagno O.F.M., former librarian of Quaracchi and Grottaferrata.

I am grateful to Father Mark Hegener O.F.M., managing director of Franciscan Herald Press, for publishing my book, and for his patience and that of his assistant Mark Mayer during the long period when it was reaching completion. The editorial task was made easier by the excellent work of Carolyn Gonzales in typing the manuscript.

Through the years of work on Bonaventure, I have felt a growing relation to the Franciscan tradition through study of its medieval spirituality and contact with many contemporary Franciscans. This relation was given a formal expression in 1970 in a ceremony of affiliation to the Holy Name Province of the Order of Friars Minor. For this affiliation and for my continued enrichment through the Franciscan tradition, I wish to express my deepest gratitude.

Finally, I wish to express my gratitude to my wife Kathryn and our children Hilary, Sara and Emily, to whom this book is dedicated and who shared my exploration into the Franciscan world

xii COINCIDENCE OF OPPOSITES

on several camping trips across Europe and in travel in the Holy Land. In addition, I am grateful for the professional editorial assistance of my wife in bringing this book to completion and in preparing the index.

(One final note: because the manuscript for this book was prepared before my recent translation of Bonaventure's *Itinerarium, Lignum vitae* and *Legenda maior* was completed, I was unable to use this translation in the present text.)

Ewert H. Cousins
Fordham University
February 1, 1978

INTRODUCTION

Throughout the history of Christianity, theologians and philosophers have had to cope with a tension of opposites. On the one hand, the God of Christian revelation is the Wholly Other, the transcendent Being who created the world out of nothing and who in his revelation has disclosed his power and majesty. On the other hand, God is intimate to the world. He has left his imprint on creation and in the Incarnation has joined himself personally to the world. In Jesus Christ, God and man, the absolute and the relative, being and nothingness are united in one single person.

In their efforts to deal with this tension, theologians — and the community of Christian believers — have often emphasized one or the other pole of these opposites. This was as true in the Middle Ages as it was before and since. For many Christians in the Middle Ages, the God they worshipped was the absolute Master of all things, the transcendent Lord who held dominion over them and who demanded their obedient service. In contrast, they looked upon themselves and the world they inhabited as distant from God — separated from him by a vast abyss. In their spiritual journeys, in their earthly pilgrimages, they felt far removed from the divine majesty.

Then in the thirteenth century a little poor man joined these pilgrims as another had joined the disciples on the road to Emmaus. And that little poor man began to sing a canticle of creatures — to call the sun his brother, water his sister and the earth his mother And he summoned all these creatures to join him in praising his "most high omnipotent good Lord," whom he saw reflected throughout creation, even in a tiny earthworm. Suddenly the eyes of the pilgrims were opened to a new perspective, as if God were made present to them and spoke to them through the flowers along the way. Never before in the history of Christianity, and never since, was God's immanence in creation sung with such depth and such charm as by Francis of Assisi. Among the pilgrims who heard Francis' song was Bonaventure, the eminent theologian and early Minister General of the Friars Minor. As a follower of Francis, he set himself the task of formulating the metaphysics and logic that stood behind this Franciscan song.

But the song of Francis has not always been heard through the centuries, and the metaphysics that explained it has been often obscured. For example, in the nineteenth and twentieth century revival of scholasticism, emphasis was placed on God's power in creating out of nothing and on the dependence of creatures on God. Although the world was seen as participating in existence through God, emphasis was not placed on the world as reflecting God. The metaphysics of separation dominated over the metaphysics of manifestation, and the principle of contradiction was used to reinforce this separation. The logic of contradiction formed a wedge between God and the world, dividing them into different spheres of being. In order to recapture the Franciscan vision in its richness, there was need to rediscover the metaphysics of manifestation, whereby God manifests himself in the world. In order to bring this metaphysics fully to light, there was need to articulate its logic.

This is what Ewert Cousins has admirably done in the present book through a detailed textual and thematic analysis of Bonaventure's thought. He identifies this logic as that of the coincidence of opposites. For him this logic does not reject the principle of contradiction, but rather subsumes it into a larger sphere. Professor Cousins does not claim that Bonaventure developed the coincidence of opposites into a formal logic as Nicholas of Cusa did later. Rather this logic lies just beneath the surface of Bonaventure's thought, awaiting a formal analysis to bring it to light. By providing such an analysis Professor Cousins has made a major contribution to Bonaventure studies and the intellectual history of the Middle Ages.

His analysis of the coincidence of opposites throws light on central aspects of Bonaventure's vision. It allows Bonaventure's thought to be seen on its own terms and with its own distinctive structure. Professor Cousins has not only stressed the importance of viewing Bonaventure's thought in its integrity, but has provided a means for achieving this. From the perspective of the coincidence of opposites, the Trinity and Christology emerge as providing the comprehensive design of his system. Once this is clarified, one can avoid the problem — often encountered in the past — of viewing elements of Bonaventure's synthesis as unrelated to this comprehensive design.

Bonaventure never intended to present to his students a philosopher's God, seen in isolation from the Christian Trinity. Rather Bonaventure's God is the God revealed by Jesus Christ, whose life is manifested in the diffusion of being, life and love — all springing from the plenitude of the Father. Out of his fountainfulness, the Father expresses himself in one, unique Word, his own personal Word and Son. In generating his Son, the Father expresses all that he is and also all that he can make and do. From the mutual and ineffable love of the Father and the Son there proceeds the Holy Spirit. Thus for Bonaventure, the Trinity is the mystery of God's dynamic fecundity, his eternal self-diffusion that issues in the divine persons, who are united in the most intimate mutuality. This Trinitarian mystery reveals a dynamic inner logic of the coincidence of opposites which, according to Professor Cousins, is the source and archetype of all other forms of the coincidence of opposites in Bonaventure's system.

This Trinitarian dynamism overflows into creation, where according to Bonaventure God is manifested in his vestige, image and similitude. It is here that Bonaventure gives a metaphysical basis for Francis' "Canticle of Brother Sun." All creatures flow out of God's self-diffusing fecundity and through the metaphysics of exemplarism, manifest God and lead men back to God. Once again it is the logic of the coincidence of opposites that helps clarify the issues, for in the mystery of creation there is a coincidence of the eternal and the temporal, the infinite and the finite.

Finally, the metaphysics of manifestation reaches its climax in the mystery of Christ, the greatest coincidence of opposites. Christ is the fulness of the divine manifestation. He is the center of the universe and the *medium* between God and man. The Word Incarnate is the very expression of God under a human form. By and in the Incarnate Word, and through the Holy Spirit, we come to the Father. Through him and in him, we discover the Franciscan sense of creation; for Christ, the Word Incarnate is the Way, the Truth and the Life, leading us back to the fulness of the Father. Here, in the mystery of Christ, Professor Cousins' analysis of the coincidence of opposites is especially rich and brings to light the climactic role that Christ plays within Bonaventure's total system.

Bonaventure's vision of reality was shaped by three factors: first, an experiential factor, derived from Sacred Scripture, the word of God, which for Bonaventure, as for his medieval contemporaries, was an ever-flowing spring and source of religious experience; secondly, an intellectual factor, that is, the theological-philosophical heritage of the Greek Fathers of the Church from John Damascene and the Pseudo–Dionysius, a heritage which Bonaventure received from his teacher Friar Alexander of Hales; and thirdly, an existential factor, namely, the person of Francis of Assisi, who in his original imitation of Jesus Christ, continually sought to prove his love by concrete action. In the light of Professor Cousins' analysis of the coincidence of opposites, we can see how Bonaventure took elements from these three sources and shaped them into one of the richest visions in the history of Christianity.

Professor Cousins' book has grown out of many years of work on Bonaventure. It is grounded in some five years of painstaking work in translating texts of Bonaventure into English. In fact, it was while translating Chapters Five through Seven of the *Itinerarium,* that he discovered the pattern of the coincidence of opposites in Bonaventure's text. This period of textual work was followed by a period of interpretative analysis which culminated in the present book. The development of his thought coincided with and received impetus from the preparations for the celebration of the seventh centenary of Bonaventure's death in 1974. These preparations involved publications and international conferences of specialists. Almost ten years ago, when I was organizing the first of these conferences, the Colloque Saint Bonaventure at Orsay, France, 1968, I asked Professor Cousins to give the inaugural address. In his paper entitled "The Coincidence of Opposites in the Theology of Bonaventure," Professor Cousins presented the basic thesis of this present book to an international group of Bonaventure specialists. The response to his paper was very positive and led him to continue his research on this theme in articles, lectures and papers at other academic conferences.

My asking Professor Cousins to lecture at Orsay in 1968 was the beginning of our deep friendship, a friendship which has expressed itself in mutual collaboration and which has grown continuously through the years. In 1969 we were together again, this time for a meeting at the Collegio San Bonaventura, International Franciscan Research Center, at Quaracchi (Florence) Italy. At this meeting Father Constantine Koser, Minister General of the Friars Minor, approved the establishment of the Commissio Internationalis Bonaventuriana. The purpose of this international commission was to stimulate research in Bonaventure for a scholarly commemoration of the seventh centenary of his death. The work of the commission concentrated on publishing five volumes of scholarly studies entitled *S. Bonaventura 1274-1974*.

Appointed one of the nine members of this commission, Professor Cousins had as his chief task to gather articles from scholars in the United States for publication in the five-volume centenary series. As chairman of the commission, I collaborated very closely with him throughout the project. In addition to continued correspondence, we worked together on two occasions at Vezelay, France, and on several occasions at Grottaferrata, near Rome, where the Quaracchi center has been transferred from Florence. We also spent a week together at Assisi doing detailed work on the text of *S. Bonaventura 1274-1974*. He was for me then — during that period of intense activity — as he is now, a faithful friend and untiring collaborator.

In 1971 at Orsay, France, he presented a paper at the second Colloque Saint Bonaventure. This was followed by a number of lectures on Bonaventure at various universities in the United States at the time of centenary, e.g., Yale, Columbia and Western Michigan University. In 1974 he was awarded an honorary degree for his work on Bonaventure by Siena College, where he gave the major address at its centenary celebration. Throughout these lectures he developed the theme of this book, with its two major implications: the use of the coincidence of opposites for understanding Bonaventure's thought, first within the context of medieval culture and then in relation to twentieth century thought.

In my opinion this theme and its implications are of cardinal importance. As we have seen, Professor Cousins' analysis allows us to see more precisely and coherently the organic structure of Bonaventure's thought and by that very fact helps us situate that thought within the context of medieval culture. But he goes beyond a limited study of texts and even the analysis of thought within its historical context. He has consistently demonstrated the open-endedness of Bonaventure's thought in its relevance to contemporary issues. His research involves a constant dialogue between history and contemporary culture. Paradoxically, it is precisely by entering deeply into historical studies that he has drawn Bonaventure into the Great Dialogue, as he calls it, over issues that transcend a specific historical milieu. But what he sees is not a superficial connection or a facile syncretism; rather it is an encounter in depth which evokes a forthright and challenging dialogue. Such a dialogue can be seen in his nuanced and critical correlations of Bonaventure with process thought and the evolutionary system of Teilhard, two areas of contemporary thought in which he has specialized and published.

These same qualities are evident in his extension of Bonaventure's thought into Christian ecumenism and the dialogue of world religions. In 1972-73 Professor Cousins spent the academic year as a resident scholar at the Ecumenical Institute for Advanced Theological Studies in Jerusalem. During this period he did research in Islamic religion as a background for medieval Christian theology and philosophy. He also explored the possibilities of Bonaventure's thought for ecumenism within Christianity and for the dialogue of world religions. Jerusalem provided a remarkable atmosphere for ecumenical research. At the Institute he worked with theologians from various Christian traditions and throughout Israel engaged in dialogue with Jews and Muslims. In this context he was able to test out concretely the possibilities and problems of the theme he was developing: Bonaventure's Christology — examined in the light of the coincidence of opposites — as a resource for Christian unity and for the dialogue of world religions. This research led to his paper entitled "Bonaventure's Christology and Contemporary Ecumenism," delivered at the International Congress on Bonaventure commemorating the centenary, in Rome, 1974. Over the last several years, as consultant to the Vatican Secretariat for Non-Christians, he has been exploring further the resources of Bonaventure's thought for the dialogue of world religions.

As collaborator and friend, I have observed the development of his thought, which he has synthesized in a tightly-reasoned, organic unity in the present book. The result of a slow, constant maturation — through many years of research, writing, lecturing, dialogue and prayer — it now brings forth its fruit. Bonaventure's insights, presented anew to our day, with such scholarly skill and creative originality by Professor Cousins, cannot, I know, but mature into a rich harvest.

January 15, 1978   Jacques Guy Bougerol, O.F.M.

Collegio San Bonaventura
International Franciscan-Dominican Research Center
Grottaferrata, Rome, Italy

CHAPTER I

HE Middle Ages produced many striking personalities who were both religious leaders and intellectual giants. In this array of religious personalities — which includes such thinkers as Anselm of Canterbury, Bernard of Clairvaux, and Thomas Aquinas — Bonaventure takes his place among the most eminent men of his era. Born in 1217 in the tiny village of Bagnoregio near Orvieto in central Italy,[1] Bonaventure became a leading figure in the complex culture of the high Middle Ages. As a master at the University of Paris, he rose to the intellectual leadership of the young Franciscan Order. When he was forty years old, he was elected Minister General of the Order at one of the most critical points in its history. For seventeen years he served as General, resolving tensions within the Order and taking an active part in the intellectual controversies of the time. Elevated to the cardinalate in 1273, he spent the last months of his life in intense work at the Second Council of Lyons, at which he died on July 15, 1274. Two centuries later, in 1482, he was canonized under Pope Sixtus IV, and in 1588 was declared a doctor of the Church by Sixtus V.

Bonaventure achieved eminence in several areas. In view of his accomplishments as Minister General, he is esteemed as the second founder of the Order, whose talents for mediation enabled him to draw together disparate factions and to establish the Order on a firm organizational basis. A gifted stylist, he was one of the most eloquent preachers and controversialists of the turbulent mid-thirteenth century, employing his oratorical skill not only to preach the Gospel, but to defend the mendicant

1

orders and theological tradition against varied attacks. As a saint and spiritual writer, he composed some of the richest and most influential treatises of mystical theology in the Christian tradition; throughout the centuries his writings have been a primary source of Franciscan spirituality. In his achievement as a philosopher-theologian, he ranks with Thomas Aquinas as one of the greatest synthetic minds in a century that was outstanding for its theological synthesis. Bonaventure achieved for the medieval Augustinian tradition a synthesis comparable to that produced by Thomas with Aristotelian philosophy.

BONAVENTURE'S INTEGRAL SYNTHESIS

Bonaventure's thought represents one of the greatest intellectual achievements of the Middle Ages. It is enormously rich and complex, like the Gothic cathedrals that flowered in the same period. There is reason to think that Bonaventure's synthesis is the most integral in the Middle Ages. It comes at the high point of scholastic development, when the logical and metaphysical tools were available and the design of the *summa* had been elaborated. With this design and these precision instruments, Bonaventure constructed a synthesis that is a microcosm of the medieval world. It is a many-faceted diamond reflecting the variety of medieval experience.

Where Thomas Aquinas' choice of materials for his synthesis was selective, Bonaventure's was expansive. Thomas chose the abstract logic of the schools and laid aside symbolism and mysticism. Whereas Thomas abandoned Augustinian illumination for Aristotelian abstraction, Bonaventure attempted to bind them together. Thomas approached God through the cosmological argument, rejecting Anselm's ontological argument and turning aside from Augustine's inner way through subjectivity. In contrast Bonaventure integrated all three in a complex approach to God that was both rational and mystical. Following this comprehensive design, Bonaventure worked out a rich integration of Plato and Aristotle, Augustine and the Greek Fathers, the

Pseudo-Dionysius and Francis of Assisi. He brought together the cosmic Logos-Christology of the Greek Fathers with the Western sense of particularity expressed in Francis' devotion to the humanity of Christ. In the theology of history, he blended cosmic Christocentricity with elements drawn from the radical eschatology of Joachim of Fiore. One might argue whether Bonaventure's desire to integrate so much was laudable or whether his performance was effective; yet one can look to his system as perhaps the richest integrative venture of the Middle Ages.

The integral nature of Bonaventure's vision is seen most strikingly in his *Itinerarium mentis in Deum*, written at the mid-point of his career, and in the *Collationes in Hexaemeron*, lectures delivered the year before his death.[2] In each of these he blended logic, metaphysics, symbolism, and mysticism. In his early works, composed during his years at the University of Paris, he employed the more austere scholastic method of commentary on Scripture, commentary on the *Sentences* of Peter Lombard, disputed questions, and a condensed *summa* under the title of *Breviloquium*.[3] In his mid-career he wrote a number of specifically mystical and devotional works, and over many years he preached numerous sermons. If one views not only the synthetic works like the *Itinerarium,* but Bonaventure's corpus as a whole, he will find a variety of literary genres which, taken together, constitute a most comprehensive medieval synthesis.

Bonaventure's thought is not only rich in itself and reflects the variety of the Middle Ages, but in a larger context it reflects one of the major currents of Western philosophy and theology. This is the Platonic, or more technically, the Christian Neo-Platonic tradition. Originating in Plato, it flowed through the Neo-Platonists and into Christian theology, where it was developed by the Greek Fathers in the East and Augustine in the West. In the East it emphasized the dynamism of God in the Trinitarian processions and God's involvement in the world through the Logos in creation. Man was seen as image of God, drawn by the Spirit in a dynamic return to his archetype. In

Augustine the image doctrine took on specifically Western qualities through a detailed psychological analysis of subjectivity. In the ninth century the Greek Fathers' tradition flowed into the West through John Scotus Erigena's translations of the Pseudo-Dionysius. Blending with Augustinian elements in Anselm and the Victorines in the twelfth century, the tradition flowed in the thirteenth century to Alexander of Hales, Bonaventure's teacher at the University of Paris. Bonaventure produced the major medieval synthesis of this tradition, integrating into it distinctly Franciscan elements.

Although this tradition was eclipsed in the late thirteenth century, it continued in mystical writings and reappeared in Nicholas of Cusa and the Platonists of the Renaissance. Eclipsed again by scientific rationalism and empiricism, it reappeared in German romanticism: in Fichte, Schelling, and Hegel. Elements of this tradition have emerged again in the twentieth century: in the theologies of Paul Tillich and Karl Rahner, in the theology of hope and in the process thought of Alfred North Whitehead and Pierre Teilhard de Chardin. Since Bonaventure was the major synthesizer of this tradition in the Middle Ages, whose genius made unique contributions, a knowledge of his thought is indispensable to understand both the history of this current and certain crucial aspects of its inner dynamics.

BONAVENTURE'S THOUGHT OBSCURED

In spite of Bonaventure's great achievement, the significance of his thought has been obscured both in the Middle Ages and in the twentieth century. During the Middle Ages, Bonaventure's thought was obscured by the shift of consciousness that occurred in the thirteenth century as a result of the Aristotelian influx in theology and the success of the Thomistic-Aristotelian synthesis. The Platonism that had formed the matrix of previous medieval theology was replaced by a newly discovered Aristotelianism, derived largely from Muslim sources and transformed by Thomas into a new Christian synthesis. In the sphere of philosophy, the Aristotelianism ushered in a new empirical cast of mind and an interest in the study of nature on its own terms. This led to a shift of consciousness in theology: on the relation of faith and reason, on knowledge of God and on God's relation to the world. In contrast with the new Aristotelianism, Bonaventure's synthesis represents the end of an era — summing up as it does the Platonic-based, more mystical theological speculation of the earlier Middle Ages.

Although Bonaventure attracted disciples, such as Matthew of Aquasparta, within a generation after his death theological questions shifted to an Aristotelian context. By the end of the thirteenth century, even within the Franciscan school issues were formulated in an Aristotelian way. In this context Duns Scotus emerged as the Franciscan champion. On major theological questions, two schools of thought developed: the Thomistic and the Scotist. These two schools tended to polarize themselves around certain issues, such as the purpose of the Incarnation. Even the Franciscan order tended to look upon Duns Scotus as its intellectual leader and guide rather than upon Bonaventure. The latter was admired as the second founder of the Order and the great theologian of Franciscan spirituality. But a certain clouding continued to obscure Bonaventure's total intellectual achievement and his position in the history of Western thought.

Again in the modern era Bonaventure's vision has been obscured, this time by the emergence of neo-scholasticism. At first glance, this may seem strange since neo-scholasticism greatly stimulated Bonaventurian scholarship. Beginning in the nineteenth century and continuing through the first half of the twentieth century, the neo-scholastic revival aroused widespread interest in medieval thought. In this climate, the ten-volume critical edition of Bonaventure's texts was published from 1882 to 1902 by a small group of Franciscan scholars known as the Quaracchi editors.[4] Judged a monumental scholarly achievement, especially for its time, the Quaracchi edition has provided a firm basis for continuing Bonaventurian studies. Yet the neo-scholastic revival was chiefly a revival of the thought of Thomas Aquinas. His thought was studied with great enthusiasm, and the Middle Ages were interpreted in the light of his synthesis. The theological issues of the twelfth and thirteenth centuries were formulated in terms of Thomas' position. Although Bonaventurian research moved apace, it never reached the quantity of Thomist scholarship, nor did the Bonaventurian vision find its way into the larger intellectual public as a philosophical or theological movement as was the case with Thomism. Hence Bonaventure's thought was obscured in being overshadowed by the sheer power and popularity of Thomism. In this situation it was difficult to see Bonaventure's world on its own terms and to assess his place in the history of Western thought.

Against this background it is not surprising to find Bonaventure interpreted as a Thomist. In the early years of neo-scholasticism there was a tendency to see Bonaventure as a Thomist, or at least as an incipient Thomist. If he did not reach the fullness of Thomas' positions, it was due to the fact that during his university period he did not have sufficient knowledge of Aristotle's texts. Later when these became available, he was too engaged in administering the Franciscan Order to assimilate them. The tendency to interpret Bonaventure as a Thomist can be seen in the scholia to the critical texts of Bonaventure, written by the Quaracchi editors and published at the end of the nineteenth century.[5] In 1924 Etienne Gilson challenged this interpretation in his book *La philosophie de Saint Bonaventure*,[6] where he maintained that Thomas and Bonaventure presented different world views, each valid in itself but each irreducible to the other. Although Gilson highlighted the differences between Thomas and Bonaventure, problems still remained. Frequently when Bonaventure's thought was studied, it was examined precisely where it had something to say to the cardinal points of Thomas' vision. In instances where Bonaventure's thought did not touch upon these points, it tended not to be examined or not to be taken with equal seriousness. Often these points of nonconvergence were the most central in Bonaventure's synthesis; hence this tendency has led to a blurring of distinctive elements in Bonaventure's vision.

Perhaps the major cause obscuring Bonaventure's vision was the neo-scholastic emphasis on philosophy. The neo-scholastic revival was primarily a revival of medieval philosophy. Scholars attempted to extract from medieval thinkers, chiefly from Thomas Aquinas, a philosophical core which could then be used to dialogue with modern philosophical issues and with such thinkers as Descartes, Kant, and Hegel. Both Thomas and Bonaventure have suffered by having their philosophy extracted from their theological synthesis, for their larger theological concern affected their philosophy. In this Bonaventure has suffered more than Thomas, since the Franciscan's philosophical elements are rooted in areas that are clearly theological: the doctrine of the Trinity and Christology. The Trinitarian perspective permeates Bonaventure's entire vision in a way that is not the case in Thomas'. It affects his doctrine of creation, his metaphysics of exemplarism and epistemology of illumination. This has led to two tendencies: to view Bonaventure's entire system solely as theology, or if philosophical elements are extracted, they tend to be examined without contact with the Trinitarian mystery that gives them vitality. The relation between philosophy and theology in Bonaventure is subtle and complex. In order to reach the heart of Bonaventure's vision without mutilating it, the philosopher must be able to sort out intricate, interpenetrating relations between philosophy and theology. In an era dominated by Thomism, which maintains a different relation between philosophy and theology, the Thomist perspective was often unconsciously imposed on Bonaventure, thus distorting both his philosophy and theology.

The neo-scholastic emphasis on philosophy, then, tended to produce a confused image of Bonaventure the philosopher and theologian. But it further tended to produce a deceptive image of Bonaventure the mystical writer, in contrast with Thomas the metaphysician. Gilson states in the conclusion of his book on Bonaventure: "Hence St. Bonaventure's doctrine marks for us the culminating point of Christian mysticism and constitutes the completest synthesis it has ever achieved. Thus it must be clear that it can never be properly comparable in any point with the doctrine of St. Thomas Aquinas."[7] There is, of course, no doubt that Bonaventure is a great mystical writer and that his synthesis integrates the mystical dimension as essential to his vision. But his mystical synthesis contains distinctive theological and philosophical dimensions which merit study on their own right. Although Gilson's treatment of Bonaventure deals precisely with these philosophical dimensions, the image of Bonaventure the mystical writer has tended to keep philosophers and theologians from investigating certain central elements in his system.

COINCIDENCE OF OPPOSITES

The basic problem in understanding Bonaventure's vision — a problem which is at the same time the source of its richness — is its integral nature. The images of Bonaventure as philosopher, theologian, and mystical writer are inaccurate in isolation. Bonaventure is all three — not in isolation, but in interrelation. To understand one of these images accurately, we must understand it in relation to the other two. In order to see Bonaventure's vision clearly, we must view it in its organic unity. We need a path, a road, a bridge that will lead us directly into the heart of Bonaventure's world view so that we can study it from the inside — in its integral wholeness, without obscurity or distortion. Once we have entered and have seen the organic structure of his thought, we are not limited merely to admire its harmony and beauty. At first glance, we might think this is all we can do, since Bonaventure is a mystic, poet, and theologian. As a mystic, he may seem beyond logical analysis; as a poet, beyond linguistic analysis; as a theologian, beyond philosophical analysis. I contend that this is not the case. If we can find the proper analytic tools, we can give a detailed systematic account of his vision in its totality and in its parts.

I believe that such a path into his vision can be found in the *coincidentia oppositorum* and that precision tools for analysis are available in the logic of the coincidence of opposites. For the last several years I have claimed in a number of articles that the *coincidentia oppositorum* is the indigenous logic of Bonaventure's vision and that it provides the single unifying structure in all the dimensions of his thought.[8] It is present in his philosophy, his theology, and his mysticism, binding together his thought as a whole. If we were to approach Bonaventure's thought through another path or attempt to analyze its structure in a different way, I believe we would not penetrate into the depth and unity of his vision. The coincidence of opposites, then, is the key to understand Bonaventure's thought. This is the thesis of the present book, and its aim is to spell out this thesis in detail by analyzing Bonaventure's texts and the structure of his thought. In the course of this study, I will maintain that by clarifying Bonaventure's vision, the coincidence of opposites enables us to situate him more accurately within the history of thought. In the light of the coincidence of opposites, we can see how he is related to his predecessors, to the controversies of the thirteenth century, and to subsequent thought, especially to some of the most central issues of the twentieth century.

CONTEXT OF BONAVENTURIAN SCHOLARSHIP

I would like to situate my work on the coincidence of opposites within the context of recent Bonaventurian scholarship, specifically within certain trends that have provided the basis for a more accurate picture of Bonaventure's thought. In this respect I am indebted to Jacques-Guy Bougerol for his study of Bonaventure's writings and the sources of Bonaventure's thought,[9] and to Ignatius Brady for his research into early Franciscan sources and his reevaluation of the critical edition of Bonaventure texts.[10] On the interpretation of Bonaventure's thought, I have found my horizons enlarged by the work of Joseph Ratzinger on Bonaventure's theology of history.[11] But I am especially indebted to the more recent work of John Quinn and Zachary Hayes. The former has clarified Bonaventure's thought against the background of the complicated issues of the past fifty years; and the latter has formulated a most illuminating distinction, which provides the framework for my own study of the coincidence of opposites.

In his monumental study published in the summer of 1974, John Quinn has surveyed some fifty years of controversy on the relation of philosophy and theology in Bonaventure.[12] This controversy created a labyrinth of complexity and confusion which could easily entrap not only the general reader but the Bonaventure specialist as well. With remarkable precision and control of Bonaventure's texts, Quinn has provided a way out of the labyrinth, presenting a lucid exposition of the various levels of Bonaventure's thought and clearly delineating the spheres of philosophy and theology. More recently Zachary Hayes has provided a striking way to see the interrelation between philosophy and theology in Bonaventure. Hayes makes a distinction between Bonaventure's philosophical and theological metaphysics. Although not found as such in Bonaventure, this distinction is implicit in his treatment of Christ the metaphysical center in the first of the *Collationes in Hexaemeron*.[13] The formulation of this distinction is an original contribution of Hayes and was presented for the first time in his paper "Christology and Metaphysics in the Thought of Saint Bonaventure," delivered in November 1974, as part of the Medieval Heritage program at the University of Chicago on the occasion of the seventh centenary of the death of Thomas and Bonaventure.[14]

Hayes acknowledges a distinction between philosophy and theology in Bonaventure, but focuses on the interrelation between the two. I believe that he has brought to light the very core of this interrelation in a way that simultaneously reveals the basis of their unity, their distinction, and the primacy of

theology over philosophy. In a strategic move, Hayes links Bonaventure's theology with a metaphysics — a metaphysics whose principles have been revealed in the mystery of Christ and the Trinity. Hayes further sees this metaphysics associated by Bonaventure with the self-diffusion of the good and the mediation between God and the world through the Trinitarian Word. And
he points to the two major texts where this metaphysics is spelled
out: namely, the sixth chapter of the *Itinerarium* and the first
of the *Collationes in Hexaemeron*.[15]

Bonaventure's theological metaphysics completes his philosophical metaphysics by bringing the principles of the latter to full
realization. For example, on the level of philosophical metaphysics, the principle that the good is self-diffusive can be known
and can be observed to have limited realizations. But through
Christian revelation this principle can be seen to have an absolute realization in the Trinitarian processions. For the Father
is revealed as the fecund source of the divinity who communicates
himself eternally and absolutely within his inner life, in the
generation of the Son and the spiration of the Spirit. Thus the
Christian revelation of the Trinity lifts the principle of the self-
diffusion of the good to an absolute level.[16] Through its absolute
realization in the Trinity, the principle itself is grasped more
clearly than was possible prior to revelation in the darkness of
man's fallen state. Not only is the principle grasped more clearly
in the light of revelation, but it is seen as an architectonic principle, which permeates philosophical metaphysics as well and
constitutes its ultimate structure and dynamism.

Thus theological metaphysics completes and clarifies philosophical metaphysics. It does not stand in opposition to philosophical metaphysics nor does it encompass a realm of mystery
whose metaphysical structure is inaccessible to man. In fact, there
is at bottom only one metaphysics, which has two levels of ac-
cessibility: one through philosophy without revelation and the
other through revelation. Without revelation man can know
something of this metaphysics, but only partially and often in

a distorted manner. However, in the light of revelation, he can penetrate into its theological level where he can grasp its principles more deeply and clearly, although not in their ultimate depth or comprehensiveness.[17]

Hayes' distinction, I believe, helps us see more sharply the difference in the methodologies of Bonaventure and Thomas. In Bonaventure, Christian revelation opens up a new level of metaphysics, which can be explored in its own right and in relation to philosophical metaphysics. This new level is not only in harmony with philosophical metaphysics but in continuity with it — related by way of absolute to relative, for in Christ and the Trinity we see manifested the fullness of principles we could grasp only relatively before. Thus Christ and the Trinity are grasped after the fashion of Platonic archetypes, in the light of whose fullness all relative participations are understood. This is in contrast with the Aristotelian approach of Thomas, who separates philosophy and theology more decisively than Bonaventure.[18] There is no basis in Thomas' system for the equivalent of Bonaventure's theological metaphysics. For Thomas, as far as man's knowledge is concerned, metaphysics does not extend beyond philosophy. Revelation does not make available to us a new level of metaphysics; it rather makes man aware of the existence of certain mysteries whose reality he can grasp only through improper analogies. Like Bonaventure, Thomas holds that there is no incompatibility between philosophy and revelation, but he does not see, as Bonaventure does, the interpenetration of the two through a common metaphysics.

In the light of Hayes' distinction, we can see the dialectical nature of Bonaventure's theological method and thus more accurately situate him within the history of thought. For example, his dialectical method is not unlike the correlation method of Paul Tillich and the method employed by Teilhard de Chardin.[19] For Bonaventure philosophical metaphysics raises questions and proceeds up to a certain point, where revelation enters in and provides the answers to the questions. Revelation thus completes the movement of reason by drawing it into a new level, that of theological metaphysics. Note that what is revealed does not remain completely obscure in contrast to the clarity of philosophical metaphysics. On the contrary, revelation illumines the *ratio* of the mystery, not exhaustively of course, but sufficiently to constitute a new level of metaphysics. Here in the light of Hayes' distinction, we can see the validity of the twelfth century theological method which sought necessary reasons (*rationes necessariae*) for the Trinity.[20] Bonaventure inherited this method from Richard of St. Victor and exercised it in applying to the Trinity the principle of the self-diffusion of the good. Opponents have criticized this method because it steps far beyond the limits of reason established by Thomas. Their objections, however, have assumed that Richard and Bonaventure were searching for necessary reasons merely on the level of philosophical metaphysics. I believe, to the contrary, that the necessary reasons are on the level of theological metaphysics and must await the revelation of the Trinity in Christ for their emergence into consciousness. Once revealed, however, they manifest their inner intelligibility which is grasped, within the realm of theological metaphysics, as necessary.

Clarification of his theological metaphysics can not only situate Bonaventure in the history of thought, but can draw him as an active participant into what has been called the Great Dialogue or Great Conversation.[21] In the great dialogue among Western thinkers, Bonaventure has much to contribute; but unfortunately, he has often not been called forward to join the dialogue of metaphysicians since he has been identified chiefly as a mystical writer and a theologian. If he has been brought into the dialogue of metaphysicians, it has often been over areas that are secondary and which have not been clearly shaped by his Trinitarian metaphysics. This has been due in large measure to the fact, which we pointed out above, that Bonaventure has been viewed primarily from a Thomist perspective, specifically from Thomas' own distinction between philosophy and theology.

Since Thomas did not employ the metaphysics of the good to explore the Trinity, he did not develop Bonaventure's notion of a theological metaphysics. On the contrary, Thomas developed a metaphysics of being which he used to explore the realm of nature and the divine substance. Applied only analogously to the Trinity, the metaphysics of being was not transformed into a new level of metaphysics within the Trinity as was Bonaventure's metaphysics of the good. Since Bonaventure's theology was usually assumed to be similar to Thomas', the metaphysical nature of Bonaventure's Trinitarian theology was left largely unnoticed. The result has been that Bonaventure's contributions to solving metaphysical problems have been often overlooked. For example, in the light of his Trinitarian metaphysics, he reached solutions to some of the most vexing problems in the history of Western thought. As we will see in the course of this book, Bonaventure can enter into significant dialogue on these metaphysical problems with such thinkers as Hegel and Whitehead precisely in the light of his theological metaphysics.[22]

The implications, then, of Hayes' distinction are significant for understanding Bonaventure and throw considerable light on my own work. For some ten years I had been studying Bonaventure's thought with the assumption of this distinction but without bringing it to self-consciousness. I am deeply indebted to Hayes for this clarification, which I consider a major contribution to Bonaventurian scholarship. Hayes' distinction provides the immediate framework of my work in the coincidence of opposites. I see myself analyzing the logic of Bonaventure's theological metaphysics — a logic which I have identified as the coincidence of opposites. This logic can be seen most vividly in Bonaventure's Christology and in his Trinitarian theology; but since his theological and philosophical metaphysics are at bottom not diverse but a single metaphysics, there is a common logic at the base of both his theology and philosophy, namely the logic of the coincidence of opposites. Seen in the light of Bonaventure's theological metaphysics, then, this same logic can be discerned in his doctrine of creation, his metaphysics of exemplarism and his epistemology of illumination. Although situated against the background of the work of Quinn and Hayes, my own research is an independent project for which I must assume complete responsibility. Hence I do not wish to imply that their work would necessarily lead them to agree with my interpretation of Bonaventure according to the coincidence of opposites.

CONTEXT OF THE COINCIDENCE OF OPPOSITES

The coincidence of opposites has had a long history in religious and philosophical thought. It appears often in primitive myths, as for example, in the sacred marriage of the Sky-God and Mother Earth.[23] It is found in both primitive and developed theologies in the union of the terrible and beneficient aspects of the divinity, as for example, in the Indian god Shiva, who is both the creator and destroyer.[24] In China Taoism speaks of the harmony of opposites — the dark and the light, the weak and the strong, the male and the female.[25] In Greece the Pre-Socratics saw a cosmic struggle between love and hate, justice and injustice.[26] Heraclitus said: "God is day and night, winter and summer, war and peace, satiety and hunger; all opposites are in him."[27] The name most closely associated with the formula *coincidentia oppositorum* is Nicholas of Cusa; for he caused the term to become enshrined in our culture; he used the paradoxical method formally and made it the characteristic perspective of his entire thought.[28] In modern times it has appeared in the dialectical idealism of Hegel and the dialectical materialism of Marx.[29] In the twentieth century, it plays an important role in the psychology of C. G. Jung.[30] More recently it has emerged in the 'death of God' theology, in the Christology of Thomas Altizer, who sees in Christ's kenotic incarnation the basis for a dialectical coincidence of the sacred and the profane.[31]

How is Bonaventure related to this long history? I believe that Bonaventure belongs squarely within this tradition and that his thought can be best interpreted in the light of the coincidence of opposites. By speaking of the coincidence of opposites in Bonaventure's thought, however, I do not wish to imply that he used the phrase or employed the method of contraries thematically as Nicholas of Cusa did. Yet, on the other hand, I mean more than the mere fact that the coincidence of opposites is implicit in his thought. This would be true of any theologian who speaks of God and creation, and especially true of a Christian theologian who sees Christ as a mediator between God and man. In Bonaventure the coincidence of opposites has more prominence than this. At times it provides the rhetorical structure of a passage. On closer inspection, the reader can see that this rhetorical structure is reflecting an underlying metaphysical principle. At times the paradoxical juxtaposition of opposites is clearly and forcefully stated by Bonaventure. For example, at certain key points in Bonaventure's writing, we read texts like the following. In the *Itinerarium,* he speaks of our amazement "at the fact that the divine Being is both first and last, eternal and most present, most simple and greatest or uncircumscribed, wholly everywhere and nowhere contained, most actual and never moved."[32] Later in the same chapter, while gazing upon Christ, he sees united in him "the first and the last, the highest and the lowest, the circumference and the center, 'the Alpha and the Omega,' the caused and the cause, the Creator and the creature."[33] Such passages can suggest to the reader a reflection or *reductio,* leading him back to the coincidence of opposites at the base of Bonaventure's philosophical and theological metaphysics.

In this study we contend that the coincidence of opposites reveals the very core of Bonaventure's thought. When this is grasped, we can better situate Bonaventure against the background of the history of religious experience and better evaluate his distinctive contributions. This becomes clear, for example, if we situate Bonaventure within the context of the research done by Mircea Eliade. In his extensive study of comparative religion, Eliade has analyzed the most fundamental religious pattern as that of hierophany, or the manifestation of the sacred. He has further analyzed hierophany as involving a coming together of opposites: of the sacred and the profane, the infinite and the finite, and eternal and the temporal. This union of opposites has been expressed throughout the history of religion by various forms of the *coincidentia oppositorum*. In *Patterns in Comparative Religion*, Eliade writes:

> This coming-together of sacred and profane really produces a kind of breakthrough of the various levels of existence. It is implied in every hierophany whatever, for every hierophany shows, makes manifest, the coexistence of contradictory essences: sacred and profane, spirit and matter, eternal and non-eternal, and so on. That the dialectic of hierophanies, of the manifestation of the sacred in material things, should be an object for even such complex theology as that of the Middle Ages serves to prove that it remains *the* cardinal problem of any religion. One might even say that all hierophanies are simply prefigurations of the miracle of the Incarnation, that every hierophany is an abortive attempt to reveal the mystery of the coming together of God and man.[34]

Eliade's reference to the theme of hierophany in medieval theology immediately calls to mind Bonaventure. Perhaps more than any other medieval theologian, his thought is primarily focused on the reflection of God in all levels of the universe and reaches a fullness in the hierophany of Christ. If, as Eliade says, hierophany is the basic religious problem, it would seem that Bonaventure's vision penetrates to the very essence of the religious sphere. And if medieval theology has brought this essential element to a high level of self-consciousness and has given it a rich expression, we can say that within medieval theology Bonaventure provides one of the most self-reflective and multi-dimensional expressions of the theophanic tradition.

Eliade's study throws light on the depth and richness of Bonaventure's thought, as seen against the background of the history of theology and comparative religion. At the same time Eliade provides a point of view from which to study Bonaventure. If theophany is the central pattern of religion and if Bonaventure's thought is primarily concerned with this issue, it would be of paramount importance that our frame of reference for studying his thought should be such that it is coherent with the structure of theophany. Our framework must neither falsify nor distort Bonaventure's theophanic vision; rather it should clarify its dimensions. That is to say that our theoretical model for gaining a self-reflective awareness of Bonaventure's thought should be compatible with the metaphysical structure of his thought. We must select the proper theoretical model for studying the metaphysics of theophany.[35] Eliade indicates that the proper model is that of the *coincidentia oppositorum*, for in theophany the opposites come together: the absolute and the relative, the infinite and the finite, the eternal and the temporal.[36]

THREE TYPES OF COINCIDENCE OF OPPOSITES

Although with Eliade we can see that hierophany is the basic religious pattern and that it involves a coincidence of opposites, we must analyze more precisely the various types of the coincidence of opposites. I believe that there are at least three large metaphysical frameworks or models which include three different forms of the coincidence of opposites: (1) unity; (2) difference; and (3) unity and difference. In the first, unity swallows up difference; opposites coincide to such an extent that they become one — in a unity where they no longer exist as opposites. This is a monistic view, in which opposites are judged either to be an illusion or to be transcended in an undifferentiated unity. An example of this form of the coincidence of opposites is found in the thought of Śankara, the great theologian of medieval India, who proposed the doctrine of *advaita,* or nondifferentiation.[37] Śankara held that the phenomenal world, with its differences, is illusory and that there is only one reality, namely Brahman, the divine ultimate reality. The fundamental opposites — Brahman and the phenomenal world — do coincide, but in such a way that the opposition is not maintained: all is swallowed up in the unity of Brahman. The sheer power and reality of Brahman overpower the phenomenal world and reveal its unreality. In the perspective of true knowledge, we realize that only

Brahman really exists. Similar monistic tendencies are found also in Western thought, but to a lesser extent than in the East. For example, among the Greeks, the pre-Socratic philosopher Parmenides affirmed that nonbeing is an illusion since only being exists; hence change and differentiation are illusions.[38] Do these monistic positions involve a true coincidence of opposites? Only in a limited sense, for although the opposites coincide, they do not remain as opposites. One so transforms the other that it reduces the original opposition to unity.

In the second class, that of difference, opposition remains; but there is no genuine coincidence. The opposites persist as opposites to such an extent that they achieve no real union. They coincide only by repelling or opposing each other or at the most by mere juxtaposition. An example of this is seen in the ancient Greek atomism of Leucippus and Democratus, in which the basic particles of the universe are radically separate and discrete, without any internal relations.[39] When they form patterns of unity, it is merely by external juxtaposition. A further example is found in the various dualistic positions, such as that of ancient Zoroastrianism, in which there are two basic principles, one good and the other evil, which war against each other. At a later period dualism emerged in Gnosticism and Manichaeism, which affirmed a radical opposition between matter and spirit.[40]

A striking example of the difference tradition is found in the Biblical affirmation of God's transcendence above the world. The Old Testament reflects the struggle of the Hebrew religious consciousness against the immanent Near Eastern gods of nature, and the triumph of the sense of God's transcendence. This Semitic sense of transcendence reaches a high point in Islam, which is the religion of God's transcendence *par excellence*. The Koran proclaims that Allah is unique and absolutely transcendent above the world.[41] Allah is wholly other, transcendent in his reality and power. It is the duty of the Muslim to worship Allah, bowing before his majesty in the prescribed prayers five times a day. The sense of the wholly otherness of God and the opposition between

God and the world are part also of the Christian heritage from its Semitic roots. Although the Incarnation affirms a coincidence of God and creation which neither Jews nor Muslims can accept, nevertheless the Christian tradition shares with the Semites the basic sense of God's transcendence and the opposition between God and creation. This theme has been strongly stressed at times in Christian history, for example in Calvin and later in Kierkegaard, whose emphasis of the infinite qualitative difference between eternity and time, God and the world, was taken up by Barth in the twentieth century.[42]

In the third framework, that of unity and difference, opposites genuinely coincide while at the same time continuing to exist as opposites. They join in a real union, but one that does not obliterate differences; rather it is precisely the union that intensifies the difference. The more intimately the opposites are united, the more they are differentiated. I call this a coincidence of mutually affirming complementarity; for the opposites complement each other, and through their union mutually intensify their individuality as opposites. An example of this can be seen in the doctrine of the complementarity of the Yin-Yang, or the female and male principles, in Taoism.[43] A similar complementarity is found in the Western personalistic philosophy of such thinkers as Martin Buber, who analyzes the mutuality involved in the I-Thou relation: the more one relates to the other as *Thou,* the more he becomes an *I.*[44] The principle of complementarity becomes a cosmic principle of evolution in the thought of Teilhard de Chardin. On all levels of the universe and at all stages of the evolutionary process, Teilhard sees a single law operating — the law of creative union, which he articulates in the terse formula: union differentiates.[45] The more a particle of matter or a human person enters into a creative union with another, the more their true uniqueness is achieved.

At the outset I would like to forestall a possible misunderstanding. I do not wish to place in radical opposition the principle of contradiction and the coincidence of opposites. I believe that the principle of contradiction applies universally across any meta-physical framework, whether that of difference, unity, or unity and difference. We can formulate the principle of contradiction as follows: A thing cannot be and not be at the same time under the same formal aspect. It is important to underscore the phrase "under the same formal aspect." In the coincidence of opposites this implies that one element, in so far as it is opposite to another, is not identical with the other; but this does not prevent a coincidence of mutual complementarity. It must be emphatically stated that the principle of contradiction does not favor the difference model more than the unity and difference model. In discussion and debate the contrary assumption is often made, and the full force of the principle of contradiction is brought against the coincidence of opposites. Such a move in argumentation, I believe, is not founded; for according to the interpretation I am giving here, the principle of contradiction applies equally to the difference model and to the unity and difference. Hence it cannot be marshalled as ammunition against the coincidence of opposites.

I believe that Bonaventure falls squarely and consistently within this third class, for his thought emphasizes both unity and difference. On all levels of his vision, one finds the coincidence of mutually affirming complementarity: in the doctrine of the Trinity, creation, God's relation to the world, man as image of God, Christology, the return of the soul to God and the realization of mystical union. For example, Bonaventure maintains the Semitic affirmation of the difference of God and the world, not merely by affirming their opposition, but as we will see later, by affirming God's transcendence precisely through his immanence. Bonaventure maintains the opposition found in the second class but always within the union of the third class. It will be the task of this book to reveal by analysis how all the levels of Bonaventure's thought are structured according to the coincidence of opposites of this third class: namely, the coincidence of mutually affirming complementarity.

Speaking in general terms, I believe that the great religions of the world can be related according to these three classes. As we indicated, Hinduism of the non-dualistic or *advaitan* type, as represented by Śankara, belongs to the class of unity, and Judaism and Islam belong to the difference class. Christianity is more difficult to place. With Judaism and Islam it forcefully rejects the monist position as being unorthodox. While sharing the Semitic affirmation of the difference between God and the world, its doctrine of the Incarnation necessarily places it at least partially within the third class: of unity and difference; for Christ is both God and man, joined through the hypostatic union. Therefore, for a Christian to state the absolute difference position of classical Islam would be in effect to deny the Incarnation. Hence a Christian cannot belong exclusively to the difference class, but must at least in the area of the Incarnation affirm unity and difference.

COINCIDENCE OF OPPOSITES IN CHRISTIANITY

In the history of Christianity theologians have dealt with this problem in various ways. Basically there are two approaches: one can begin from the difference side or from the unity-and-difference side. Bonaventure and the Christian Neo-Platonic tradition begin from the latter, taking the Incarnation as the paradigm of the entire theological structure. While affirming difference, they see difference primarily within unity. Hence, I believe that the coincidence of opposites of mutually affirming complementarity is the inner logic of this position. The other approach begins from the difference side and moves toward the unity-and-difference of the Incarnation. Within this approach, I discern two major subdivisions: the two-leveled system of the Aristotelian-Thomistic tradition and the more dialectic approach of classical Protestantism. Thomas sees two levels. The natural level, known by reason, belongs to the difference class. Using Aristotelian principles of act and potency, Thomas affirms the difference between God and the world; for the world being in potency and hence contingent is radically dependent upon God who is pure act. However, there is a higher realm, the supernatural, which is made known through divine revelation and accepted by faith.[46] This realm, since it includes the Incarnation, reflects the third class: of unity and difference. Through grace it is possible for man to be lifted up to this realm, thus overcoming his radical difference and participating in the divine life of the Trinity made available by Christ. Classical Protestantism rejected the natural-supernatural universe and affirmed the difference between God and man in terms of man's sinfulness.[47] Christ bridges the gap between God and man and effects the reconciliation of the sinner, but the relation between God and man in this tradition remains much more dialectical than in the Thomistic position.

In contrast, then, to both the Thomistic and the classical Protestant tradition, Bonaventure takes his point of departure from the unity-and-difference class, seeing the element of difference — both metaphysical differences and the separation due to sin — within the larger framework of the unity of opposites. This is why there is a different logic in his system from that of Thomism and classical Protestantism. Based on the bi-polarity of act and potency, Thomas' system is permeated with the logic of difference. Classical Protestantism is also permeated with the logic of difference because of its dialectical relation between sin and grace. In both cases the bi-polar model highlights difference because it does not contain within itself a mediating principle. In contrast to these bi-polar models, Bonaventure employs a Trinitarian model, in which a third element acts as mediating principle unifying the opposites. The Trinitarian model is the classical Christian model of the coincidence of opposites, for it contains both bi-polarity and a unifying mediating principle. From one point of view, the Spirit is seen as the unity of the Father and the Son; from another point of view the Son is seen as the mediating principle between the Father and the Spirit. In each case unity and bi-polarity are affirmed by the triadic model. The Trinitarian model, with its logic of the coincidence of opposites, permeates Bonaventure's entire system — not only the area designated by Thomists as supernatural, but the natural order as well; for Bonaventure sees vestiges of the Trinity everywhere. Bonaventure's system is built from its foundation to its summit according to the architectonic design of the Trinitarian model, with the logical structure of the coincidence of opposites.

If this analysis is correct, we can see the importance of using the proper model in exploring Bonaventure's thought. If we were to begin with the difference model, from the perspective of Thomism or of classical Protestantism, then we would fail to touch the basic philosophical and religious experience out of which Bonaventure's thought grows. Furthermore we could easily criticize his thought unjustly since we would have the wrong expectations, derived from our different model. We might feel that he is confusing the natural and the supernatural, philosophy and theology, faith and reason; or we might feel that his doctrine of man as image of God is ungrounded because it cannot bridge the abyss between the transcendent God and sinful man. I believe that some of the misunderstanding and criticism of such Bonaventurian doctrines as illumination, exemplarism, and the immanence of God in creation have been due to viewing his thought through an improper model.

In the present book I am focusing on the understanding of Bonaventure's thought, since I believe that it has been obscured by being viewed from alien perspectives. I am making a generic plea that it be viewed on its own terms and a specific claim that it belongs to the class of unity and difference. Even if I successfully defend this position, there remains the further question: Is Bonaventure's system true? There are, of course, two stages to the study of a man's thought: understanding and evaluation. If we have understood his thought on its own terms and within its own logic, our task is only half completed; for we must evaluate, judge, critically reflect upon its validity. This is a demanding and complex process, involving not only a judgment according to norms, but a clarification and justification of the norms employed. In the case of Bonaventure this is further complicated by the fact that it involves both philosophical and theological norms.

I will not make this normative question central to the thesis of this book, nor will I treat it systematically. Nevertheless it will inevitably permeate the entire presentation, since as a philosopher and theologian Bonaventure was himself in search of truth and felt that he had to a large measure found truth. Although I will be concerned directly with the accuracy of interpreting Bonaventure, I will be constantly dealing with the truth-dimension of what he had to say, since throughout I will be touching the reasons he gave for the truth of a position. As a philosopher he gave metaphysical and epistemological reasons for his claims, and as a theologian he rooted himself in Scripture and tradition. Although I personally believe that Bonaventure's system is valid according to philosophical and theological norms, I will not undertake to defend that position within this book, but will simply allow the reasons to unfold implicitly as I pursue the task of establishing the coincidence of opposites of complementarity as the proper framework for interpreting Bonaventure's thought.

BONAVENTURE AND THE NEO-PLATONIC TRADITION

The thesis of this book has a larger ambit than its central claim that Bonaventure is to be interpreted according to the coincidence of opposites of complementarity. As we have indicated, Bonaventure does not stand in isolation but reflects the Christian Neo-Platonic tradition. This tradition runs through the Greek Fathers, the Pseudo-Dionysius, Anselm, the Victorines, Alexander of Hales, and Bonaventure. It continues in subsequent thought, in Nicholas of Cusa and the Platonists of the Renaissance, surfacing again in German romanticism and reappearing in various forms in the twentieth century. Although there is considerable variety in this current as it passes through diverse thinkers and different ages, I believe that it has sufficient common elements to allow it to be identified as a unified current, at least in a generic way. Furthermore, I make the same claim for this current that I have made for Bonaventure: that it belongs to the class of unity and difference, as described above, and that its indigenous logic is the coincidence of opposites of complementarity. Here again there is considerable diversity in the various thinkers, but I believe a basic common unity. Hence, if one penetrates into this current at a significant point, for example in Bonaventure's elaborate medieval synthesis, and if one brings to light the logic of the coincidence of opposites, then he can understand more clearly this tradition's inner dynamics and its underlying unity as it flows through various thinkers even to the present day.

In the light of the history of Bonaventurian scholarship, the central thesis of this book — that Bonaventure should be interpreted according to the coincidence of opposites — is a rather bold, perhaps even pretentious claim. Through the centuries Bonaventure has not been studied in this way — largely, I believe, because of the obscuring of his thought and the failure to see him as part of a continuing tradition. Two centuries after Bonaventure, Nicholas of Cusa brought the coincidence of opposites to self-consciousness, but scholars were not inclined to return to Bonaventure and examine his thought in the light of the coincidence of opposites. Still later in this current, Hegel brought to self-consciousness the dynamic aspect of the coincidence of opposites in his dialectic and, not unlike Bonaventure, made the Trinity the basis of his entire system. Once again this did not occasion a reexamination of Bonaventure's thought. Now, aided with this accumulated self-consciousness and with the additional research of Jung and Eliade in the twentieth century, it is possible to see more clearly the coincidence of opposites in Bonaventure — not as an isolated thinker, but as representative of a continuing tradition.

If one discerns a continuing tradition whose logic is the coincidence of opposites, then Bonaventure can more easily be situated within the history of thought. In the light of the coincidence of opposites, we can more clearly see his relation to the Greek Fathers, especially to the Pseudo-Dionysius, to Anselm and the Victorines. The coincidence of opposites throws considerable light on Bonaventure's positions in thirteenth century controversies: his critique of Aristotle and his reaction to Islamic influence. It illumines his relation to the Christian mystical tradition, to the Pseudo-Dionysius and to Meister Eckhart.

We will begin our study by giving a summary of Bonaventure's life and an exposition of the general outlines of his thought. Against this background we will embark upon a systematic analysis of his texts as these reveal the presence of the coincidence of opposites found in his thought. This will throw further light on the interpretation of his vision, his sources, and the controversies of the thirteenth century. We will then attempt to situate Bonaventure's use of the coincidence of opposites within the subsequent history of thought, with special attention to Nicholas of Cusa.

This will lead us to contemporary theology and philosophy — to such issues as the dynamic nature of God, the relation of God to the world, the religious meaning of secular culture, the dynamics of history and the emergence of the future, the relation of Christianity to world religions. We might be surprised to discover how contemporary Bonaventure is. For he has much to say of relevance in a dialogue with Tillich, Rahner, Whitehead and process theology, Teilhard de Chardin, Pannenberg, Moltmann, Metz, and Panikkar. An analysis of Bonaventure's thought from the standpoint of the *coincidentia oppositorum* will not only throw light on the structure of his thought in its historical context, but will draw us into the heart of universal issues that are as burning today as they were in Bonaventure's world of the thirteenth century.

CHAPTER II

Bonaventure's Life and Thought

 N MANY instances there is no discernible correlation between an author's thought and the physical setting of his birthplace. This is not so in the case of Bonaventure's birthplace, Bagnoregio.[1] Not only is it in a setting of striking physical beauty but the very structure of the setting reflects the structure of Bonaventure's thought. Situated in the Etruscan country about sixty miles north of Rome, between Viterbo and Orvieto, Bagnoregio is perched high on the crest of a spur of land jutting into the Tibur valley. About seven miles to the west lies Lago di Bolsena, a deep blue lake that shines like a jewel in the crater of an extinct volcano. On its eastern slope, this volcano stretches in a plateau which after several miles divides into what appear to be fingers of land separated from each other by deep gorges. Extending towards the Tibur, these fingers break off abruptly into the valley below. Bagnoregio is built along the thin edge of one of these fingers. Scanning the horizon, the visitor has a breathtaking sense of the vastness of space — deep gorges plunging down on each side, massive cliffs rising across the gorges, directly ahead the steep drop off into the Tibur valley and in the distance lofty mountains in the direction of Todi. Towards the southeast stretch the mountains of the Sabine country north of Rome, where on a clear day can be seen Mount Soracte, immortalized in an ode of Horace. This setting easily awakens a sense of joy in nature — of awe at its power and at the same time peace in its harmony. Bagnoregio seems to be the midpoint of a vast and ordered cosmos, the center of the earth as it were; for it lies on a pinnacle of land rising from the valley, ringed about by a

sweeping circular horizon whose outlines are traced by massive mountains.

This natural setting would be spectacular enough, but added to it is the fact that the very tip of the finger stands alone in the shape of a conical hill, on the crest of which lies the ancient center of Bagnoregio, now abandoned and in ruins — a medieval ghost town. Erosion, landslides, and earthquakes have for centuries eaten away the thin spur of land on which Bagnoregio is situated. In 1695 a disastrous earthquake shook the city, causing massive landslides along the ridge behind the ancient center.[2] This led to the decline of the center and the shifting of the life of the city to the other section towards the plateau. The result is that Bonaventure's Bagnoregio now stands in solemn isolation, unchanged for centuries, a silent reminder of the medieval world in which Bonaventure lived. Although a number of homes here have been restored and are inhabited, the visitor has the impression at times that he is wandering through a city whose life had stopped as abruptly as that of Pompeii. He walks along deserted streets, peers into gutted buildings, visits the ancient cathedral in which Bonaventure worshipped as a boy, and observes a wall at the side of the gorge — the only remains of the home that tradition assigns to Bonaventure's family.[3] Standing on the edge of the inhabited section of the city and gazing across the eroded land to the ancient center, the visitor sees Bonaventure's Bagnoregio — the bell tower of the cathedral rising above the silent homes and city gate.[4] From this observation point, the simple medieval atmosphere of the city unites with the grandeur of the natural setting. Bonaventure's Bagnoregio clearly becomes the focal point at the center of the vast circular sweep of the horizon.

Although we know relatively little about Bonaventure's early years in Bagnoregio, we can see how this landscape could shape his vision. It would be indeed surprising if a young boy, as sensitive as Bonaventure, could grow up in that setting without being moved by its power and symbolism. In the sweeping landscape of Bagnoregio there is a natural resonance with the distinctive elements of Bonaventure's thought. Sketched in the book of nature at Bagnoregio are the outlines of the philosophical-theological vision he elaborated in his later years. Here in Bagnoregio is the basis of his Franciscan sensitivity to nature — not in gentle Umbrian colors, but in sweeping cosmic dimensions. Most of all, the landscape of Bagnoregio contains the symbolism of the center, which will play so important a role in the evolution of Bonaventure's Christology. As we will see shortly, the notion of Christ the center emerged through the years as a major theme in Bonaventure's thought. I will eventually argue that the symbol of the mandala — a circle and center — permeates Bonaventure's thought and is the key to understand its structure.[5] One could find few settings in which the mandala design is more immediately apparent in the landscape than in that of Bagnoregio.

BOYHOOD AND EDUCATION

It was in this setting that Bonaventure was born in the early part of the thirteenth century. The date of his birth is not known with certainty. Although traditionally considered to be 1221, this was challenged by Giuseppe Abate in 1949-1950, who proposed convincing evidence that Bonaventure was born not later than 1217, the date which has been subsequently accepted by a majority of Bonaventure scholars.[6] Knowledge of his family is limited to sparce details. His father was John di Fidanza, who seems to have been a doctor of medicine and a man of some means. His mother was Maria di Ritello, sometimes called simply Ritella. Their son was not baptized Bonaventure, but apparently John after his father; his name was changed to Bonaventure only after he entered the Franciscan Order.[7]

Although practically nothing is known of his boyhood, one event is recorded by Bonaventure himself: namely, his miraculous cure through Francis of Assisi. When years later he was commissioned by his Order to write the life of Francis, Bonaventure said in his introduction: "I was snatched from the jaws of death through his invocation and merits, when I was a boy, as I still vividly remember. If I refused to publish his praises now, I fear I would be accused of being ungrateful."[8] In his shorter life of St. Francis, he states in greater detail: "God's numberless favors granted through Francis in various parts of the world do not cease to abound, as I myself who have written this life have verified through my own personal experience. For as I lay seriously ill while still a child, I was snatched from the jaws of death and restored to perfect health owing to a vow made by my mother to the blessed Father Francis."[9] A tradition grew up that this cure was performed by Francis personally, as is depicted in the bas-relief on a monument to Bonaventure in Bagnoregio, which shows his mother presenting him as a very young child to Francis, while his father stands imploringly in the background. The tradition further recounts that Francis took the child in his arms, offered him to God, and in a prophetic vision exclaimed, "O, la buona ventura!" (Oh, good luck). After this the boy was no longer called John but Bonaventura.[10] However, a recent examination of the evidence concludes that the cure occurred after Francis' death and canonization, perhaps between 1228 and 1231, that is, when Bonaventure was between eleven and fourteen years of age.[11]

On Bonaventure's early education we have the testimony of Sixtus IV in 1482 that he received his preliminary schooling with the Franciscans at their friary in Bagnoregio.[12] It had been thought that he entered the Franciscan order in Italy and did his novitiate perhaps at Orvieto. However more recent scholarship holds that he entered the Order only after going to the University of Paris and completing the course there for the master of arts. According to this reckoning, he would have gone to Paris in 1234 or 1235, becoming a master of arts in 1243 and beginning his theological studies as a novice in the Franciscan Order in Paris the same year. However, according to the regulations of the Order at that time, he was received as a member of the Roman Province.[13]

Having arrived in Paris in 1234 or 1235, Bonaventure began

an involvement with the University which would last continuously
for over twenty years, during his period as a student and professor,
and which would continue intermittently throughout his life.
When he was a student in the faculty of arts, Bonaventure continued the contact with the Franciscans he had begun in Bagnoregio. By the time he reached Paris, the Franciscans were solidly
established there and on their way to becoming a major force in
the University. Having arrived in Paris in 1217, the Franciscans
were first housed in a small building belonging to the Benedictine
abbey of Saint-Denis.[14] When vocations increased their number,
it was necessary to provide education, especially in Scripture in
view of their mission of preaching. The friars began walking the
great distance from Saint-Denis to the University each day until
that became impractical. There is evidence that by 1224 they were
established in Paris and had increasing contact with the university
world.

In 1230 the friars obtained from the Benedictines of the abbey
of Saint-Germain a cluster of houses within the city walls, where
they could dwell but without the possibility of expansion. Through
the assistance of the king, St. Louis, who was attracted to the new
order, the friars acquired from the abbey a large area of land
near the original houses. By 1240 the friars were able to begin
construction there on what would become their major house of
studies in the Order. Called in French the "Grand Couvent des
Cordeliers," the house was situated on the left bank, on the edge
of the city walls — in the present city of Paris, near the Boulevard
Saint-Germain, at the site of the school of medicine, between Rue
Monsieur-le-Prince, Rue Racine and Rue de l'Ecole de Médecine.
During the Middle Ages the Couvent des Cordeliers flourished as
a major center of the University of Paris; it was here that the
great Franciscan masters taught: Alexander of Hales, Bonaventure, and Duns Scotus. With its cloister and thirteenth century
church, it remained a center of Franciscan learning until its dis-
appearance at the time of the French Revolution.

The status of the young Franciscan group in Paris was enormously bolstered when the most illustrious professor of the University, Alexander of Hales, entered the Order in 1236.[15] A native of Gloucestershire in England, he was about fifty at the time and at the height of his career, a man of great learning and prestige. By bringing with him his doctoral chair to the Couvent des Cordeliers, he established the school of the Friars Minor as officially part of the University of Paris. With the presence of a *magister regens* of the University, the friars had the right to open a public school of theology. This was a decisive event for the Franciscans, for it definitively oriented them towards higher academic studies.

THEOLOGICAL STUDENT AND PROFESSOR

Alexander's entrance into the Franciscan Order occurred shortly after Bonaventure's arrival at the University and during his course at the faculty of arts. After his own entrance into the Order, in 1243, Bonaventure studied theology under Alexander until the latter's death in 1245. This was a most important relation for Bonaventure, for from Alexander he received the substance of the tradition that he was to shape into his own synthesis — especially the currents flowing from the Pseudo-Dionysius and the Victorines. Even in developing his own thought, Bonaventure considered himself a disciple of Alexander, as can be seen by his attitude of respect, his reference to his "master" and "father" and his affirmation that he did not want to deviate from his master's opinion.[16] Alexander's appreciation and respect for Bonaventure is summed up in a tradition which is recounted in the following quotation from the bull of canonization of Sixtus IV: "Bonaventure was great in learning, but no less great in humility and holiness. His innocence and dove-like simplicity were such that Alexander of Hales, the renowned doctor whose disciple Saint Bonaventure was, used to say of him that it seemed as though Adam had never sinned in him."[17]

Although Bonaventure was undoubtedly attracted to the Franciscans by the learning of Alexander of Hales and other scholars of the convent at Paris, he was also drawn by the simplicity of

Francis. He saw in the development of the Franciscan Order a reflection of the primitive Church. In the following statement, written some twenty years after his entrance into the Order, in response to a critic of the Rule, we can see an expression of the ideal of simplicity and learning that marked his own life as a friar:

> Do not be upset that in the beginning the friars were simple and unlettered. This ought rather to strengthen your faith in the Order. For I acknowledge before God that what made me love the life of Blessed Francis so much was the fact that it resembled the beginning and growth of the Church. As the Church began with simple fishermen and afterwards developed to include renowned and skilled doctors, so you will see it to be the case in the Order of Blessed Francis. In this way God shows that it was not founded by the prudence of men but by Christ.[18]

After entering the Order, Bonaventure pursued his theological studies under Alexander of Hales and John of La Rochelle. After their deaths in 1245, he continued under Odo Rigaldus and William of Melitona. In 1248 Bonaventure was licensed as a bachelor of Scripture, *baccalarius biblicus,* and for the next two years lectured on the Bible.[19] From 1250 to 1252, as a *baccalarius sententiarius,* he lectured on the sentences of Peter Lombard, producing his *Commentary on the Sentences.* In 1252 and 1253 he was engaged in disputations and preaching. In 1253 or 1254 he was awarded by the Chancellor of the University the licentiate and doctorate, which gave him the right to teach not only at Paris but throughout Christendom. Because of the struggles between the secular masters and the mendicants, some think that Bonaventure was not formally accepted into the guild of masters as a *magister regens* until 1257, but there is evidence indicating that he was recognized as such at the earlier date.[20] As regent master of the Franciscan school, he lectured on Scripture, determined questions, and preached. During the period from 1254 to 1257, he composed commentaries on the gospels of Luke and John, on Ecclesiastes, and the Book of Wisdom; he also produced three sets of disputed questions: on the knowledge of Christ, on the Trinity, and on evangelical perfection. In the course of the same period he composed his condensed *summa,* the *Breviloquium.* During this time, when he was intensely engaged in lecturing and writing, he rose to the intellectual leadership of the Franciscan Order.

Bonaventure's position at the University became embroiled in a dispute between the secular masters and the new mendicant orders.[21] Both the Dominicans and the Franciscans had acquired two chairs of theology at the University. The secular masters, who were the entrenched authorities at the University, resented the rise of the new mendicant orders and opposed their acquisition of power. A statute was issued limiting the number of chairs in the Dominican and the Franciscan houses to one each. The Franciscans complied, but the Dominicans resisted. Furthermore, when the secular masters decided to suspend classes in protest over police violence against some students, the mendicants refused to comply and continued teaching. This complex situation directly concerned both Thomas and Bonaventure because it jeopardized their status as regent masters. The political situation broke into open controversy when a secular master, William of Saint-Amour, wrote *De periculis novissimorum temporum,* attacking the very foundations of the new Orders. William claimed that the mendicants were false prophets and that their way of life was contrary to morality and religion. Bonaventure answered in his disputed questions on evangelical perfection and Thomas in his *Contra impugnantes Dei cultum et religionem.* William's book was condemned by Pope Alexander IV; through successive interventions of the pope the dissensions at the University were brought to a close, and the status of the mendicant orders in the structure of the University was recognized.

MINISTER GENERAL OF FRANCISCAN ORDER

Before these problems had reached a final solution, an event occurred that changed the course of Bonaventure's life. On February 2, 1257 he was elected Minister General of the Friars Minor.[22] This meant that he had to abandon his academic career at the

University and for the next seventeen years devote himself to administering the Order and solving the complex problems it faced. Not the least among these was the very problem that led to his election. For some time the Order was being polarized into two camps: On the one hand were the Spirituals, who maintained that the primitive ideal of Francis should be lived without adaptation or evolution. These took their inspiration from Francis' original companions who still dwelt in the hermitages of the Rieti valley and on Mount La Verna. Emphasizing the simplicity of Francis, the Spirituals adhered to a strict poverty, rejected learning, and feared the organizational structure that came with the expansion of the Order. On the other hand, another camp was formed by those who accepted the need for interpretation and adaptation of the Rule, the cultivation of learning — even in the great universities — and the more elaborate organization of the Order demanded by its expansion.[23]

To complicate the situation, the Spirituals began to interpret their position in the light of the theology of history of Joachim of Fiore, the twelfth century Calabrian abbot who prophesied that an age of the Spirit would begin in 1260 and last to the end of the world.[24] In this age the ecclesiastical structures of the past would be superceded by the reign of the Spirit. Joachim prophesied further that this age would be ushered in by a new Order, which would be contemplative and spiritual. This latter prophecy the Spirituals saw fulfilled in Francis and themselves as faithful followers of the primitive ideal. Joachim's influence reached even the Franciscan General, John of Parma, who had been aligned with the Spirituals. This created an awkward situation, since Joachim's thought was considered heretical, having been condemned by the Fourth Lateran Council and by Alexander IV in 1255 in his condemnation of the *Liber introductorius in evangelium aeternum* of the Friar Gerard of Borgo San Donnino. This same pope secretly ordered John of Parma to resign his office of General. Because he was highly respected by the Order, he was asked at the chapter in Rome to name his successor. Salimbene gives the following account: "Those who had responsibility for the election, seeing his anguish of soul, said to him reluctantly: 'Father, you have made visitations of the Order and you know how the friars live and what they are. Show us one suitable friar to whom this Office should be entrusted, show us who should succeed you.' John of Parma immediately named Brother Bonaventure of Bagnoregio and said that he knew no one in the Order better than he. Immediately all agreed upon him and he was elected."[25] After being chosen General, Bonaventure found himself in the awkward position of having to participate in the trial of John of Parma, his predecessor and friend. The picture of the trial that has come down to us is not clear since the only account we have is by Angelo Clareno, whose reporting reflects his allegiance as a Spiritual and Joachite.[26]

Through his years as Minister General, Bonaventure had to deal with problems arising from the tension between the Spirituals and those who favored adaptation. While attempting to remain faithful to the spirit of Francis, he pursued policies that established the Order along institutional lines.[27] In interpreting the Rule in general, and specifically in matters of poverty, he allowed for adaptation and evolution that would harmonize with the expansion of the Order. Having been trained at the University of Paris, he himself saw no incompatibility between learning and the simplicity of Francis. As Minister General he fostered the traditions of learning: in his interpretation of the Rule, in his own lecturing and writing, and in his cultivation of centers of study, for example, the Couvent des Cordeliers at Paris. Although he was highly respected by all for his holiness, his policies naturally fell under the criticism of the Spirituals. Yet through his personal sanctity and his gifts of reconciliation, he was able to prevent a rupture within the Order and to develop a workable rapprochement between the primitive ideal and the necessities of organic development.

Two and a half years after his election, in October 1259, he retired to La Verna, the mountain where Francis had received the stigmata, in search of peace and contemplation. While meditating there, he had an extraordinary insight into the symbolic meaning of the vision Francis had at the time he received the stigmata: the vision of the six-winged Seraph in the form of the crucified. This insight he developed in detail in the *Itinerarium mentis in Deum*.[28] This experience at La Verna made a profound impression on him and marked a new direction in his writing. From this time on his writings reflect a greater integration of Franciscan elements with the content and form of the scholastic tradition he had received at the University of Paris. After La Verna the mystical dimensions of his thought emerge more clearly and symbols play a greater role in his style. In the next several years he wrote a number of mystical and spiritual treatises: *Lignum vitae, De triplici via, Soliloquium, De perfectione vitae ad sorores*. Shortly after his La Verna experience, he was commissioned by the chapter of Narbonne to write a new biography of Francis in order to settle the controversy in the Order arising from several different and even conflicting biographies. To gather material he traveled in Italy, visiting the scenes of Francis' life and interviewing his original companions. Out of this research he produced the *Legenda major* and the *Legenda minor*, which he presented to the Order. These were accepted as the official biographies; by a decree of the chapter of Paris in 1266, all other lives of Francis were ordered to be destroyed.[29]

CONTROVERSY, CARDINALATE, COUNCIL

Not all of Bonaventure's concerns were over internal matters within the Order. In 1269 the old controversy against the mendicants flared up again with an attack by Master Gerard of Abbeville. Bonaventure responded with a refutation entitled *Apologia pauperum*. Before this Bonaventure had become involved in another problem which would grow into the major controversy of the last years of his life. While residing at Mantes-sur-Seine, Bonaventure kept in close contact with Paris, frequently preaching at the University, where certain philosophical and theological

problems were disturbing the faculty and students. Aristotelianism had made a continuous inroad in the teaching of the faculty of
arts, where there emerged a certain radical Aristotelianism supported by the interpretations of the Islamic philosopher Averroes.[30]
The adherents of this radical Aristotelianism taught positions in
philosophy that seemed clearly incompatible with the Christian
faith: such as, the eternity of the world and the denial of personal immortality. Against this growing Latin Averroism, as it
has come to be called, Bonaventure began to launch an attack in
two Lenten series of lectures delivered at the University of Paris:
on the Ten Commandments in 1267 and on the gifts of the Holy
Spirit in 1268. Bonaventure's strategy was to attack this radical
Aristotelianism in the light of his Neo-Platonic synthesis of
Augustine, the Pseudo-Dionysius, and certain Franciscan themes.
In contrast, Thomas Aquinas also refuted this radical Aristotelianism, but in the light of his own Aristotelian synthesis. Bonaventure's attack on the new trends reached its peak in the *Collationes
in Hexaemeron,* a series of twenty-three lectures delivered at
the University during April and May 1273. Although this series
has a sharply focused polemic thrust, it is, in fact, Bonaventure's
final *summa,* which is remarkable for the intricacy of its structure,
the power of its imagery and rhetoric, and its mature synthesis
of his scholasticism and Franciscanism. It is Bonaventure's crowning work and, from many points of view, his finest intellectual
achievement.

   This series of lectures was never completed. On May 28 he
received at Paris the news that Pope Gregory X had named him
cardinal bishop of Albano. Although Bonaventure had previously
refused an appointment by Pope Clement IV to the archbishopric
of York, this time the pressures were sufficiently strong for him to
accept. He set out immediately to meet the Pope in Italy and
received the cardinal's hat in the convent of Mugello, near Florence. With the Pope he proceeded to Lyons in order to prepare
for the Second Council of Lyons which was to convene in May
of the following year. At Lyons Bonaventure was consecrated

bishop on November 11, 1273. He continued as Minister General of the Order until after the opening of the Council of Lyons, when on Pentecost, May 19, a chapter was held at Lyons at which Bonaventure resigned and Jerome of Auscoli, who later became Pope Nicholas IV, was elected as his successor.

Bonaventure took an active part in the preparation of the Council and in its execution.[31] Pope Gregory had created Bonaventure cardinal in order to have him as his personal advisor in matters pertaining to the Council. According to the Pope's design, the Council had three major items on its agenda: the liberation of the Holy Land through a crusade, the union of the Greeks and the Latins, and the reform of the Church. In the matter of Church reform, Bonaventure played an important role, working on the constitution *Religionum diversitas*. In the reunion of the Greeks and Latins, Bonaventure had chosen, at Gregory's bidding, a legation composed of Franciscans to travel to Constantinople and negotiate the sending of a Greek representation to the Council. At the Council itself, Bonaventure preached at an extraordinary session on May 28, when it was officially announced that the Greeks were sending delegates. After their arrival on June 24, he preached again at the solemn ecumenical ceremony on June 29 which signaled the tenuous reunion of the East and the West. Neither of these sermons is now extant. Although it has been said that Bonaventure presided over the Council, this is highly unlikely since the Pope himself was present. It is probable, however, that Bonaventure presided over several meetings between the Greek delegates and the Latins.

In the midst of these labors, Bonaventure died on Sunday, July 15, just two days before the termination of the Council. He was buried on the same day at the Franciscan church in Lyons, in the presence of the Pope, the cardinals, and prelates of the Council. The scene is recorded by a chronicler as follows: "Greeks and Latins, clergy and laity, followed his bier with bitter tears, grieving over the lamentable loss of so great a person."[32] The next day when opening the fifth session of the Council, the

Pope spoke of the great loss sustained by the Church in the death of Bonaventure, and out of gratitude for all his labors, ordered all priests and prelates throughout the world to offer Mass for the repose of his soul. Two centuries later Bonaventure was canonized, on April 14, 1482, by Pope Sixtus IV; and a century after that, on March 14, 1588, he was declared a Doctor of the Universal Church by Pope Sixtus V, with the title "Doctor Seraphicus."[33]

If we scan Bonaventure's life, we see that a single theme permeates the whole, both his personal life and his public career. Bonaventure was a man of peace — but a peace acquired not through inactivity, but through the creative integration of opposites. He was a man *in whom* polarities were reconciled and *through whom* they were reconciled in others. His life embodied many forms of the coincidence of opposites. He united the simplicity of Assisi with the sophistication of the University of Paris, the mystical contemplation of La Verna with the ecclesiastical politics of the Council of Lyons. He combined the humility of a friar with the dignity of a cardinal, the speculation of a theologian with the practicality of an administrator, a high degree of sanctity with the most technical learning of his time. His writings reflect the same coincidence of opposites; they include mystical works as well as scholastic treatises, and works that combine the two. In the controversies that spanned his intellectual career, he attempted to bring together disparate camps: the secular masters and the mendicants, Platonists and Aristotelians, Joachites and traditional eschatologists. Within the Franciscan Order he emerged as the leader who through his own integration of sanctity and learning, of mysticism and practicality, was able to maintain unity within the Order and guide it in a direction that would preserve the primitive ideal while adapting to the practical necessities of change and evolution. He was able to hold together the Spirituals and the moderates and to unite the ideal of Francis with changing circumstances in the area of poverty, study, and the interpretation of the Rule. The same spirit of reconciliation animated his work for the Church as a whole, as is seen during the final months of his life in his efforts to bring about the union of the East and the West at the Council of Lyons.

STRUCTURE OF BONAVENTURE'S THOUGHT

The same coincidence of opposites that permeates Bonaventure's life is found throughout his thought. This is true both of the diverse traditions he brought together in his system and also of the system itself. As a medieval synthesizer, Bonaventure attempted to unite the Patristic tradition with the scholasticism of the Middle Ages. Even in dealing with the past, he drew together a number of diverse strands. He united the East and the West by integrating Augustinianism with the theology of the Greek Fathers that was channeled into the West through the Pseudo-Dionysius. This complex integration of earlier traditions he blended with the new Franciscanism of his own era. On the philosophical level, he attempted to integrate the Platonism of the Fathers with the Aristotelianism of the scholastics. In the theology of history he tried to unite the classical Augustinian vision with the problematic eschatology of Joachim of Fiore. The way in which he brought these diverse strands together was through the coincidence of opposites. Bonaventure's thought is organized around three dominant themes: the Trinity, Christ, and the reflection of God in the universe. All three of these themes contain as their inner logic the coincidence of opposites, which also unites them among themselves. In the following section we will explore the general outlines of Bonaventure's thought, observing how these three themes provide the architectonic design of his synthesis. Throughout the remainder of the book we will analyze these three themes according to the coincidence of opposites in order to reveal the all-pervasive logic of Bonaventure's thought.

Perhaps the best way to view Bonaventure's synthesis is to compare it to a Gothic cathedral. Much of his building materials he received from the past, chiefly from Augustine and the Pseudo-Dionysius. He drew philosophical elements from Platonism, Neo-

Platonism, and the new resources of Aristotle.[34] As a thirteenth century synthesizer, he shaped this material into an integral whole, using the tools of scholastic logic and the architectonic design of the *Commentary on the Sentences* and the *summa,* which his teacher Alexander of Hales was so instrumental in developing. He produced an intellectual edifice resembling the great Gothic cathedrals of the same period — for example, Notre Dame of Paris, Rheims, Chartres — in its lofty thrust, its interlocked design, and its rich complexity. But we notice immediately that this edifice reflects the spirit of Francis of Assisi. Bonaventure had captured the simplicity of Francis and had restructured it, while preserving its authenticity, in the sweeping grandeur of his intellectual edifice. The Franciscan experience provides not only a spirit permeating the whole, but also essential elements in the design that give distinctive contours to Bonaventure's structure.

Bonaventure drew his doctrine of God from sources that go back to the Greek Fathers. Following the Greek tradition, his doctrine of God is dynamic and emphatically Trinitarian, with the Father seen as the source of dynamism and unity in the Godhead. Unlike the Augustinian tradition in the West, Bonaventure does not make a sharp distinction between the divine nature and the Trinity. Consequently he is able to draw a continuous line from the dynamism of the Father to creation. From the Pseudo-Dionysius came the central emphasis on emanation and the notion that the good is self-diffusive. This strong, dynamic, Trinitarian emanationism is the foundational element in Bonaventure's system, providing the base for the doctrine of exemplarism, according to which the entire created universe reflects the Trinity. Exemplarism is the characteristic doctrine of Bonaventure's synthesis and the most systematically elaborated. With roots both in the Greek Fathers and in Augustine, Bonaventure's exemplarism is articulated chiefly according to the latter's formulation of the divine ideas and the world as a vestige of the Trinity.

While Bonaventure's doctrine of God was derived chiefly from the Greek tradition, his doctrine of man was taken from Augustine.

Viewing man as the image of God, Bonaventure articulated his position through the Augustinian inner way and the analysis of man's faculties of memory, understanding, and will. His doctrine is based explicitly on Augustine's texts, although it reflects in a generic way the Greek Fathers' doctrine of man as image of God. Bonaventure followed Augustine in his analysis of human psychological experience, penetrating through various levels until he reached the reflection of God in the depths of the soul. However, he did not follow Augustine in the path of personal autobiography recorded in *The Confessions,* but rather in the more structural psychological analysis of the *De Trinitate,* which is reflected in the third chapter of Bonaventure's *Itinerarium,* with its analysis of the memory, understanding, and will as an image of the Trinity.[35]

Bonaventure drew from Augustine not only for his doctrine of man as image of God, but also for his doctrine of the world as vestige of the Trinity.[36] By reflecting the divine power, wisdom and goodness, all creatures are vestiges of the Father, Son, and Holy Spirit. Although he drew his formulation from Augustine, he was articulating a different religious experience. Augustine's experience centered on individual subjectivity, on the soul as image of God, on the inward journey to discover God in the depths of the psyche. Augustine's writings do not express a strong cosmic sense, nor a sustained consciousness of the presence of God in the material world. This is undoubtedly due to many factors, one of which is very likely the lingering influence of his early Manichaeism. In sharp contrast, Francis of Assisi was in tune with the entire cosmos; he took great joy in creation and sensed God's presence throughout nature. With Francis, Bonaventure was conscious of God's creatures, and contemplated the reflection of God across the vast expanse of the universe.[37] When he drew from the exemplarism of the Greek Fathers and Augustine, it was to give a philosophical-theological articulation of this Franciscan religious experience. In so doing, he made exemplarism the focal point of his entire system. All other elements — the emanation of the Greek Fathers and the image doctrine of Augustine — were shaped

Exemplarism ?

in such a way as to highlight exemplarism and to support the Franciscan religious experience.

FRANCISCAN RELIGIOUS EXPERIENCE

We can compare the Franciscan experience of God's reflection in the universe to the experience one has within a Gothic cathedral. The sunlight pours through the great stained glass windows in a brilliant array of colors. The cathedral is illumined with blues, reds, greens, yellows in intricate designs — a kaleidoscope of colors and forms. The circular rose windows and the vaulted windows of the nave and apse become aglow with a riot of colors that are at the same time as harmonious as a symphony. In a similar way Francis saw God reflected in creatures: in brother sun and sister moon, in brother fire and sister water, in the power of the wolf and the gentleness of the dove. The fecundity of God is revealed in the variety of creatures — from the grandeur of the heavens to the simplicity of a fly. The pure rays of the divinity penetrate into the universe, which acts as a prism refracting the light into a myriad of colors.[38]

The spirit of Francis' *Canticle of Brother Sun* is captured in Bonaventure's *Itinerarium mentis in Deum,* which is a systematic contemplation on the reflection of God throughout the universe and in human experience. No other writer in the Middle Ages has expressed so profoundly God's splendor shining through creatures. This is the dominant and all-pervasive theme in Bonaventure's writings, which he expresses in a wealth of poetic and mystical imagery, as well as metaphysical and theological concepts. For example, in the following passage from the *Collationes in Hexaemeron,* he uses a cluster of images, including that of light shining through a window:

> . . . the entire world is a shadow, a road, a vestige, and it is also 'a book written without' [Ez. 2:9; Ap. 5:1]. For in every creature there is a shining forth of the divine exemplar, but mixed with darkness. Hence creatures are a kind of darkness mixed with light. Also they are a road leading to the exemplar. Just as you see that a ray of light

entering through a window is colored in different ways according to
the different colors of the various parts, so the divine ray shines forth
in each and every creature in different ways and in different properties;
it is said in Wisdom: 'In her ways she shows herself' [Wis. 6:17].
Also creatures are a vestige of the wisdom of God. Hence creatures are
like a kind of representation and statue of the wisdom of God. And in
view of all of this, they are a kind of book written without.[39]

Not only does Bonaventure use luxuriant poetic and mystical
images to express this theme, but he reserves for it some of his
most forceful rhetoric. For example, the following passage appears
in the *Itinerarium* immediately after his contemplation of God in
the sevenfold characteristics of creatures:

> Therefore, whoever is not enlightened by such great splendor in created
> things is blind; whoever remains unheedful of such great outcries is
> deaf; whoever does not praise God all these effects is dumb; whoever
> does not turn to the First Principle after so many signs is a fool. Open
> your eyes, therefore; alert the ears of your spirit, unlock your lips
> and apply your heart that you may see, hear, praise, love and adore,
> magnify and honor your God in every creature, lest perchance, the
> entire universe rise against you.[40]

To share this vision of Bonaventure, we must enter the religious
experience of Francis; otherwise we would remain, as it were,
outside the Gothic cathedral, looking merely at the exterior of
the stained glass windows. We would see only the abstract design
on a drab and utterly uninteresting surface — without a hint
of the warmth and dazzling colors within. This has often happened to Bonaventure. Coming upon him for the first time,
some have read him from the outside, and found him dry and
abstract like the exterior of the stained glass windows. As in the
case of the cathedral, if we enter within, then everything is transformed. If we enter into the Franciscan religious experience, then
his thought begins to glow with an interior radiance, and all the
complex elements in its structure can be seen to support this
experience. Just as the interior of the cathedral is shaped by the
gigantic pillars and soaring arches within and supported by the
flying buttresses without, so Bonaventure has constructed a lofty
theological edifice from materials supplied by Augustine and the

Pseudo-Dionysius and has strengthened it by the buttresses of Platonism and Aristotelianism.

But we can view a Gothic cathedral from many points of view. For example, we can be moved by the sacred atmosphere within and the warmth of the colors of the stained glass windows. Or we can study certain structural elements in their limited functions, such as the arches within and the flying buttresses without. Or we can leave the cathedral, withdraw some distance and view the design of the whole, grasping in a single glance the contours of the towers, the facade, and the total mass of the building. It is important to withdraw and view the overall design of the whole, otherwise we would have only a limited and even distorted view of the cathedral. In the case of Bonaventure, if we remained within the glow of the Franciscan religious experience at the interior of his thought, we might interpret him exclusively as a spiritual writer and mystical theologian who gave articulation to the religious experience of his founder. On the other hand, if we were to examine some of the structural supports in isolation, we might interpret him exclusively as a philosopher — a Platonist or Aristotelian — without seeing these elements in the overarching theological design that gives them significance. For Bonaventure, as for his medieval contemporaries, the basic architectural framework of his system was theological.

The primacy of theology in the design of Bonaventure's synthesis has been widely acknowledged; yet in practice it has been obscured by two tendencies. At times scholars have extracted philosophical elements and studied them in isolation from the theological context that shapes their meaning. Such a procedure would do violence to any medieval theologian, but especially to Bonaventure, who has built philosophy and theology into a closely interlocked structure. Others have not fallen into this trap but have examined philosophical elements against the background of Bonaventure's theology. Yet their emphasis has kept his theology precisely in the background, allowing its contours to remain vague, without the sharp delineation their importance deserves.

The rise of neo-scholasticism in the late nineteenth and early twentieth centuries — with its strong emphasis on medieval philosophy — gave great impetus to these two tendencies. To counteract these tendencies, one must back away, as it were, and view Bonaventure's thought as a whole — on its own terms, with its own structure, and with its own distinctive outlines. We must withdraw and observe from a distance, where we can grasp the master design and discern the contours of the whole.

THE TWO TOWERS OF THE CATHEDRAL

When we do this, the outlines of Bonaventure's thought become clear. We observe that theology provides his unifying theme, and further that his theology has a distinctive design. In his theology two elements stand out sharply — like the towers of a Gothic cathedral — giving the ultimate shape to the whole. These two elements are his Trinitarian theology and Christocentricity. In his doctrine of the Trinity and of the centrality of Christ, Bonaventure's thought reaches its culmination and achieves its distinctive design.

Yet if we look more closely, we will observe that these two towers are not symmetrical as are, for example, the towers of Notre Dame of Paris. Rather they are like the towers of Chartres, developed in different periods and reflecting diverse styles. The design of Bonaventure's Trinitarian theology was present from the beginning, from his writing of the *Commentary on the Sentences*. It was inherited from his teacher Alexander of Hales and from the Victorines, who, in turn, received it from the Pseudo-Dionysius and ultimately from the tradition of the Greek Fathers. Even from the beginning Bonaventure's Trinitarian theology was systematic, self-reflective, and intricately elaborated.

On the other hand, his Christocentricity emerged gradually, from Bonaventure's Franciscan roots. Latent in the early period, it reached self-consciousness in his meditation on Francis' vision at La Verna and concrete literary form in the *Itinerarium*. It reached its highest development in the *Collationes in Hexaemeron*.

Yet, unlike Chartres, this tower is left unfinished. The foundations, the design, and even the beginnings of the superstructure are there; but they lack the systematic analysis and critical self-reflection that is characteristic of his Trinitarian theology.

If we study these two towers, we will grasp the distinctive lines of Bonaventure's theological superstructure. In this comprehensive design, we will observe how the other elements of this thought are shaped to perform their distinctive functions within a unified whole. We will see how this design harmonizes with his Franciscan religious experience and how it gives it a foundation and an ultimate expression. The dynamic Trinity is the source of exemplarism; for as the Son expresses the Father, so creation expresses the Son and is rooted in the power and unity of the Father. Furthermore, the exemplaristic universe reaches its culmination in the Incarnation and the mystery of Christ as the center of creation. As expressing God, all of creation strives towards the maximum expression which is realized in Christ. Under these two mysteries of divine expressionism, all other aspects of Bonaventure's thought are subsumed: his doctrine of creation, his notion of man as image of God and the world as vestige, his Platonism and his Aristotelianism, and his adaptation of the eschatology of Joachim of Fiore.

I believe that the best way to present Bonaventure's thought is through this overarching design since the unity of his vision can be maintained throughout. Furthermore, in studying these two poles, we can discern the evolution of Bonaventure's thought — an evolution which does not alter its unity, but rather fulfills it. The Trinitarian pole reflects his anchoring in the theological tradition, and the Christocentric pole reflects the emergence of a new consciousness of the mystery of Christ on the part of the Christian community. Emphasizing the humanity of Jesus in his passion and as the center of the universe, this new consciousness was germinating for centuries in the spirit of Western Europe. In the personality of Francis, it reached a remarkable embodiment; and in the course of Bonaventure's life, it emerged gradual-

ly into awareness until it became the second tower giving final
balance and harmony to his theological system.

In dealing with the evolution of Bonaventure's thought, we will
divide his writings into three periods: The first period, during
his teaching years at Paris from 1248 to 1257, reflects the academic-
scholastic world of the University. Here we will concentrate on
the *Commentary on the Sentences,* the disputed questions *De
mysterio Trinitatis,* and the *Breviloquium.* In the second period,
from 1257 to 1267, Bonaventure composed his mystical works.
Here we will draw chiefly from the *Itinerarium* and the *Lignum
vitae.* In the final period, 1267–1273, he was engaged in controversies through his three series of *collationes.* Our chief focus
of attention here will be the final series, the *Collationes in
Hexaemeron.*

TRINITARIAN DESIGN

Even in the first period, during Bonaventure's teaching years
at the University of Paris, 1248–1257, his Trinitarian theology is
found in its essential features. As early as the *Commentary on
the Sentences* (1250–1252), the basic elements are present and
systematically developed. Aspects of his teaching on the Trinity
are elaborated in greater detail in the disputed questions *De
Trinitate* and *De scientia Christi* (both in 1254). In the *Breviloquium* (1254–1257), which draws this period to a completion, the
Trinitarian theology is again integrated in a *summa* structure,
similar to that of the *Commentary.* Although reflecting the refinement of the intervening years, the design of the doctrine remains
substantially that of the *Commentary.*[41]

This Trinitarian design contains the following elements: (1)
The Trinity is conceived according to the Greek model and not
the Latin model. Like the Greek Fathers, Bonaventure focuses on
the Father as dynamic source and not on the persons as relations
as Augustine had done. Bonaventure also integrated the Latin
or Augustinian model of the Trinity into his thought, but it always remained subordinated to the Greek model. (2) The Trini-

tarian processions, then, are seen as the expression of the Father's fecundity. In this perspective, Bonaventure developed a highly elaborated doctrine of the generation of the Son, as Image and Word of the Father. (3) Bonaventure makes a self-conscious link between the Trinity and creation. The world issues ultimately from the fecundity of the Trinity and reflects the Trinity, according to various categories of representation: vestige, image, similitude. (4) This Trinitarian theology is the basis for Bonaventure's spirituality, in which the soul as image of the Trinity returns to its Trinitarian source.[42]

FATHER AS "FONTALIS PLENITUDO"

Bonaventure's characteristic notion of God is that of dynamic and fecund source. This fecundity is realized not only in God's act of creation, but within his inner Trinitarian life. Hence the mystery of the Trinity is seen precisely as the mystery of the divine fecundity rooted in the Father as source. This basic element in Bonaventure's Trinitarian design is present at the very beginning of the early period. In the second distinction of the *Commentary on the Sentences,* Bonaventure relates fecundity not only to the divine nature but to the Trinity itself.[43] According to Bonaventure, supreme happiness, perfection, simplicity, and primacy all demand that there be a plurality of persons in God. At the base of these reflections is the notion of self-diffusive, self-transcending, self-communicating love that Bonaventure inherited from Richard of St. Victor and the Pseudo-Dionysius.[44] In his fourth point, namely primacy, Bonaventure makes the formal connection between self-diffusive fecundity and the person of the Father, although this connection is understood also in the case of happiness, perfection, and simplicity. He writes of primacy:

. . . but the more primary a thing is, the more it is fecund and the principle of others. Therefore just as the divine essence, because it is first, is the principle of other essences, so the person of the Father, since he is the first, because from no one, is the principle and has fecundity in regard to persons.[45]

Later, in distinction 27 of the first book of the *Commentary*, Bonaventure deals with the fecundity of the Father in greater detail.[46] He analyzes the Father's personal property of *innascibilitas,* which means that the Father cannot be begotten nor proceed from another. Bonaventure claims that *innascibilitas* has both a negative and a positive meaning. Negatively it indicates a lack of source; but positively it indicates fecundity. Once again he applied the principle, which this time he cites from Aristotle.[47] The more primary the principles are, the more powerful or fecund they are. Therefore the Father, as absolutely primary, is absolutely fecund. Bonaventure refers to this absolute fecundity of the Father as *fontalis plenitudo,* or fountain-fullness. This focusing on the Father as fecund source situates Bonaventure within the tradition of the Greek Fathers, who called the Father the *pyge,* the primordial fountain-spring of the divinity.[48]

Thus in the first book of the *Commentary on the Sentences,* we see Bonaventure's characteristic Trinitarian theology: dynamic fecundity associated with the inner Trinitarian life and grounded in the person of the Father. This design is not only present, but is highly self-conscious and analyzed with a precision that will not be equaled in his later works. Undoubtedly his Trinitarian theology was highly developed so early in his career because he had inherited an ancient tradition. Stemming from the Greek Fathers, this tradition reached Bonaventure in a highly developed form, with distinctly Western embellishments made by the Victorines and his teacher Alexander of Hales. To this tradition Bonaventure made his own creative contributions, but these are visible at the outset and do not show a significant growth.

In the other writings of his early period, Bonaventure's basic Trinitarian design is present in various ways. In the disputed questions *De scientia Christi,* the notion of Father as fecund source remains largely a silent presupposition behind the explicit issues, which deal with the Word in relation to the world. In the disputed questions *De mysterio Trinitatis,* Bonaventure treats the themes of fecundity and primacy explicitly and at considerable length. Finally in the *Breviloquium,* he sketches this basic Trinitarian design with remarkable consciousness and clarity.[49]

In his later writings Bonaventure will not change or substantially develop his dynamic view of the Trinity, based on the Father as *fontalis plenitudo.* His Trinitarian synthesis of Chapter 6 of the *Itinerarium* (1259) presents the same view with a remarkable blend of compactness and complexity.[50] Yet even here his basic position is not more self-conscious than in the *Commentary.* In fact, the notion of primacy is not explicitly mentioned, nor does he speak of the Father's *fontalis plenitudo.* Rather the mystery of Trinitarian fecundity is presented through the Pseudo-Dionysian notion of the good as self-diffusive. This notion of the self-diffusive good is the basis for his exploration of the Trinity in *Collatio XI in Hexaemeron* (1273).[51] In the later writings one can detect a shift from the notion of primacy and *fontalis plenitudo* to the notion of self-diffusive good. If one holds, as does this writer, that the notion of primacy and the Father as *fontalis plenitudo* are prior to the notion of self-diffusive good, then he can say that the basis of Bonaventure's Trinitarian theology was more thoroughly explored in his earlier than in his later writings.

SON AS IMAGE AND WORD

The second element in Bonaventure's Trinitarian theology consists in the dynamic Trinitarian processions, with special focus on the generation of the Son as Image and Word. This element derives directly from the *fontalis plenitudo* of the Father. Because the Father is the fecund source — the good that is absolutely self-diffusive — he expresses his fecundity absolutely in the generation of the Son and the spiration of the Holy Spirit. Thus the divine fecundity is realized in an absolute way within the inner life of the Trinity. This frees God's fecundity from dependence on the world, since God does not have to create in order to realize his fecundity. Bonaventure's position has profound theological and metaphysical implications, for it allows for a transcendent

God who is not static or removed from the world. His transcendence consists precisely in his dynamic self-communication,
but this self-communication is realized fully only at the heart of
the divinity itself. His is a fecundity that breaks the bounds of
all limitations and realizes itself adequately only in the generation of the Word and the spiration of the Holy Spirit. Thus
God's fecundity does not have to be fitted on the Procrustean
bed of creation. At the same time, his transcendent fecundity is
the wellspring of creation and of his immanence in the world.
The problem of how to balance God's fecundity, his transcendence,
and his immanence has throughout the history of thought plagued
such thinkers as Plotinus, Avicenna, Hegel, and Whitehead. By
seeing transcendence itself as fecundity and by situating fecundity
within the Trinity, Bonaventure has safeguarded God's transcendence and at the same time has provided a solid basis for
God's immanence in the world.[52]

That the divine fecundity is fully expressed in the Trinitarian
processions is stated early in Bonaventure's writings, for example,
in the first book of the *Commentary*:

> It can nevertheless be said . . . that the Father's power is manifested
> in the production of the Word, and consequently the entire divine
> power, since the power of the Son and the Holy Spirit is one and they
> are equal in power.[53]

Bonaventure develops this theme in great detail in the disputed
questions *De mysterio Trinitatis.* In dealing with problems over
infinity and the Trinity, Bonaventure states in several ways that
the divine fecundity is perfectly expressed in the Trinitarian
processions.[54] Later, in the *Itinerarium,* he will state this point
more forcefully; yet the position itself will remain essentially
the same as found in the earlier writings. In the *Itinerarium* he
proceeds by stating that God must be self-diffusive in the highest
degree. This means that there must be within the divinity
Trinitarian processions, since no other diffusion would meet the
demands of maximum self-diffusion. Bonaventure writes:

For the diffusion that occurred in time in the creation of the world
is no more than a pivot or point in comparison with the immense
sweep of the eternal goodness. From this one is led to think of another
and a greater diffusion — that in which the diffusing good communicates to another his whole substance and nature.[55]

The boundless fecundity of the Father expresses itself in the
generation of the Son, as Image and Word. This is the focal point
of Bonaventure's entire theology. It was in treating the generation of the Son that Bonaventure made his famous observation:
"This is our whole metaphysics: emanation, exemplarity, consummation."[56] It is in the Son that the fecundity of the Father
finds its perfect Image; and it is from the Son, as Word, that all
creation issues, and it is to him, as exemplar, that it reflects back
and returns. In his early writings Bonaventure develops these
themes in great depth and detail. Throughout the Trinitarian
sections of the *Commentary,* Bonaventure discusses the Son as
perfect Image and the most expressive Word of the Father.[57] In
the disputed questions *De mysterio Trinitatis,* he states a theme
that will occur often in his later writings:

> The Father . . . generates the Word, which is the Father's likeness
> equal to him in all things. Hence just as the Father in understanding
> himself understands whatever he can understand, so in speaking the
> Word, he says whatever he can say and whatever can be said in the
> deity. Hence neither he nor any other of the persons in the Trinity,
> has another word to say in view of the fact that in that Word was
> said whatever can be said.[58]

The Son is the complete and adequate expression of the Father,
his first and final Word. In the Son the Father expresses himself
and all he can make. This position requires a doctrine of the
divine ideas and their relation both to the Word and to creatures.
This doctrine is developed with great precision in the *Commentary*
and in the disputed questions *De scientia Christi* and becomes the
matrix of all of his later writings.[59]

TRINITY AND CREATION

As we have just seen, we cannot discuss Bonaventure's doctrine
of the Word without touching the relation of the Word to crea-

tion. Yet it is wise to draw this point into sharper focus. The connection between the Trinity and creation cannot be over-stressed since it is the cornerstone of Bonaventure's entire world view. It is why he sees universal exemplarism and vestiges of the Trinity everywhere. For Bonaventure creation is not a mere external act of God, a making of an object on the fringe of the divine power. Rather creation is rooted in the fecundity of the inner Trinitarian life. True, the divine fecundity cannot express itself adequately in finite creation; yet in generating the Word as adequate Image of himself, the Father expresses in the Word all that he can make. The act of creation *ad extra* — while remain-ing free and not dependent on creatures — springs ultimately from the eternal fecundity of the Father and is an overflow of that fecundity. This connection between the Trinity and creation is already quite self-conscious in Bonaventure's early writings. For example, we find a sharp formulation in the disputed ques-tions *De mysterio Trinitatis* where he speaks of two types of *fontalitas,* or dynamic source of production: one at the source of the Trinitarian processions and the other at the source of crea-tion. For Bonaventure the prior is the root of the latter:

> But this *fontalitas* is in a certain way the source of another *fontalitas.* Because the Father produces the Son and through the Son and with the Son produces the Holy Spirit, therefore God the Father through the Son with the Holy Spirit is the principle of all creatures. For unless he produced them from eternity, he could not through them produce in time.[60]

By connecting the Trinitarian processions with creation, Bona-venture provides the background for the vestige-image doctrine which he develops so richly in the *Itinerarium* and the *Collationes in Hexaemeron.* All of the finite world of creation reflects the power, wisdom, and goodness of God and hence is a vestige of the Trinity. Rational creatures reflect God in a special way since they have him as their object; they are also images of the Trinity in their memory, intelligence, and will. Although the panorama of creation as vestige-image is sketched in striking colors in Bonaventure's later writing, the elements of the doctrine are sharply analyzed in his early period. The classical source for Bonaventure's divisions on this point is found in the first book of the *Commentary*.[61] Here Bonaventure distinguishes *umbra, vestigium,* and *imago* according to: (1) the manner of representing God, whether from a distance and obscurely or from near at hand and distinctly; (2) the aspect of God that is involved, whether as general cause, or as efficient, formal, and final cause, or as the object of the memory, understanding, and will; (3) whether general aspects of God are grasped or personal properties; (4) the classes of creatures, namely, all creatures reflect God as cause and as triple cause, but only rational creatures have God as object. This division, which is merely summarized here, is remarkably precise and can be used to answer questions of interpretation that arise over passages in the later writings, e.g., in the *Itinerarium* or the *Collationes in Hexaemeron.*

This exemplaristic Trinitarian vision forms the context for Bonaventure's spirituality. In *Collatio I in Hexaemeron,* he describes his vision as: creation emanating from the Word, reflecting the Word, and returning to the Word — and through the Word to the Father.[62] In the disputed questions *De mysterio Trinitatis,* he expresses the same vision. Although the stages of the soul's ascent are not sketched out so systematically as in the *Itinerarium,* the generic outlines of the vision are present:

> Hence this alone is eternal life: that the rational spirit, which flows from the most blessed Trinity and is an image of the Trinity, return by way of an intelligible circle by memory, understanding, and will, through divine likeness of glory to the most blessed Trinity.[63]

This brings to a close our treatment of the Trinitarian pole of Bonaventure's theology. As we suggested in the beginning, his Trinitarian theology stands like the tower of a Gothic cathedral, giving distinctive shape to the contours of his thought. The Trinitarian pole reveals the following design: At the base is the notion of the Father as *fontalis plenitudo,* from whose fecundity the Trinitarian processions flow as the absolute expression of the

self-diffusive fullness of the divinity. Creation is an overflow of
this goodness and has its roots within the dynamism of the Trinitarian life. The world, then, reflects its archetype as Trinitarian
vestige. As images of the Trinity, rational creatures have God as
their object and are in a process of return to their divine source.
This design was present from the outset of Bonaventure's writings.
Although the Trinitarian theology of the later period shows the
marks of a mature mind, with enriched depth and complexity,
in his early writings the basic Trinitarian design is explored
in an analytic-critical manner that in certain areas is not equaled
later.

EVOLUTION OF CHRISTOCENTRICITY

In contrast with his Trinitarian theology, Bonaventure's
Christocentricity does not emerge into prominence until the
middle period, and then undergoes a development that reaches
its climax in the *Collationes in Hexaemeron.* In order not to
overstate our case, we must distinguish two dimensions of Bonaventure's Christocentricity: the Trinitarian and the Incarnational.
His doctrine of the Trinity itself contains a strong Christocentric
dimension, or it might be more accurate to say a strong Logos-
centered dimension. The Son is the center of the Trinity, the
persona media, the exemplar of all creation, the light illumining
human knowledge and the medium of man's return to the
Trinity.[64] We are not claiming that this Trinitarian dimension
emerged late or that it underwent a significant evolution. Since
this dimension is essential to the design of his Trinitarian theology,
we maintain that it was present and, in fact, was richly developed during the early period.

If, however, we shift our attention to the Incarnational dimension, we can detect an evolution. But again we must distinguish.
One dimension of Bonaventure's Christocentricity deals with the
hypostatic union as such and is concerned with the mystery of
Christ as the union of the divine and the human. The hypostatic union is explored as the basis of Christ's mediatorship be-

tween God and man and as the root of the doctrine of redemption. This dimension of Bonaventure's thought is, of course, developed extensively in his early writings, e.g., in the third book of the *Commentary on the Sentences,* in the *Breviloquium,* and in the disputed questions *De scientia Christi.*[65] This first dimension of Bonaventure's Incarnational Christocentricity forms the basis for the second dimension, which sees Christ as the dynamic center of the soul's journey into God, the center of the universe, and the center of history. It is this latter dimension that we claim emerged at the middle period, underwent a development, and reached its climax in the final period.

It is necessary to specify more precisely what we mean by the second dimension of Christocentricity. In this dimension Christ operates as a dynamic center — drawing into an integrated whole all the elements of the individual soul, of the physical universe, and of history. This dynamic center is the incarnate Christ in his concrete particularity, in the mystery of his humanity, involved in the process of transformation through death and resurrection. We can call this a *cosmic* Christocentricity since Christ is the center of the three major dimensions of the created cosmos: the soul, the physical universe, and history. All lines of the cosmos converge in Christ the center and through him are transformed and return to the Father. This cosmic Christocentricity presupposes the other two Christological poles — the Trinitarian Logos and the hypostatic union — and brings these to an integrated completion. The Trinitarian Logos-centricity is universalistic in the sense that the entire cosmos reflects the Logos. On the other hand, the mystery of the incarnate Logos is particularistic in the sense that it occurs in a particular place and time. Cosmic Christocentricity unites these two poles, for it is precisely the particularity of the historical Jesus that integrates into an organic and dynamic energy system the entire cosmos — the physical universe, history and the spiritual energies of mankind.

The dimension of cosmic Christocentricity is of paramount importance to the historian and systematic theologian. First, for the sake of clarity, since it is a distinctive dimension of Christology, it must be carefully distinguished from other dimensions. Secondly, cosmic Christocentricity is as ancient as the New Testament, appearing, for example. in the cosmic hymn of the letter to the Colossians.[66] In the twentieth century it has emerged in a new form in the evolutionary vision of Teilhard de Chardin. Throughout the intervening history it has been prominent in certain theologians and lacking in others. Thirdly, from a systematic point of view it can serve as a link between the universalistic and particularistic tension in Christology. In my opinion, cosmic Christocentricity always remains implicit as a necessary logical link between the universalistic and particularistic poles of Christology, and will tend to emerge in the thought of a theologian even if he is unconscious of its presence or resists its force. Hence, I believe, a number of tensions in theology both in the past and today can be clarified and in certain cases resolved through the dimension of cosmic Christocentricity. In this task Bonaventure's contributions can be especially helpful.

Cosmic Christocentricity emerges strikingly in the *Itinerarium*, the piece that ushers in the second period of Bonaventure's writings. Retiring to La Verna in 1259 for peace and spiritual renewal, Bonaventure meditated on Francis's vision of the six-winged Seraph.[67] In a flash he realized that the vision symbolized both the goal of the soul's ascent into God and the stages of its progress. For our concerns here, it is important to note that the vision is Christocentric (for the Seraph is in the form of the Crucified) and that the *Itinerarium* unfolds in a Christocentric perspective. For example, in the prologue, Bonaventure states that, in the soul's journey into God, the way is only through a most ardent love of the Crucified.[68] Later after presenting the tabernacle as a symbol of the soul, he meditates on Christ as the mercy seat at the center of the Holy of Holies, or the innermost chamber of the soul. In Chapters Six and Seven, he depicts Christ the center as the medium of the soul's passage into the seventh or mystical stage. Gazing on the mystery of Christ the center, we see united

in an extraordinary way cosmic opposites; and thus we are drawn
into the seventh stage, by seeing united "the first and the last,
the highest and the lowest, the circumference and the center, the
'Alpha and Omega,' the caused and the cause, the Creator and
the creature, that is, 'the book written within and without.' "[69]

The Christ of the *Itinerarium* is the center of the soul and the
center, the focal point, and the means of the soul's journey into
God. He is the center around which all the activities of the
soul are focused: sensation, memory, understanding, willing. It
is through Christ as center — as crucified, incarnate Logos —
that all our activities are led back to their root in the eternal
Logos. And it is through Christ the center — as goal and medium
of passage — that the soul progresses on its journey into God.
In the *Itinerarium* Christ can be considered as the center of the
universe as well as the center of the soul, since two of the wings
of the Seraph symbolize the material world. However, when
we analyze the *Itinerarium*, it becomes clear that the emphasis
is on Christ the center of the soul and not as center of the universe. And it is only by extending the journey of the soul to the
history of the universe that we can see in the *Itinerarium* Christ
as the center of history.[70]

The notion of Christ the center of the soul is developed in
great detail in the *Lignum vitae* (1260), written not long after
the *Itinerarium*. Christ crucified is depicted as the tree of life,
which branches out and blossoms in rich foliage, flowers, and
fruit, symbolizing the moral virtues. By meditating on the humanity of Christ and the events of his life, by learning from
him, and identifying with him, our souls can blossom forth in
the virtues of humility, piety, confidence, patience, constancy.[71]
Thus in the *Lignum vitae* Christ is the center of the moral life
of the soul, just as in the *Itinerarium* he had been depicted as the
center of the mystical life of the soul. In each case the Christocentricity is presented in a symbol: the six-winged Seraph and the
tree of life. By analyzing these symbols in great detail, Bonaventure draws the moral and mystical energies of the soul to focus

on Christ the center and through this centering to develop towards a rich and integrated spiritual life.

In the middle period, Bonaventure developed the theme of Christ the center of the soul. In the final period the emphasis shifted to Christ the center of the universe and history. In the *Collationes in Hexaemeron,* Bonaventure's crowning piece of the final period, his Christocentricity comes to full flowering and receives its strongest rhetorical expression. In the first of the *Collationes,* which serves as an overture of the entire series, Bonaventure develops the theme of Christ as universal center.[72] He is the center of all the sciences: metaphysics, physics, mathematics, logic, ethics, jurisprudence, and theology. The sciences study the entire expanse of reality — from the generation of the Son in the Trinity, through creation, to the return of creatures to the Father. On every level, Christ is the center: metaphysical center in his eternal generation, physical center in his incarnation, mathematical center in his passion, logical center in his resurrection, ethical center in his ascension, juridical center in the final judgment, and theological center in eternal beatitude. Although the notion of Christ the center of the soul is present within the *collatio,*[73] the emphasis here is on the panorama of the universe and the crucial events of salvation history.

It is interesting to compare this Christocentric vision with the panorama of the universe presented from the viewpoint of the Trinity in the *Itinerarium,* Chapter One, n. 14.[74] In the *Itinerarium* Bonaventure contemplates creation from seven vantage points and in each discerns the divine power, wisdom, and goodness manifested in creatures. Thus the treatment of the universe in the *Itinerarium* remains within the Trinitarian vestige pole of Bonaventure's thought and is not explicitly subsumed into the Christocentric pole, as is richly done in the first *Collatio in Hexaemeron.*

In the first *Collatio* Bonaventure depicts Christ as the center of both the universe and history. He is the center of history in the great events that shape salvation history: his incarnation,

crucifixion, resurrection, ascension, and judgment. This notion
of Christ the center of history unfolds as a basic theme throughout
the *Collationes* and plays an important role in Bonaventure's
eschatology. Ultimately the notion of Christ the center of history derives from the Trinitarian and the Incarnational dimensions of Bonaventure's thought. As Ratzinger says:

> It is precisely the figure of Jesus Christ, the middle person in the
> Trinity as well as the mediator and middle between God and man, who
> gradually becomes the synthesis of everything that is expressed for
> Bonaventure in the concept of center. Christ becomes the center. And
> as a consequence of this general interpretation of Christ from the no-
> tion of center, He becomes also the 'center of time.'[75]

Because Christ is the center of history, Bonaventure's notion
of time differs from that of Aristotle and the Joachites.[76] His
Trinitarian dimension of Christocentricity differentiates him
from Aristotle. For Bonaventure time is involved in the emanation and return of creatures. All things emanate through the
Logos and all things return through the Logos to the Father.
Since the Logos is the Alpha and the Omega, time must have
a beginning and an end. Hence the world cannot be eternal, as
Aristotle had held, nor is time merely the measure of motion in
an endless series of generation and corruption of forms.

While the Trinitarian dimension of his Christocentricity differentiates Bonaventure from Aristotle, it is chiefly the Incarnational dimension — developed into its cosmic Christocentric form
— that differentiates him from the Joachites. To explain the
ages of history the Joachites used a Trinitarian theory. After
the ages of the Father and of the Son, a third age will come —
the age of the Spirit, which will dissolve the forms of the previous
age and usher in a spiritual era. In contrast, for Bonaventure
Christ remains the middle person of the Trinity, the dynamic center of the Trinitarian processions. The Logos is completed, not
superseded in the Spirit. And as incarnate Logos, he is the center
through which the incarnational structures of history are not
dissolved, but transformed. Thus for Bonaventure the historical
process remains at its core Christocentric.

This brings to a close our brief survey of the Christocentric pole of Bonaventure's thought. His Christocentricity is profoundly conceived, forcefully presented, and comprehensively expanded: Christ is the center of the soul, of the universe, and of history. Yet one wishes that he had given to his cosmic Christocentricity the same self-reflective, analytical, and critical scrutiny that he gave to his Trinitarian theology. There are, of course, many reasons for this lack. First, he did not have the leisure or the academic setting in his last years that he enjoyed during his period at the University of Paris. Secondly, the literary genres of the mystical treatises and the *collationes* do not lend themselves to the type of analytic-critical reflection that characterizes the scholastic genres of the early writings. Thirdly, although his Christocentricity arises in the meditative calm of La Verna, it becomes caught up later in polemic turmoil in the *Collationes in Hexaemeron* — against the Averroists and the Joachites. In the heat of controversy the polemic side of his position emerges rather than the critical-analytical. Fourthly, his Trinitarian theology had come to him as a developed tradition, with sharply formulated positions, questions, and analytic tools — in one tradition from the Greek Fathers, in another from Augustine, and with the technical embellishments that emerged out of the twelfth century Trinitarian discussions. His cosmic Christocentricity did not come to him in that way. What he inherited from the past was not accompanied with critical apparatus. And the distinctive quality of his Christology arose out of the much more recent tradition of Francis. In Bonaventure's time it had not yet been shaped into a synthetic vision and formulated as an intellectual position. In this Bonaventure himself was a pioneer. He took two elements found in Francis: the sense of the universal presence of God in nature and the imitation of Christ. These he fused into a doctrine of universal Christocentricity. Although one can appreciate the many historical forces that shaped Bonaventure's Christocentricity, one wishes that after reading the *Collationes in Hexaemeron,* he could turn back to the *Commentary* and find a series of distinctions on Christocentricity — with sharply defined terms, divisions, and critical dialogue with objections. And one wishes that as a companion piece to the disputed questions *De scientia Christi,* one could find a series *De Christo medio.*

If Bonaventure had given his Christocentricity such an analytical-critical treatment, his synthesis would have been more complete. And he would provide us with more effective tools to solve some of the speculative problems that are inherent in the Christian vision: How to relate the Trinitarian mystery to the mystery of Christ? What are the implications of a thoroughgoing Christocentricity? For systematic theology? For Christian spirituality? For the relation of Christ to culture and Christ to time? For the relation of Christianity and other religions? We will examine these questions in the last two chapters of this book when we explore Bonaventure's relevance to contemporary thought and ecumenism.

This, then, is the architectonic design of Bonaventure's synthesis, with a sketch of the various elements that are integrated within its structure. This entire structure has a single logic: that of the coincidence of opposites. This is clearest in the major structural elements of the design, especially in the two towers: the Trinity and Christocentricity. In our study of the Trinity, we will discover a number of forms of the coincidence of opposites: between the manifesting and nonmanifesting aspects of the divinity; between unity and plurality in the divinity; in the dynamic movement from the Father to the Son, to the union of the Spirit. In the other pole of Bonaventure's thought, in the mystery of Christ, we will see the most remarkable coincidence of opposites: God and man, the cause and the caused, the Alpha and the Omega; furthermore, we will see how the opposites of the universe are bound together in Christ the universal center. These two mysteries provide the two poles within which we can explore the coincidence of opposites in the Franciscan religious experience. In the reflection of God in creation we will see a union of the highest and the lowest, the absolute and the relative, the eternal and the temporal. It is the purpose of the remaining chapters of this book to study systematically the various types of the coincidence of opposites in Bonaventure's system: especially in the mysteries of the Trinity, Christ, and the reflection of God in creation.

CHAPTER III

Itinerarium Mentis in Deum

N STUDYING the coincidence of opposites in Bonaventure's thought, two paths are open to us. We can do a thorough analysis of those texts in which the coincidence of opposites is most evident, for example, in the last three chapters of the *Itinerarium* and in the first of the *Collationes in Hexaemeron*.[1] Or we can study Bonaventure's thought systematically, treating in succession the Trinity, God and the world, and Christology. The first approach has the advantage of marshaling the most persuasive evidence to convince the reader of the main thesis of this book, for in these texts the coincidence of opposites is quite apparent. In them Bonaventure presents the basic Christian mysteries from the standpoint of the coincidence of opposites, by way of the rhetorical structure of the passages, the logic of the thought and the use of powerful symbols. Furthermore, in these two texts the coincidence of opposites is applied not to isolated or minor points, but to the major areas of Christian belief: to the Trinity, the divine nature, God and creation, Christ and redemption. The coincidence of opposites not only operates in each era, but functions as the overall logic, binding together the various areas into a single unified whole. In both of these texts, then, we get a condensed but panoramic view of Bonaventure's thought, revealing the coincidence of opposites as the all-pervasive logic of his system.

The organic nature of these texts presents a problem. If we anchor ourselves here, where the coincidence of opposites is clearest, how can we do an extended systematic analysis of each area of Bonaventure's thought? How can we range over the entire body of his texts, drawing together the complex details of his vision? The very organic structure of the key passages militates against this. For it makes it difficult to assimilate a large body of material which has been divided into separate units by extended analysis. If, however, we took the second approach, we could avoid this problem. We would simply give a systematic exposition of Bonaventure's major doctrines, through texts drawn from all parts of his writing, and then interpret these doctrines according to the coincidence of opposites. While allowing us to be more analytic, this approach has the disadvantage of cutting apart elements that are united in Bonaventure's system. Besides, it weakens the case for this book's thesis, since it highlights my personal interpretation rather than Bonaventure's own textual evidence.

To resolve this dilemma, I will take both approaches, hoping to reap the benefits of both while using each to compensate for the limitations of the other. I will begin with a study of Chapters Five through Seven of the *Itinerarium,* where we will see Bonaventure analyze the divine nature, God and the world, the Trinity, Christ and the spiritual ascent according to the coincidence of opposites. This will provide us with firm textual evidence for the thesis of this book and also allow us to see at the very outset, in a condensed synthetic form, how the coincidence of opposites operates in the major areas of Bonaventure's thought. Then in the next chapter, we will embark on a systematic approach, studying Bonaventure's doctrine of the Trinity and the relation of God to the world. Here we will draw from a wide range of texts, some of which reflect the coincidence of opposites, while others simply present a position which can be interpreted in that way. In the following chapter (Chapter Five) I will explore the second key text, the first lecture of the *Collectiones in Hexaemeron,* which contains a study of Christ through the coincidence of opposites. In this text the two approaches coincide, since Bonaventure studies in a systematic fashion various aspects of the mystery of Christ; and with Christ as a focal point he views the coincidence of opposites in the major areas of his system.

These two approaches to the coincidence of opposites in Bonaventure are themselves related as opposites. For one deals with a *maximum*: the vast amount of texts in Bonaventure's corpus, for example, the *Commentary on the Sentences,* the *Breviloquium,* the disputed questions, the *collationes,* and the other works in the ten volumes of the Quaracchi edition. The other deals with a *minimum*: two relatively brief passages in which the coincidence of opposites is sharply presented. I believe that this *minimum* coincides with the *maximum.* These passages are so concentrated and touch such depth that they manifest the basic structure of Bonaventure's total system. Each is a microcosm in which we can view the macrocosm of Bonaventure's vision. His texts can be interpreted in this way precisely because the coincidence of opposites at the base of his thought shines in his rhetoric. He has a tendency to express his entire vision in a rhetorical form that is microcosmic/macrocosmic.[2] In a short treatise, a single lecture, a chapter, even at times in a paragraph, he expresses his entire vision, not by a comprehensive listing of details, but by penetrating to the point where opposites come together. This is the case in the two key passages under study; they are microcosms through which all of his texts can be interpreted. This is especially the case in the second passage, in which Bonaventure focuses on Christ as the coincidence of opposites. As center of the universe, the medium of all benefits, and the vehicle of our spiritual transformation, Christ becomes, as it were, the center of a circle through which pass all lines connecting points situated on the circumference as opposites. For Bonaventure Christ is the microcosm of the universe. Because this passage deals with Christ the microcosm, it becomes a microcosm itself in which his entire thought is reflected and through which his many texts can be interpreted.

SETTING OF *"Itinerarium"*

The *Itinerarium* ushers in the second period of Bonaventure's writing career. He tells us that he received the idea for the piece

while at La Verna in 1259, meditating on Francis' reception of
the stigmata.[3] It is not clear whether he wrote the text during
his stay there or shortly after. Having been elected Minister
General two and a half years before, Bonaventure was required
to leave his academic career at the University of Paris. This
brought to a close the first period of his writing, which consisted
chiefly of treatises composed in the scholastic mode: the *Commentary on the Sentences*, commentaries on Scripture, disputed
questions, and the *Breviloquium*. The *Itinerarium* is a transi-
tional piece, marking not only a passage into the mystical and
spiritual writings of the second period, but a pivotal point in
his personal life and in his entire writing career. He was profoundly moved by the religious experience and intellectual insight he had at La Verna and which provided the wellspring
of the treatise. Some new integration took place in his person,
on the spiritual and intellectual levels, which was reflected in
the text of the *Itinerarium* and in his subsequent writings.

From this time on the spiritual dimension is more prominent.
Not only does he write explicitly mystical treatises, but spirituality is more integrally fused with his theology and philosophy.
Mystical images abound, becoming the vehicle to express theological and philosophical concepts. This new spiritual dimension
is distinctly Franciscan, with a sharp focus on the suffering of
Christ. The latent Christocentricity in Bonaventure's thought begins to emerge in the *Itinerarium* and to take its place along with
the Trinitarian theology of the previous period. La Verna integrates the theology of the Greek Fathers with the Christocentricity of Francis, the scholasticism of Paris with the spirit of
Assisi. Lying as it does geographically between Paris and Assisi,
La Verna became for Bonaventure the point of confluence between the two major currents in his life, drawing together the
Neo-Platonic theology, cast in a scholastic form at Paris, with
the spiritual world of Assisi, with the compelling personality of
Francis and his single-minded devotion to Christ.

The text of the *Itinerarium* is remarkably dense, compact and integral. It is brief, only about thirty-five pages, yet it condenses an entire world view elaborately explicated. It is a microcosm of medieval culture, reflecting not only Bonaventure's vision but the wide spectrum of medieval learning and experience. Its literary genre defies classification. Commentators have tried to designate it as a mystical or theological treatise; yet the extensive philosophical stratum of the work prevents such a simple classification.[4] It is a mystical, a theological, and a philosophical work; but it is also more, because it integrates these levels into a single whole. Through the centuries the *Itinerarium* has been Bonaventure's most popular and widely read work. In some respects it is the most representative, although the *Collationes in Hexaemeron*, which resembles the *Itinerarium* in its integral structure, is longer, more elaborate, and represents the most mature articulation of Bonaventure's vision.

In the prologue to the *Itinerarium*, Bonaventure describes the setting in which he conceived the treatise. He says that he went to La Verna "thirty-three years after the death of the Saint [Francis], about the time of his passing," that is, his death.[5] Since Francis died on October 4, 1226, the year would be 1259 and the time would be late September or early October. The purpose of his visit, he says, was to gain peace: "I withdrew to Mount La Verna as to a place of quiet, there to satisfy the yearning of my soul for peace."[6] The peace which he sought was the deep spiritual peace preached by Jesus and Francis: "This is the peace which our Lord Jesus Christ preached to us and which he gave to us. This message of peace our father Francis ever repeated, announcing peace at the beginning and at the end of every sermon, making every greeting a wish for peace, every prayer a sigh for ecstatic peace, like a citizen of that Jerusalem about which the Man of Peace, who was peaceable with those that hated peace, exhorts us concerning it: 'Pray ye for the things that are to the peace of Jerusalem.' "[7]

Following Francis, Bonaventure desired to gain this peace: "Inspired by the example of our blessed father, Francis, I sought after this peace with yearning soul — sinner that I am and all unworthy, yet seventh successor as Minister to all the brethren in the place of the blessed father after his death."[8] In referring to himself as General and successor to Francis, Bonaventure seems to be expressing his weariness from the burdens of his office and the heavy responsibility he felt in leading the Order in the spirit of Francis. At this point he had been Minister General for more than two years. During this time he had found himself in the role of peacemaker in the center of crises and controversies. He had to balance factions and develop a policy that would assure the peaceful and organic growth of the Order. His very election as General had grown out of the struggle with the Spirituals, who were arming themselves with the heretical thought of Joachim of Fiore. While attempting to keep peace within the Order, Bonaventure had to preside over the trial of his predecessor John of Parma. In the midst of severity on one side and laxity on the other, he had to maintain a policy — in such matters as poverty and studies — that would be faithful to the original ideals of Francis and yet allow for development. Even before his election, his life had been caught up in turmoil at the University of Paris, where the controversy between the secular masters and the mendicants had threatened his status as a professor. Just as these problems were being resolved, he was thrust into another group of problems as General. So for the last several years, his life had been continually caught up in tensions and struggles. And he must have been weary of the countless administrative details that were suddenly thrust upon one whose previous life had been devoted to intellectual pursuits. No wonder that Bonaventure "sought after this peace with yearning soul."[9]

However, there may have been a deeper reason. He may have felt a need to return to his Franciscan sources by making a pilgrimage to one of the most sacred Franciscan shrines. What better place than La Verna, the very spot where Francis received the climactic grace of his life, the vision of the six-winged Seraph and the marks of the stigmata! Here on this sacred mountain, where Francis' way of life was crowned by final divine approval, perhaps Bonaventure could contact the roots of his Franciscanism, both for himself personally and for his role as General. Perhaps he would discover the primordial roots that would unite on a deeper level in his personal life his intellectual past at the University with the spirituality of Francis. Here, too, he might touch that primitive wellspring of Francis' spirit that would enable him as General to guide the Order faithfully in its ongoing development. In the vision of the Seraph, Bonaventure found the peace he was seeking — a peace that was not static, but a creative integration of opposites that led to new productivity in his life and in his work for the Order and the Church.

Mount La Verna and the Stigmata

La Verna is indeed a holy mountain. Even to this day it stands stark and wild, rising out of the valley in a single mass, topped by a wall of gray stone jutting out of the forest that blankets its sides. It is situated in Tuscany about thirty miles north of Arezzo and about fifty miles southeast of Florence, near the town of Bibbiena. From its summit, which rises 4280 feet above sea level, one enjoys a panoramic view of the Tuscan landscape. Although the countryside reflects the soft beauty of Tuscany, La Verna itself conveys a numinous quality — an otherworldly atmosphere that evokes awe. One feels that this is indeed a spot where God has broken into the world. In view of its physical grandeur and sacred atmosphere, it rightly takes its place among other holy mountains of the Judeo-Christian tradition: such as Mount Sinai, Mount Carmel, and the mountain above Subiaco containing Benedict's cave.

This mountain was given to Francis as a gift by Count Orlando dei Cattani, of the castle of Chiusi in Casentino. In 1213 Francis and Brother Leo attended a festival to celebrate the knighthood of one of the Counts of Montefeltro. On this occasion Francis preached a sermon and greatly attracted Count Orlando, who went to him privately for spiritual advice. Knowing of Francis' love of nature and desire to spend time in wild, secluded settings, the Count offered him the mountain of La Verna as a gift. According to the following account from *The Considerations on the Holy Stigmata,* Orlando said to Francis:

> "Brother Francis, I have a mountain in Tuscany which is very solitary and wild and perfectly suited for someone who wants to do penance in a place far from people or who wants to live a solitary life. It is called Mount Alverna. If that mountain should please you and your companions, I would gladly give it to you for the salvation of my soul.'
>
> Now St. Francis had a most intense desire to find some solitary place where he could conveniently devote himself to contemplation. So when he heard this offer, he first praised God who provides for His little sheep, and then he thanked Count Orlando, saying: 'Sire, when you go home, I will send two of my companions to you, and you can show them that mountain. And if it seems suitable for prayer and penance, I very gladly accept your charitable offer.'"[10]

A few months later two companions of Francis, with an escort from Count Orlando's castle, climbed La Verna, built some small cells there and in the name of Francis took possession of the mountain. In 1224 Francis spent several weeks at La Verna with some of his companions, fasting and praying in preparation for the feast of St. Michael the Archangel, September 29. Sometime around the feast of the Exaltation of the Cross, September 14, he received the vision of the six-winged Seraph in the form of the crucified, which left in his body the marks of the stigmata. The following account is from Bonaventure's biography the *Legenda major*:

> On a certain morning about the feast of the Exaltation of the Holy Cross, while he was praying on the mountain side, he saw a Seraph, with six wings that were fiery and shining, descend from the height of heaven. And when in swift flight the Seraph had reached a spot in the air near the man of God, there appeared between the wings the figure of a man crucified, with his hands and feet extended in the form of a cross and fixed to a cross. Two wings were lifted above his head, two were extended in flight and two covered his entire body . . .
>
> The vision vanished, leaving in the heart of the saint a wonderful ardor and no less wonderful imprint of the marks in his flesh. For immediately in his hands and feet there began to appear the marks of the nails, just as he had seen them but a little before in the vision

of the man crucified. His hands and feet seemed to have been pierced
through the center by nails. The heads of the nails were round and
black; and the points were oblong, twisted and almost bent back so
that they broke through and protruded from the flesh. His right side
also, as if pierced by a lance, was covered with a red wound from which
flowed his sacred blood, moistening his habit and trousers.[11]

Thirty-five years later Bonaventure meditated on this vision
at La Verna. A short distance from the site of the vision, a small
chapel, the Oratory of St. Bonaventure, marks the traditional
spot where the Minister General retired to meditate and where
he received the inspiration for the *Itinerarium*. "Moved by a
divine impulse," Bonaventure writes, "I withdrew to Mount La
Verna as to a place of quiet, there to satisfy the yearning of my
soul for peace. While I abode there, pondering on certain spiritual ascents to God, there occurred to me, among other things,
that miracle which in this very place had happened to the blessed
Francis — the vision he received of the winged Seraph in the form
of the crucified."[12] While meditating on the vision, Bonaventure
had the seminal insight that would unfold in the writing of the
Itinerarium: the six wings of the Seraph symbolized the six stages
of the mind's ascent into God. Actually as Bonaventure described
it, the insight had two points: (1) the vision expressed the goal
of the spiritual ascent, namely the mystical ecstasy given to Francis; and (2) it symbolized the stages of the journey by which the
mind reaches that goal. This twofold aspect of the insight is, I
believe, highly significant and will be studied in some depth when
in a later chapter I treat the six-winged Seraph as a mandala symbol.[13] Bonaventure described his insight as follows: "As I reflected on this marvel, it immediately seemed to me that this
vision suggested the uplifting of Saint Francis in contemplation
and that it pointed out the way by which that state of contemplation can be reached."[14]

STRUCTURE OF "ITINERARIUM"

The vision of the six-winged Seraph in the form of the crucified provides the structural design of the *Itinerarium*. As Bona-

venture says: "The figure of the six wings of the Seraph, therefore, brings to mind the six steps of illumination which begin
with creatures and lead up to God."[15] Bonaventure first treats
the wings as pairs and sees them symbolizing three stages: the
lower pair symbolizes the material world; the middle pair, the
soul; and the upper pair, the consideration of God himself. Bonaventure's journey, then, is also an ascent leading from the lowest
to the highest, from the material world to God. After the ascent
through the three levels, the soul reaches the stage of mystical
ecstasy, symbolized by the vision as a whole. The Seraph, then,
is not a static symbol, but the symbol of a journey which is also
an ascent. The title of the piece, *Itinerarium mentis in Deum
(The Itinerary of the Mind into God)* indicates this. In the Latin
of Bonaventure's era the term *itinerarium* signified a number of
things related to a journey: in general, it meant what pertains
to a journey; more specifically, it meant a plan or a description
of a journey; in ecclesiastical terminology it meant a prayer for
a safe journey, or it indicated a pilgrimage to the Holy Land,
either the pilgrimage itself or a description of the pilgrimage.[16]
In the title, Bonaventure apparently intended to convey all of
these meanings, since in various ways they are reflected in the
treatise.

Although Bonaventure merely mentions in passing the classical mystical symbol of the ascent of the holy mountain,[17] it is
suggested by his focusing on Mount La Verna, on Francis' vision
on the mountain and his own ascent of the mountain in order
to achieve peace. He also makes brief mention of the symbol of
the ladder, with specific reference to Jacob's ladder, viewing all
of creation as a ladder on which we can climb to God.[18] In the
middle of the *Itinerarium* Bonaventure employs the symbol of the
tabernacle to represent the journey within the depths of the soul.
Step by step he leads the reader into the various precincts of the
tabernacle, entering ever more deeply into the sacred areas until
he arrives at the Holy of Holies.[19] In a manner quite typical of
his style, Bonaventure uses a number of distinct symbols, each

expressing a different facet of meaning but each blending into the others and supporting the others. Thus the six-winged Seraph, the mountain, the ladder, and the tabernacle, each in its own way expresses the motif of the journey, or pilgrimage, of the soul into God.

Bonaventure's plan of the journey contains three major stages: the material world, the soul, and the consideration of God. He further divides each of these into two, making a total of six, thus corresponding to the original consideration of the six wings of the Seraph. This division, then, becomes the outline of the whole treatise and provides the topics of each chapter. Thus Chapter One deals with the material world as seen exteriorly; Chapter Two, with the material world as received into our senses; Chapter Three deals with the soul in its faculties of memory, intellect, and will; Chapter Four, with the soul as reformed by grace; Chapter Five treats the consideration of God as Being; and Chapter Six, the consideration of God as Good. This leads to the seventh and final chapter, which treats the end of the journey, the summit of the ascent. Here one enters *into* God (*in* Deum) in the ecstasy of mystical union.

This is not merely a journey into the future with our gaze fixed on a distant goal. Rather we see the goal present at each stage of the way; we gaze at the landscape around us, meditating on God's reflection there as we progress towards the goal. In fact, it is precisely by seeing the reflection of God at each stage that we advance towards union with him. The chief symbol which Bonaventure uses to express God's presence in the universe is the mirror: all of creation is a mirror in which God is reflected. Our meditation on this mirror (*speculum*) is a speculation (*speculatio*), or a gazing into the *speculum*.[20] Thus the *Itinerarium* provides a method of meditation to cultivate the distinctive Franciscan religious experience of the presence of God in creation. To revert to the image I used in the previous chapter, the *Itinerarium* presents a sustained meditation on the reflection of God in the universe, like the reflection of light through the stained glass

windows of a Gothic cathedral.[21] This meditation takes us through
the philosophical and theological levels of Bonaventure's thought:
from the epistemology of illumination, to the metaphysics of exemplarism and ultimately to the doctrines of the Trinity and
Christocentricity, which provide the two structural poles of the
treatise. It is especially in these two latter doctrines that the
coincidence of opposites appears.

STAGES OF THE JOURNEY

Although the coincidence of opposites comes to the fore only
in the last three chapters, it is prepared for in the prologue when
Bonaventure introduces the image of Christ crucified drawn from
Francis' vision. In the *Itinerarium* the Christ image rises to a
new prominence in Bonaventure's thought. Emerging as the
focal point of the entire treatise, it continues to be a dominant
image in his later writings, undergoing an evolution towards the
elaborated Christocentricity which we described above.[22] Immediately after sketching the symbolism of the six wings of the
Seraph, Bonaventure states: "The road to this peace is through
nothing else than a most ardent love of the crucified, the love
which so transformed Paul into Christ when he was rapt to the
third heaven that he declared: 'With Christ I am nailed to the
Cross. It is now no longer I that live, but Christ lives in me.' "[23]
This love, he continues, so absorbed Francis that it shone through
his flesh in the stigmata. Bonaventure then begins to blend
symbols: Christ crucified is the door through which we enter;
he is the lamb in whose blood we must be washed. "That is to
say, no one can enter by contemplation into the heavenly Jerusalem unless he enters through the blood of the lamb as through
a door."[24] Having established the centrality of Christ in the
prologue, Bonaventure will return to this theme at key points
in the treatise, especially in Chapters Six and Seven, where he
deals with Christ as the mystery of the coincidence of opposites,
who having passed from death to life can lead us to pass over
into the mystical joy of the final stage of the ascent.

With Christ as the road and the door, Bonaventure begins the ascent through the six stages symbolized by the six wings of the Seraph. The first stage deals with the reflection of God in the material world. Bonaventure says that he is beginning at the lowest rung of the ladder of creatures: "Let us place our first step in the ascent at the bottom, setting the whole visible world before us as a mirror through which we may pass over to God, the Supreme Creative Artist."[25] Meditating on various aspects of material creatures, he sees them as vestiges of the Trinity. In reflecting the power, wisdom, and goodness of the divinity, they point to the Father, Son, and Holy Spirit. The metaphysical and theological roots of the vestige doctrine are not developed here, but are treated later in the *Itinerarium* and at length elsewhere in his writings.[26] Here in the first stage of the ascent, Bonaventure meditates on material things in their weight, number, and measure; their mode, species, and order; their substance, power, and activity; their origin, development, and end.[27] From various aspects of visible creation, he rises to the power, wisdom, and goodness of God, "in so far as he is existing, living, intelligent, purely spiritual, incorruptible, and immutable."[28] The chapter reaches its climax in a panoramic view of material creation seen from seven perspectives — origin, greatness, multitude, beauty, plenitude, activity, and order. For example, he considers the greatness of things "looking at their vast extension, latitude and profundity, at the immense power extending itself in the diffusion of light, and the efficiency of their inner uninterrupted and diffusive operation, as manifest in the action of fire."[29] Seen in this panoramic sweep, the greatness of things "clearly portrays the immensity of the power, wisdom and goodness of the Triune God, who, uncircumscribed, exists in all things by his power, presence and essence."[30]

In the second stage of the ascent, Bonaventure meditates on the process of sensation. "It should be noted that this world, which is called the *macrocosm*, enters our soul, the *microcosm*, through the portals of the five senses in so far as sense objects

are apprehended, enjoyed and judged."[31] According to Bonaventure's theory of sensation, a similitude of the object is generated in the medium and then impressed on the organ. Through
this impression we are led back to the starting point, the sense
object to be known. Bonaventure sees in this process a reflection
of the Trinity. "If, therefore, all knowable things must generate
a likeness of themselves, they manifestly proclaim that in them,
as in mirrors, can be seen the eternal generation of the Word, the
Image, and the Son, eternally emanating from God the Father."[32]
Drawing from Augustine, Bonaventure meditates on various kinds
of numbers — such as are found in sounds, in gesturing and danc-
ing — as these lead us to God. At this point he sums up the first
two stages of the ascent by stating that the contemplative man
can rise from material creatures to God, "for creatures are
shadows, echoes, and pictures" of the eternal Source and Light.[33]
Although Bonaventure does not develop these stages according
to the coincidence of opposites, it is implicit in the doctrine of
exemplarism that underlies these two chapters. The coincidence
of opposites between God and creatures will emerge into self-
consciousness in Chapter Five.

Turning from the material world and sensation, Bonaventure
penetrates within himself to explore the image of God in the soul.
"Enter into yourself," he says, bidding us follow the path that
Augustine had charted.[34] In the depths of the soul's faculties —
in the memory, intellect, and will — he finds a reflection of God.
The memory here is taken in the Platonic sense of the depths of
the soul where the eternal truths reside and in the mystical sense
of the ground of the soul which reflects the presence of God.
When we know a first principle, we seem to grasp it in our memory
since we see it as eternally true, as if we always knew it and
are now remembering it. When our intellect knows truth, it
does so in the light of the eternal Truth; and when our will desires
or judges something as good, it does so in the light of the absolute Good. "See, therefore," Bonaventure says, "how close the
soul is to God, and how, through their activity, the memory leads

us to Eternity, the intelligence to Truth and the elective faculty
to the highest Good."[35] If we consider the relation of these
faculties to one another, we will see that they reflect the Trinity.
"For from the memory comes forth the intelligence as its off-
spring; . . . from the memory and the intelligence is breathed
forth love, as the bond of both."[36] Thus when the soul meditates
upon itself in this way, it rises as if through a mirror to the reflection of the divine processions; to the Father generating the
Word and with the Word spirating the Spirit, who is Love
breathed forth.

In the fourth stage, Bonaventure deals with the restoration of
the fallen image through Christ. It is strange, he observes, that
given the fact that God is so close to the soul, so few are concerned
with perceiving God within themselves. Distracted by cares, clouded by sense images, drawn away by concupiscence, the soul cannot reenter into itself as image of God. It lies fallen, immersed
in the things of sense, in need of someone to lift it up so that
it can see its true self as image of God, with the eternal Truth
shining within itself. Christ has come and lifted up the soul,
restoring the fallen image. Eternal Truth itself took on human
form in Christ and became "a ladder restoring the first ladder that
had been broken in Adam."[37] In this chapter the image of Christ
emerges again with the same prominence it had in the prologue.
The entire chapter is focused on Christ's work of redemption,
viewed not as satisfying for sin but as restoring the image of God.
In this Bonaventure is echoing not the Anselmian satisfaction
tradition, but the Greek Fathers' notion of the restoration of the
image in man through Christ the Image of the Father. Through
Christ, Bonaventure says, the image of our soul is "clothed over
with the three theological virtues, by which the soul is purified,
enlightened and perfected."[38] Through Christ the spiritual senses
are restored so that like the bride in the Canticle of Canticles,
the soul can respond to her beloved. At this stage the study of
Sacred Scripture is especially helpful, just as philosophy was in
the previous stage; for Scripture is concerned chiefly with Christ's

work of restoration. It is concerned principally with charity, with
the two commandments: love of God and love of our neighbor.
At this point Bonaventure begins to view Christ as a coincidence
of opposites, in a manner which will emerge more sharply in the
following chapters. Speaking of the two commandments of love,
Bonaventure says:

> These two are signified by the one Spouse of the Church, Jesus Christ,
> who is at one and the same time our Neighbor and our God, our
> Brother and our Lord, our King and our Friend, Word incarnate and
> uncreated Word, our Maker and our Re-maker, 'the Alpha and the
> Omega', who is also the supreme Hierarch, who purifies, enlightens,
> and perfects his spouse, that is, the whole Church and every sanctified
> soul.[39]

COINCIDENCE OF OPPOSITES

Having meditated on the reflection of God in the material
world and within the soul, Bonaventure now turns to God himself. In Chapter Five he considers God as Being and in Chapter
Six, God as Good; this leads to the passage into mystical ecstasy
in Chapter Seven. In these last three chapters the coincidence of
opposites clearly emerges, having been foreshadowed by the brief
reference to Christ quoted above. The last three chapters form
a single literary unit, bound together by a common symbolism
and by the rhetorical and logical structure of the coincidence of
opposites. In Chapter Five Bonaventure bids the reader to gaze
in wonder upon the coincidence of opposites in the divine nature; and in Chapter Six he directs us to contemplate the coincidence of opposites in the Trinity. He then bids us look at Christ.
If we have been struck by the opposites in the divine nature,
we will be stunned by Christ, in whom the first principle is united
to the last, God with man, the eternal with time. If we have
been struck by the coincidence of unity and plurality in the
Trinity, we will be amazed at Christ, in whom personal unity
coexists with a trinity of substances and a duality of natures. When
we gaze upon Christ, the highest and the lowest, the Alpha and
the Omega, we will celebrate our Pasch with him and make our

Passover into mystical elevation. In the beginning of the seventh
chapter, Bonaventure describes how with Christ crucified we pass
from death to life, how our understanding is put at rest and our
affection passes over entirely into God. With its Christological
focal point, then, the coincidence of opposites provides a multi-
dimensional structure for the last three chapters of the *Itinerarium*. It sets up a rhetorical structure, which becomes a dialectical
method of arriving at metaphysical understanding, which in turn
becomes a technique of negative theology to achieve a transition
to a mystical elevation.

The symbol that binds together the last three chapters is that
of the tabernacle or temple.[39] This is one of the three major symbols of the *Itinerarium*. The symbol of the journey, implied in
the title, acts as a generic or overarching symbol which has two
specifications: first there is the six-winged Seraph in the form of
the crucified, which Bonaventure develops in Chapter One and
which is the chief symbol of the first part of the *Itinerarium*.
Balancing this as the chief image of the second part is the symbol
of the tabernacle or temple, which he introduces in Chapter
Three and which he develops at length in Chapters Five and Six.
He draws his description of the tabernacle from Exodus[41] and
follows the tradition of the New Testament and of Christian
mystical writers of seeing the temple as symbol of the soul.[42]
Just as God is present in the temple, so he is present in the soul.
As we enter more deeply into ourselves, we penetrate ultimately
into the Holy of Holies, where we gaze upon the divine light
shining in our souls and contemplate Christ, who is the Mercy-Seat
situated at the center of the Holy of Holies over the Ark.

The symbol of the Seraph and that of the temple are related as
opposites. The first is external and implies height, for the Seraph
appears as an image external to St. Francis, in an outdoor setting,
on the top of a mountain. The second is interior and connotes
depth, for Bonaventure brings us within the temple, even to its
innermost chamber. Yet both symbols converge in Christ. For
the Seraph is in the form of the crucified, and at the innermost

center of the temple we encounter Christ as the Mercy-Seat. Thus
through the symbols of the *Itinerarium* Bonaventure implies that
Christ effects the coincidence of the external and the internal,
the highest and the deepest.[43]

We will now embark upon a more detailed analysis of the symbol of the temple as providing the image context for the coincidence of opposites in Chapters Five through Seven. After taking
the reader on a journey through the sense world, Bonaventure
bids him enter within himself — into the tabernacle or temple.[44]
In turning into ourselves, we leave the outer area, the court or
atrium — that is, the world of sense — and enter within the tabernacle — that is, into our own minds. The tabernacle is divided
into two sections: the anterior chamber or the sanctuary and
the Holy of Holies. The anterior chamber is separated from the
Holy of Holies by a veil, before which is placed the candelabra.
The anterior section symbolizes our mind and the candelabra the
divine illumination shining in the soul. Behind the veil is the innermost part of the tabernacle, the Holy of Holies, containing the
Ark of the Covenant, above which are two Cherubim, each facing
the Mercy-Seat, which is placed above the Ark. The Holy of
Holies symbolizes the presence of God in the depth of the soul;
the Cherubim symbolize two basic attitudes of contemplating
God; and the Mercy-Seat symbolizes Christ.[45]

FIRST CHERUB: BEING

As symbols the Cherubim play a central role in setting up the
rhetorical structure of the passage. Bonaventure describes their
meaning as follows:

> By these Cherubim we understand the two kinds or degrees of con-
> templating the invisible and eternal things of God: the first considers
> the essential attributes of God; the second, the proper attributes of the
> persons.[46]

The Cherubim, then, become the symbols for the fifth and sixth
levels of contemplation in the *Itinerarium*:[47] the fifth considering
God as Being and Unity, the sixth as Goodness and Trinity. Bona-

venture describes the point of view symbolized by the first Cherub as follows: "The first method fixes the soul's gaze primarily and principally on Being Itself, declaring that the first name of God is 'He Who is.' "[48] This is grounded in the Old Testament and in God's revelation of himself to Moses as "I am Who am." It looks chiefly to the unity of the divine essence. Hence John Damascene, following Moses, says that *He who is* is the first name of God.[49] Bonaventure entitles his fifth chapter: "The Consideration of the Divine Unity through its Primary Name which is Being."[50]

Bonaventure guides us in how to take the attitude of the first Cherub and so to contemplate God in the unity of his essence. First we are led through a dialectic of being and non-being. Echoing Anselm's ontological argument,[51] Bonaventure states that being itself is so certain that it cannot be thought not to be. Being and non-being are related as absolute opposites. They are in full flight from each other. Complete nothingness contains nothing of being, and being itself contains nothing of non-being. Although opposites, they coincide, since non-being is the privation of being. Non-being can be grasped only through being; being in potency can be grasped only through being in act. What first comes into the intellect, then, is being as pure act — unlimited, unmixed with potency — and this is the divine being.[52]

Paradoxically, there is a coincidence of opposites in human blindness. In the darkness of the human situation, we mistake being for non-being and non-being for being. When we look at the highest being, we think we are seeing nothing. Accustomed to particulars and universals, we do not see the being that is beyond all categories. We are like the bat in the sunlight. Conditioned to the darkness of being and the phantasms of material things, we seem to be seeing nothing when we gaze on the light of being itself. We do "not understand that this very darkness is the supreme illumination of our mind, just as when the eye sees pure light, it seems to be seeing nothing."[53]

From the darkness of the human situation, Bonaventure turns to the pure light of being itself. Having grasped being itself as

pure act, he proceeds to derive its attributes. By negating all
forms of non-being, he deduces that being itself must be first,
eternal, most simple, most actual, most perfect, and supremely
one.[54] A further study of the attributes indicates that they embody
a coincidence of opposites:

> You have here something to lift you up in admiration. For being itself
> is both the first and last; it is eternal and yet most present; it is most
> simple and the greatest; it is most actual and most changeless; it is
> most perfect and immense; it is supremely one and yet omnifarious.[55]

These are opposites, it is true, and strike us with wonder;
yet more striking still is the fact that each opposite is derived
from the other:

> Admiring all these things with a pure mind, you will be flooded with
> a still greater light when you behold further that pure being is pre-
> cisely the last because it is the first. For since it is first, it does all
> things for itself, and thus the first being is of necessity the ultimate
> end, the beginning and the consummation, 'the Alpha and the Omega'.[56]

This pattern of the derivation of one opposite from another is
carried through the entire set. Being itself is most present precisely because it is eternal. As eternal, it has neither past nor
future, but only present being. And it is greatest precisely
because it is most simple. As the most simple, it has the greatest
concentration of power; hence it is the greatest. Further, it is
most changeless precisely because it is most actual. As pure
actuality, it cannot acquire anything new or lose anything it already has. Because it is most perfect, it is immense, or without
measure. Since it has all perfections, it is beyond encompassing
because one can think of nothing better, nobler, of higher dignity
beyond it, and consequently of nothing greater. Finally, it is
omnifarious, or possessing all aspects of the multiplicity, precisely
because it is one. For the one is the all-embracing principle of
the multitude, the efficient, exemplary, and final cause of all
things.[57]

Throughout his contemplation of God as being, Bonaventure's
thought has moved along two axes: one axis running between

polar attributes within the divinity, the other running between God and the world. In concluding the fifth chapter of the *Itinerarium,* Bonaventure describes the coincidence of opposites between God and the world.[58] If we were to use the categories of immanence and transcendence, we could express Bonaventure's coincidence principle in the following formula: The greater the transcendence, the greater the immanence. This principle is expressed by Bonaventure by means of a set of graphic images. Precisely because God is eternal, Bonaventure says, he is the center and circumference of all time, encompassing all duration and existing at its very center. Precisely because he is most simple and the greatest, he is wholly outside all things. Hence he is "an intelligible sphere, whose center is everywhere and whose circumference is nowhere."[59] Further, precisely because God is most perfect and beyond measure, he "is within all things without being contained by them, outside all things without being excluded, above all things without being aloof, below all things without being dependent."[60]

Second Cherub: the Trinity

Having viewed God in the unity of his nature, Bonaventure turns to the opposite and views God in the plurality of persons in the Trinity. Through the image of the two Cherubim — placed opposite each other, facing each other and turned to the Mercy-Seat — Bonaventure graphically portrays the coincidence of opposites of unity and plurality in God. It is true that there is a coincidence of unity and plurality in the axis that runs between God and the world; but within the Godhead itself, unity and plurality coincide in a more profound and mysterious way in the Trinitarian unity of one nature in a plurality of persons.

From the standpoint of this second Cherub, we are to gaze upon God as the Good. While the first Cherub is associated with the Old Testament, with Moses and the revelation of God as Being, the second is associated with the New Testament, the revelation of the Trinity and Christ's statement to the rich young man that only

God is good.[61] While John Damascene, following Moses, says that *He who is* is God's primary name, Dionysius, following Christ, says that God's primary name is Good.[62]

In Chapter Six Bonaventure derives the Trinitarian processions from a consideration of the Good. Beginning again with the Anselmian principle of the *Proslogion*,[63] Bonaventure states that what is absolutely the best cannot be thought not to be, since it is better to be than not to be. Bonaventure then unites this Anselmian principle with the Pseudo-Dionysian axiom that the Good is self-diffusive.[64] Hence the highest good is most self-diffusive. From this Bonaventure shows how the supreme self-diffusiveness of the divinity requires the procession of the Son and the Holy Spirit.[65] Bonaventure's logic is simple and direct; it moves in a straight line from the fecundity of the divinity, from what Bonaventure calls elsewhere the *fontalis plenitudo*.[66] From this supreme fecundity comes the supreme communication, from which follows supreme sharing and intimacy:

> By reason of their supreme goodness, the three persons must necessarily have supreme communicability; by reason of that, supreme consubstantiality; and by reason of supreme consubstantiality, they must have supreme conformability. Then by reason of all these, they must have supreme coequality, and hence supreme coeternity. Finally, from all the foregoing taken together, they must have supreme mutual intimacy, by which one person is necessarily in the other by reason of their supreme interpenetration, and one acts with the other in absolute indivision of the substance, power, and activity of the Most Blessed Trinity itself.[67]

At first glance, it might seem that Bonaventure's straight-line logic has avoided the coincidence of opposites in the Trinity. But such is not the case. Bonaventure warns the reader not to think that he has actually grasped the incomprehensible. For in these six characteristics, there is a coincidence of opposites that can lead us to a state of stunned admiration. For side by side in the Trinity are supreme communicability with individuality of persons, supreme consubstantiality with plurality of hypostases, supreme similarity with distinct personality, supreme equality with ordered procession, supreme coeternity with emanation, supreme mutual intimacy with a sending forth.[68]

CHRIST: COINCIDENCE OF OPPOSITES

Having described the attitudes of the two Cherubim, Bonaventure now bids us to observe that the Cherubim face each other, with their faces turned to the Mercy-Seat.[69] This symbolizes that we must admire the characteristics of the divine essence and the persons not only in themselves, but also in comparison with Christ; for Christ embodies an extraordinary coincidence of opposites.

If you are the first Cherub and wonder at the coincidence of opposites in the divine nature, turn towards the Mercy-Seat, Bonaventure says, and stand in amazement.[70] Bonaventure here sets up a point for point parallel between the coincidence of opposites in the divine nature and the more striking expression in Christ. If we were amazed that the divine being is the first and the last, we will be amazed that in Christ the first principle is joined to the last. "God is joined with man, who was formed on the sixth day" of creation.[71] If we were amazed that divine being is eternal and most present, we will be more amazed at Christ; for in him "the eternal is joined with time-bound man, born of the Virgin in the fullness of time."[72] If we wondered at the divine being as the most simple and the greatest, then we will wonder at Christ, in whom the most simple is joined with the most composite. If we wondered at the divine being as the most actual and never moved, then we will be amazed at Christ, the most actual, who nevertheless underwent supreme suffering and died. If we wondered at the divine being as most perfect and beyond measure, we will be amazed at Christ, who though most perfect and beyond measure, is joined with the least and insignificant. If we wondered at the divine being as both supremely one and yet encompassing all things, we will be amazed at Christ; for the supremely one that encompasses all things is "joined to an individual that is composite and distinct from others, that is to say, to the man Jesus Christ."[73]

If as the second Cherub we wondered that in the Trinity there is a coincidence of unity and plurality, we will be amazed at Christ. Bonaventure does not draw a one-to-one correspondence between the list of opposites in the Trinity and those in Christ. After listing the opposites of unity and plurality in the Trinity, he bids the reader:

> . . . face toward the Mercy-Seat and be amazed that in Christ a personal unity coexists with a trinity of substances and a duality of natures; that an entire accord coexists with a plurality of wills; that a mutual predication of God and man coexists with a differentiation of eminence; that co-exaltation over all things coexists with a differentiation of dignities; and finally that co-domination coexists with a plurality of powers.[74]

Christ, as coincidence of opposites, serves as our means of passing over from intellectual contemplation to mystical ecstasy.[75] First we see Christ as both the image of the invisible God and the model of our own humanity. By identifying ourselves with him as man, we see our humanity wonderfully exalted. In Christ we see united "the first and the last, the highest and the lowest, the circumference and the center, 'the Alpha and the Omega,' the caused and the cause, the Creator and the creature, that is, 'the book written within and without.' "[76] In Christ we arrive at a perfect reality.

As the mind gazes upon Christ, the mediator of God and man, it must transcend not only this visible world, but even itself. Christ, in whom is embodied the coincidence of opposites, becomes the way and the door for our passage.[77] At this point, Bonaventure introduces another type of coincidence of opposites: the passage from opposite to opposite — from death to life, from earth to heaven, from intellectual contemplation to mystical elevation. Bonaventure evokes the entire Paschal mystery by seeing Christ as the one who dies and rises to draw us beyond sin, beyond the limits of the world, beyond ourselves into mystical union with God. Our instrument for making the passage is the cross.

> He who turns his full countenance toward this Mercy-Seat and with faith, hope, and love, devotion, admiration, joy, appreciation, praise

and rejoicing, beholds Christ hanging on the cross, such a one cele-
brates the Pasch, that is, the Passover, with him. Thus, using the rod
of the cross, he may pass over the Red Sea, going from Egypt into
the desert, where it is given to him to taste the hidden manna; he
may rest with Christ in the tomb, as one dead to the outer world, but
experiencing, nevertheless, as far as is possible in this present state as
wayfarer, what was said on the cross to the thief who was hanging
there with Christ: "This day thou shalt be with me in Paradise."[78]

In making this passover, we abandon all intellectual activity,
go beyond opposites, beyond being and nonbeing to the shining
ray of divine darkness. Quoting the Pseudo-Dionysius, Bonaventure says:

> . . . let yourself be brought back, in so far as it is possible, to unity
> with him who is above all essence and all knowledge. And transcending
> yourself and all things, ascend to the super-essential gleam of the
> divine darkness by an incommensurable and absolute transport of a
> pure mind.[79]

By entering into the Paschal mystery and by contemplating the
marvelous coincidence of opposites in Christ, we reach the point
where all opposites disappear; for we have ceased to think in
concepts or to engage in intellectual contemplation. Rather,
with Christ we have entered into an affective union with the
Father:

> Let us, then, die and enter into this darkness. Let us silence all our
> care, our desires, and our imaginings. With Christ crucified, let us
> pass 'out of this world to the Father,' so that, when the Father is shown
> to us, we may say with Philip: 'It is enough for us.'[80]

On the one hand, the mystical level is a negation of the opposites, for here all opposites coincide and find their reconciliation.
Yet on the other hand, the soul itself is not absorbed into the
divinity. In Bonaventure's thought the soul remains an image; it
retains its identity and its otherness. It is united to God as
lover to the Beloved, and hence as opposite to opposite. It is
precisely Christ as eternal Word that grounds the individuality
of the human soul and supports its autonomy even in the con-
suming fires of the divine union.

METAPHYSICAL AND THEOLOGICAL ROOTS

The coincidence of opposites in these three chapters of the *Itinerarium* leads us to make a systematic study of the coincidence of opposites throughout Bonaventure's thought. This passage prompts us to make a *reductio,* tracing the lines of his thought back to their underlying metaphysical and theological principles. Taking this approach, we come to the two roots of Bonaventure's logical and rhetorical interest in the coincidence of opposites: the dynamic Trinity and the mystery of Christ the center. These are bound together by two principles: (1) expressionism in his Trinitarian theology; and (2) exemplarism in his doctrine of creation.

Bonaventure's doctrine of opposites is rooted in his Trinitarian theology and precisely in his doctrine of the Son as expressive Image of the Father. In his boundless fecundity the Father generates the Son as the expression of himself.[81] In this expressionism there are the two opposites — the Father and his Image — and their coincidence precisely in imaging. Hence at the very base of Bonaventure's thought, in the inner life of the mystery of the Trinity, there is an archetype for all of the opposites within the created universe.

It is on this expressionism that Bonaventure's exemplarism is based. For in generating the Son, the Father produces in the Son the exemplar and pattern of all that can be created. Hence the Son is his Art through which he creates the universe, and the universe is by its very nature a theophany. As vestige, image, similitude of God, it reflects God. It has two modes of otherness: first, it participates in the positive otherness of autonomy of the Image of the Father; and as a creature it is caught up in the otherness of non-being. These two modes of otherness coincide in man in a striking way. On the one hand, he shares in the divine imaging of the Son and, on the other, in the darkness of non-being.

The coincidence of nothingness and absoluteness in man is well illustrated in Bonaventure's epistemology of illumination.[82]

The created things we know are changeable and our minds are fallible. Yet we do have certain knowledge which is unchangeable and infallible. What makes this possible is the fact that our minds are grounded in the *Verbum increatum*. In our certain knowledge we are illumined and supported by the eternal Word, who grounds us in his unchangeableness and infallibility. In even our most casual judgments of first principles, our changeable mind coincides with the unchangeable Mind that is the cause of all things.

Because exemplarism and illumination involve a coincidence of opposites, the first four chapters of the *Itinerarium* can be reread from the standpoint of the coincidence of opposites. Through illumination in the image and exemplarism in the vestige, God and the universe are related as a coincidence of opposites. On the basis of these principles studied systematically, we can apply to the first four chapters the insight of the fifth, that God is "wholly within all things and wholly outside them."[83]

It is in Christ that the exemplaristic principle of creation coincides with the expressionistic principle of the Trinity. As limited, the universe cannot fully express its divine exemplar. But the Exemplar himself enters time and history in the most intimate personal union with human nature, the *minor mundus*. In so doing, he raises the macrocosm of the universe to approximate, insofar as it can, the fullness of imaging and expressionism that is realized in the consubstantial generation of the Son from the Father.

These principles of expressionism and exemplarism we will study systematically as the basis of Bonaventure's doctrine of the coincidence of opposites. In the following chapter, we will see them within the doctrine of the Trinity and in relation to creation. In the subsequent chapter we will see them at work in the mystery of Christ the center. Thus we will see that the concentrated passage in the *Itinerarium* presenting the coincidence of opposites is, in fact, a microcosm revealing the structure of Bonaventure's thought as a whole.

CHAPTER IV

THE TRINITY AND CREATION

I
N THIS stage of our study, we shift our attention from Bonaventure's texts to his system. As described at the outset of our last chapter, our method of studying the coincidence of opposites in Bonaventure involves a twofold approach: (1) an analysis of specific texts where the coincidence of opposites is expressed; (2) an analysis of Bonaventure's system, drawing out of its structure implicit coincidences of opposites. This second approach is also rooted in texts in the sense that we will draw our knowledge of Bonaventure's system from his own writings. But these texts will be selected with an eye to reconstructing his system rather than to obtaining textual evidence for the coincidence of opposites in his thought. Having reconstructed his system from his texts, we will then analyze his system from the standpoint of the coincidence of opposites.

Although different in their starting point and immediate function, these two approaches are by no means unrelated. For example, in our previous chapter we studied Chapters Five to Seven of the *Itinerarium* as a textual expression of the coincidence of opposites. In our present chapter we will study Bonaventure's doctrine of the Trinity and God's relation to the world from a systematic point of view. However, some of the texts which we will use to reconstruct his system will be drawn from Chapter Six of the *Itinerarium* and also from the first of the *Collationes in Hexaemeron,* where the coincidence of opposites is also expressed. These more explicit texts will serve the double purpose of establishing his system and of guiding us into the coincidence of opposites in its structure. Finally, since these

97

two explicit texts gave a comprehensive synthesis of Bonaventure's thought, they can serve as a check and corroboration of our own analysis of the coincidence of opposites in Bonaventure's system.

In our survey of Bonaventure's thought we claimed that there are two major poles: the Trinity and Christocentricity.[1] This is true from the standpoint of the design of Bonaventure's system and its major components. However from the standpoint of its structure, the doctrine of the Trinity is foundational; for it provides the basis of all the other elements in the system: the doctrine of creation, of God's relation to the world, of man as image and the world as vestige, of Christ the center and the return of all things to God. It is also the foundation of all the coincidences of opposites in Bonaventure's thought. The Trinity constitutes the primordial and archetypal coincidence of opposites, and as such, is the source of the polarities within Bonaventure's system. If God were not Trinitarian, then we would not find the coincidence of opposites as a dimension of reality. Therefore we begin our systematic study with Bonaventure's doctrine of the Trinity and then move into his doctrine of creation. In the next two chapters we will explore the coincidence of opposites in the Christocentric pole of his thought.

THE DYNAMIC TRINITY

The most characteristic aspect of Bonaventure's doctrine of the Trinity is that it is dynamic. For Bonaventure God is dynamic not merely in a general way as opposed to being static; nor is he dynamic primarily in the act of creation and his involvement in the world; rather he is dynamic primarily in his inner Trinitarian life. Bonaventure sees the Father in the Trinity as the fecund source of the divinity, the *fontalis plenitudo*, or fountain-fullness, out of whose plenitude the Son is generated and through the Son the Spirit is spirated. The dynamism of the Trinity is imparted to the world in the act of creation and in the return of all things to the Father.

This notion of the dynamic Trinity shapes the structure of Bonaventure's system and imparts coherence to its components. For example, it lies at the base of such a characteristic doctrine as exemplarism. In Bonaventure's doctrine of universal exemplarism, all creatures reflect God and can provide a path leading the soul into God. Exemplarism, then, is the matrix for Bonaventure's study of the relation of the world to God, of all things emerging out of God and returning to God. Yet exemplarism is not the foundational stratum of Bonaventure's system. Beneath exemplarism and supporting it ontologically lies Bonaventure's doctrine of expressionism. Within his inner life, God is dynamic and expressive: the Father expresses himself in generating the Son, who is his perfect Image and Word. In generating the Son, the Father produces in the Son the ideas or *rationes aeternae* of all that he can create. These *rationes aeternae* within the Son are the ontological foundation of creation *ad extra* and of exemplarism. Without Trinitarian expressionism, then, Bonaventure's system would be incomplete, for it would lack its ultimate ontological grounding.

Furthermore, without an awareness of Trinitarian expressionism, one could easily misinterpret internal elements of his system. For the Trinity does not merely provide a base for creation, but imparts its dynamism to creation. In the light of their Trinitarian foundation, then, Bonaventure's vestiges and images are not static representations of God, but dynamic realities sharing in the Trinitarian expressionism. In view of this, I suggest the following hermeneutic principle for exploring Bonaventure's thought. Using his own method of *reductio,* one should lead back to their dynamic Trinitarian source all elements within Bonaventure's system in order to grasp them in their depth and organic context.

Bonaventure's doctrine of the dynamic Trinity is the key element for situating him within his specific historical tradition. For example, Bonaventure is usually called an Augustinian to distinguish him from the thirteenth century Aristotelian camp.

Although I believe this designation is accurate, it must be nuanced. Bonaventure's Trinitarian theology is much closer to that of the Greek Fathers, which takes its point of departure from the Father as dynamic source of the Trinitarian processions. In contrast Augustine in Books V–VII of the *De Trinitate* begins with the common divine nature and sees the persons as mutual relations.[2] The Greek Fathers' tradition flowed into the West through John Scotus Erigena and his translations of the Pseudo-Dionysius. It passed through the Victorines and Alexander of Hales to Bonaventure. This tradition did not flow in the same way to Thomas, whose Trinitarian theology remains basically Augustinian.[3] Thus in the area of Trinitarian theology it is Thomas, and not Bonaventure, who is the Augustinian. Yet Bonaventure integrates into his system the characteristic Augustinian doctrines of Trinitarian vestige and image. It is very important to recognize that Bonaventure is heir to two major traditions: one from Augustine and the other from the Greek Fathers. In him they reach a new synthesis, which has remarkable depth and power. The classical Augustinian doctrines of vestige and image are given a dynamic Trinitarian base. Although the dynamic Trinity is not absent from Augustine, it is overshadowed by his own doctrine of the persons as relations. What Bonaventure has done, then, is to achieve a synthesis of certain Western and Eastern Trinitarian traditions with the dynamic Trinity as the principle of unity.

Bonaventure's dynamic Trinity is the key to understanding his positions in major controversies of the thirteenth century since it stands behind his attitude towards Aristotle. Bonaventure attacks Aristotle because the latter rejects exemplarism and consequently the mediation between God and the world. From this follow Aristotle's major errors: that God does not know particulars, nor has foreknowledge, nor providence, that the world is eternal, and that there is no personal immortality.[4] Because exemplarism is rooted in Trinitarian expressionism, Bonaventure's ultimate critique of Aristotle is founded in his dynamic doctrine of the Trinity. I believe that Bonaventure saw a specific incompatibility between Aristotle's eternal world and his own doctrine of the dynamic Trinity.

The doctrine of the dynamic Trinity situates Bonaventure in a larger historical current that spans the centuries from Plato to the present. This is the current studied by Arthur Lovejoy in his book *The Great Chain of Being* under the notion of fecundity. In this current God is seen as the fecund source, who communicates his goodness. As Lovejoy points out, this notion of God contrasts with the notion of God as self-sufficient absolute, unmoved mover, the changeless ultimate reality that stands apart from the world.[5] Although Bonaventure has integrated the self-sufficient absolute into his system, he stands clearly in the tradition of fecundity because of his dynamic doctrine of God. Once we situate Bonaventure there, we can see affinities between him and Plotinus, Hegel, and Whitehead. In this larger context, it is much easier to see how he dealt with the problems of fecundity and God's relation to the world. Although he shares much with others in this tradition, he differs with many on crucial points. As we will see in Chapter Eight, his genius led him to penetrate deeply into the problematics of divine fecundity and to arrive at solutions that not only make his thought relevant to the present, but enable him to make creative contributions to current debates.

FECUNDITY AND SELF-DIFFUSION

We shall now examine Bonaventure's dynamic Trinity in detail and bring to light its inherent coincidences of opposites. As we have indicated, the root of Bonaventure's doctrine lies in his conception of the Father as dynamic, fecund source of the Trinitarian processions. In examining the Father, Bonaventure employs two principles: the principle of fecund primordiality and the principle of the self-diffusion of the good. Both of these principles he applies to the divinity in relation to creation and to the Father in the Trinity. The first of these principles he draws from the *Liber de causis* and the second from the Pseudo-Dionysius. I believe that these are not two distinct principles, but two aspects of the same principle, which can be stated as follows: God as self-sufficient absolute must necessarily be fecund and self-communicating. This principle is Bonaventure's way of uniting the two conceptions of God which Lovejoy judges have been incompatible throughout the history of Western thought: namely, self-sufficiency and self-communication. For Bonaventure God's self-sufficiency and self-communication are so intimately united that his principle can be stated as follows: *Because* God is absolutely self-sufficient, he is absolutely self-communicating. It is clear that this is an instance of the coincidence of opposites. Since self-sufficiency and self-communication are not merely juxtaposed but require each other, this is an example of the coincidence of mutually affirming complementarity.

In the very early phase of his writing, in the second distinction of the first book of the *Commentary on the Sentences*, Bonaventure states this basic principle under the aspect of fecund primordiality: "the more primary a thing is, the more fecund it is and the principle of others."[6] Having stated this as a universal philosophical principle, he proceeds to apply it first to the divine essence as fecund source of creatures. Bonaventure states: "The divine essence, because it is first, is the principle of other essences."[7] In the very next clause, he applies the principle to the Father in the Trinity. Just as the divine essence is fecund because it is first, he states, "so the person of the Father, since he is first, because from no one, is the principle and has fecundity in regard to persons."[8]

Later in distinction 27 of the first book of the *Commentary*, Bonaventure examines the fecundity of the Father in greater detail and again applies the same philosophical principle.[9] This time it is in the context of an analysis of the Father's personal property of *innascibilitas*. Bonaventure claims that *innascibilitas* has a negative and a positive aspect: negatively it means that the Father has no source; positively, that the Father is fecund.

When Bonaventure applies the principle this time, he cites Aristotle as his source. The Quaracchi editors point out that Bonaventure is drawing from propositions 1, 16, 17, and 20 of the *Liber de causis*. Like his contemporaries, Bonaventure thought the *Liber de causis* was by Aristotle. However shortly after 1268 Thomas Aquinas read William of Moerbeke's Latin translation of Proclus' *Elements of Theology* and concluded that the author of the *Liber de causis* was an Arabian philosopher familiar with Proclus' treatise. This opinion has received support from modern scholarship.[10]

Referring to Aristotle, Bonaventure writes:

> A further reason for this opinion is found in the dictum of the Philosopher which states that the more primary causes are, the greater power they have, and that the first cause has greater influence and that the cause that is absolutely first has an influence in every respect. Therefore if we see in the order of causes, among which is the order of essence, that primacy involves in a cause the highest influence and a greater influence according to essence; in a similar way, where there is an order of person, primacy in the first person is the reason for the production of other persons. And since innascibility signifies primacy, it follows that it signifies fountain-fullness [*fontalem plenitudinem*] in relation to the production of persons.[11]

Bonaventure here is operating according to the coincidence of opposites, for he is uniting as opposites two personal properties which tradition has assigned to the Father: innascibility and paternity. Bonaventure interprets these as opposites which not only coexist but which mutually require each other. As *innascibilis*, the Father is unborn, unbegotten; he has no origin, no source. As unbegotten, he begets the Son so that in the Trinity there are polar opposites: the unbegotten and the begotten. The mediating element between the unbegottenness of the Father and the begottenness of the Son is the paternity of the Father: that is, his power to generate. But does this power to generate flow out of his unbegottenness? Bonaventure answers in the affirmative. In the technical terminology of the schools, innascibility is not merely a negative notion, but includes within it the positive note of generating fecundity. Thus the Father begets precisely because he is unbegotten. Such a mutual interpenetration, which is a mutual affirmation, is an example of the type of coincidence of opposites we described above as characteristic of Bonaventure's thought.[12]

That innascibility and fecundity are related as opposites can be seen from the fact that throughout much of the history of philosophy and theology these two notes have been considered, if not incompatible, at least in tension in God. This is the issue behind the conflict of Neo-Platonism and Arianism with the Christian Trinity. If God is unbegotten, he cannot be begotten, the Arians claimed. The Neo-Platonists contended that the One must be transcendent; lower beings might emanate from the One, but emanation is not an aspect of the One in itself; hence there is not an emanation within the One of another consubstantial with the One. The theme of Lovejoy's book *The Great Chain of Being* is the conflict of these two aspects of the divinity throughout Western history: the changeless absolute — which coincides with innascibility — and the divine fecundity.[13] How can Bonaventure affirm both and actually integrate them? Through the logic of the coincidence of opposites. Since he has opted for the coincidence of opposites as the basic logic of his system, it is completely consistent that his doctrine of the Father should participate in the coincidence of opposites. Actually it would be more accurate to say that the coincidence of opposites which operates throughout his system is ultimately rooted in his affirming the coincidence of innascibility and fecundity in the Father.

Bonaventure continues to develop the theme of fecund primordiality in his other writings of the early period: the disputed questions *De mysterio Trinitatis* and the *Breviloquium*.[14] Later he develops the same idea from the standpoint of the self-diffusion of the good in the *Itinerarium* and the *Collationes in Hexaemeron*. Drawing from the Pseudo-Dionysius, Bonaventure employs the principle that the good is self-diffusive. This principle applies both to God's diffusion in creatures and to the Father's diffusion in the Trinitarian processions. In the *Itinerarium* Bonaventure combines the Dionysian principle with Anselm's logic of the *Prologion*:

> Behold, therefore, and observe that the highest good is unqualifiedly that in comparison with which a greater cannot be thought. And this good is such that it cannot rightly be thought of as non-existing, since to be is absolutely better than not to be. And this good exists in such a way that it cannot rightly be thought of unless it is thought of as triune and one. For good is said to be self-diffusive, and therefore the highest good is most self-diffusive.[15]

Bonaventure then seeks for the highest self-diffusion, which he claims must be "actual and intrinsic, substantial and hypostatic, natural and voluntary, free and necessary, unfailing and perfect."[16] This highest self-diffusion is found only in the Trinitarian processions. Without the Trinitarian processions, we would not find in the divinity the highest good, "because it would not be supremely self-diffusive."[17]

GOD'S TRANSCENDENCE AND FECUNDITY

Bonaventure's doctrine of God's fecundity brings us to the heart of metaphysical issues. We will examine these briefly here and explore them later in Chapter Eight in Bonaventure's dialogue with process thinkers over God's fecundity in relation to the world.[18] In the *Itinerarium* and the *Collationes in Hexaemeron,* Bonaventure examines the metaphysical implications of God's fecundity seen in relation to creation. He claims that the highest good must be self-diffusive in the highest degree. This highest self-diffusion must be realized in the Trinity and cannot be realized in creation. For, as Bonaventure writes in the *Itinerarium,* "the diffusion that occurred in time in the creation of the world is no more than a pivot or point in comparison with the immense sweep of the eternal goodness."[19]

Later in the *Collationes in Hexaemeron,* Bonaventure analyzes this issue more systematically. The highest diffusion must be eternally actual, which is not the case in the diffusion of creatures. It must be integrally complete, but the full beauty of exemplarity is not given to creatures, for only the Son can say: "All things that the Father has are mine."[20] This diffusion must be ultimate, so that "the one producing gives whatever he can give; but creatures cannot receive whatever God can give." Bonaventure again uses the image of a point: "Just as a point adds nothing to a line, not even a million points, so the goodness of creation adds nothing to the goodness of the Creator, because the finite adds nothing to the infinite."[21] Finally the diffusion must be by way of perfect love. Here Bonaventure draws from Richard of St. Victor showing that God's love in order to be perfectly realized must be realized in the divine persons; for it is implied in Bonaventure, and spelled out in Richard, that God's love cannot be perfectly expressed towards creatures, but only within the Trinity.[22]

Bonaventure has penetrated to the heart of one of the most vexing metaphysical problems in the history of thought: How can God be both transcendent and immanent in the world? Following the coincidence of opposites, he has resolved the problem by grounding God's transcendence in his self-diffusion, which is, in fact, the ultimate basis of his immanence. Precisely because God transcends the world through his actualized self-diffusion in the Trinity, he can be immanent in the world without being dependent on the world. Thus since God does not need the world to activate his fecundity, his transcendence and immanence can coincide in his self-diffusiveness.

By liberating God from the world, Bonaventure is able to posit the fullness of fecundity within the inner life of the Trinity and thus establish a balanced coincidence of opposites within the divinity itself. For if God were absolutely self-sufficient in himself and only relatively self-communicating in relation to the world, then there would not be a true coincidence of opposites within God; for his self-communication would not be realized on the absolute level of his self-sufficiency. By establishing a coincidence of opposites within the divinity, Bonaventure has produced a dipolar doctrine of God, to use a term from twentieth century process thought.[23]   However, unlike Whitehead's and Hartshorne's dipolar God, Bonaventure's dipolarity is not dependent on God's relation to the world, but is realized within God's inner life.   Thus Bonaventure proposes a coincidence of opposites that goes beyond the coincidence of the primordial and the consequent nature of God in the Whiteheadian system.   According to Bonaventure, God is dipolar independently of the world; for in the innascibility of the Father there is both a self-sufficient and a self-communicating pole.   It is true that the self-communicating pole is the ground of his communication in the world; but even without the world, God's self-communicating pole is actualized in an absolute way in the Father's generation of the Son and the spiration of the Spirit.

SILENCE AND SPEECH

Having established the dipolarity of God through Bonaventure's doctrine of the Father, we can now ask a further question: Does the dipolarity of the Father have a mystical dimension? Following Bonaventure's lead, we have examined the innascibility of the Father in the light of metaphysical principles: the fecundity of primordiality and the self-diffusion of the good. And we have brought to light the metaphysical coincidence of opposites in self-sufficiency and self-communication. Does the innascibility of the Father also involve a mystical coincidence of opposites? Does it include the opposites of silence and speech, of darkness and light? Does it involve that aspect of the divinity which theologians, and especially mystics, have designated through silence, darkness, incomprehensibility, the abyss of the divinity, the non-manifesting aspect of God? Although Bonaventure did not formally develop this aspect of God in his treatment of innascibility, which we have been studying, I believe that it is implicity within the logic of his system and in conformity with the tradition he represents. From this point of view, the generation of the Son, the utterance of the Word by the Father, springs from the depths of silence in the abyss of the divinity. Thus the Father has a manifesting side and a non-manifesting side, a side of emanating light, and a side of darkness. If we thus extend Bonaventure's system according to the logic of the coincidence of opposites, we can clarify the nature of the apophatic tradition in which he stands. I would propose that there are two levels of apophatic or negative theology; one which negates the limited aspect of the finite world as commensurate with the infinite; and a second, which goes beyond the manifesting side of the divinity in order to enter into the non-manifesting side. This second form of apophatism is rooted in the Trinity and moves from contact with the Son, as Word and Image of the Father, into the silence and darkness of the Father, seen as the unbegotten abyss of the Godhead. I claim that both forms of apophatism operate in Bonaventure's thought, and that if we bring to light the second stage, we can arrive at a new interpretation of the final chapter of the *Itinerarium*.

The seventh and final chapter of the *Itinerarium* brings the reader to the level of mystical ecstacy after contemplating the sense world, the soul, and God himself as being and the good. In Chapter Five Bonaventure contemplates God as one and as being, in Chapter Six as the good and as Trinity. The seventh chapter, as the last stage of the ascent, leads to mystical contemplation. The seventh stage is usually interpreted according to the first form of apophatism; for Bonaventure says here that the mind must, "in beholding these things, transcend and pass over, not only this visible world, but even itself."[24] I would propose that the seventh chapter contains also the second level of apophatism and that the silence encountered there is not merely a subjective state of the mystic, but refers to an aspect of the divinity: to the silence of the Father as the abyss of the divinity.

I propose that the *Itinerarium* represents a blending of two forms of mysticism: the Trinitarian light mysticism of the Greek world epitomized in the Pseudo-Dionysius and Augustine, and the Christocentric mysticism of the early Franciscan milieu. Bonaventure integrates these two currents by seeing Christ as the *medium* who leads to the Father. More specifically in Chapters Six and Seven of the *Itinerarium*, Bonaventure integrates the Trinitarian and the Christocentric strands by seeing them as embodying two different types of the coincidence of opposites: the one and the many in the Trinity and the *maximum-minimum* in Christ. In Chapter Five we contemplate the coincidence of opposites in God as one and as being; in Chapter Six we contemplate the coincidence of opposites in God as the good and as Trinity; and finally we turn to Christ the greatest coincidence of opposites. The mediation of Christ as the coincidence of opposites leads us into the silence and darkness of mystical ecstacy. Chapter Seven begins with Christ as the passage and proceeds to give an extended quotation from the *Mystical Theology* of the Pseudo-Dionysius.[25] Bonaventure closes with the following statement:

> Let us, then, die and enter into this darkness. Let us silence all our care, our desires and our imaginings. With Christ crucified, let us pass 'out of this world to the Father,' so that, when the Father is shown to us, we may say with Philip: 'It is enough for us.'[26]

We note that Bonaventure has moved from a consideration of the Trinity as the self-diffusive good into darkness and silence, or we could say, from the Father as self-diffusive good to the Father as the unbegotten silent abyss of the divinity. Although in the *Itinerarium* Bonaventure does not explore the innascibility of the Father — which he had explored in the first book of the *Commentary on the Sentences* — if we add to the *Itinerarium* this other aspect of the Father, we can see that Christ, as coincidence of opposites, functions on a double level of apophatism between Chapters Six and Seven: Christ as the greatest coincidence of opposites leads us beyond the realm of sense, beyond our own selves, beyond the Word and its generation into the unbegotten depths of the silence of the Father.

I realize that the textual evidence in the *Itinerarium* is not completely suasive and that I had to bring to bear notions developed elsewhere in Bonaventure. Furthermore I developed my interpretation by extending the logic of his system beyond the point that he explored himself. My final framework is frankly a reconstruction of my own — yet a reconstruction which I claim is compatible with Bonaventure's system, implicit within it and even demanded by its logic. If this attempt to complete Bonaventure's system is not unfounded, then it can throw light on Bonaventure's relation to the various strands of the Christian mystical tradition and can raise certain questions on the norms for judging orthodoxy. Seen in the light of our reconstruction, Bonaventure may be in greater accord with the apophatic mysticism of the Pseudo-Dionysius, Eckhart, and even Gregory of Palamas than is usually acknowledged. And these theologians, in turn, seen in the light of our reconstruction of Bonaventure, may be less out of line with Christian orthodoxy than Latin theologians have been inclined to concede. On the other hand, this reconstruction may provide a framework for delineating similarities and differences between Christian and Oriental mysticism. Once the Trinitarian basis of Christian apophatic mysticism is established, one can more readily see relations with even the extreme apophatism of Zen Buddhism and the monism of non-dualistic Vedanta. In this sense, the Bonaventure system could contribute to the pioneer work that Raymond Panikkar is doing in using the Trinity as a basis for relating Christian and Oriental mysticism.[27]

COINCIDENCE OF OPPOSITES IN THE SON

Having examined the coincidence of opposites in the Father, we turn now to the Son. In the Father we found a coincidence of opposites that can be read in metaphysical terms of self-sufficiency/self-communication and in mystical terms of darkness/light, silence/speech. This is the most basic coincidence of opposites in Bonaventure's system and the source from which all others flow. Out of the Father's fecundity and self-communicating goodness the Son is generated; out of his silence, the Word is spoken. In fact, it is the Son who actualizes the Father's fecundity and establishes his self-communicating pole. In a special way, then, the Son, and not the Father, is the center of Bonaventure's attention and the focus of his more explicit treatment of the coincidence of opposites. For Bonaventure Christ is the center or *medium,* the *persona media* of the Trinity and the dynamic *medium* of the Father's expression. This is the theme developed explicitly in the first of the *Collationes in Hexaemeron.*[28] Thus in the case of the Son we have a single text in which Bonaventure deals with the coincidence of opposites explicitly and at the same time systematically. Since we will examine this text in detail in our next chapter, we will merely summarize here the various types of the coincidence of opposites realized in the Trinity through the Son.

For Bonaventure the dynamic Trinity involves a complex pattern of the coincidence of opposites centered in the Son. In a large body of texts Bonaventure studies the Trinitarian processions as the expression of the divine creativity.[29] The Son is the Father's Image and Word, and the Spirit is the breath and love of the divinity. Through the Son the Father's creativity expresses itself and flows back to its source in the unity of the Spirit. Thus the Trinitarian processions issue in a type of dynamic circle of divine creative energy, which remains within the inner life of the divinity and which binds the persons together in a most intimate union. Through the Son there is activated a type of *exitus* from the Father and a *reditus* in the Spirit, which has its counterpart in the *exitus* and *reditus* of creatures. In each case the Son is the *medium* of this going out from and return back to the source.

If this dynamic circle within the Trinity is viewed from a more static perspective, then the Son can be seen as the middle person of the Trinity, uniting within himself the polar aspects of the Trinity: the Father's unbounded creativity and the Spirit's pure receptivity. In a most suggestive text in the first of the *Collationes in Hexaemeron,* Bonaventure, speaking of the Son as the *medium metaphysicum,* states:

> This must necessarily be the center of the persons: for if there is a
> person who produces and is not produced and a person who is produced

and does not produce, there must necessarily be a central person who is produced and produces.[30]

Note that Bonaventure sees the Son as the middle person of a creative process, for he focuses here exclusively on productivity. The Father, as the person who produces, is seen as the opposite pole of the Spirit, who is produced but does not produce. Between the productive and the receptive poles of the divinity, the Son is the center (*medium*) for he embodies within himself both productivity and receptivity. This touches a crucial issue in Trinitarian theology. Throughout the centuries, many have asked the tantalizing question: If the Father is the unbounded productive source, why does he not produce an infinity of persons, or at least a greater number than two? Bonaventure holds that the unbounded productivity of the divinity must issue in the two Trinitarian processions, for only in this way can there be realized the maximum self-diffusion of the good.[31] This implies that Bonaventure's norm for maximum productivity is not mere production of large numbers, but the greatest expression of opposites. Hence for Bonaventure the Trinity is the archetype of maximum creativity which is realized by the consubstantial production of opposites and not in an infinite series of divine persons or of subordinated emanations within the realm of creatures. Thus the dynamism of this archetype is calculated by its capacity to produce opposites to the maximum degree and not by its ability to produce successive instances that can be counted arithmetically. Within this dynamic archetype the Son is the center, for in and through him the maximum coincidence of opposites is realized.

The Trinity is not only the archetype of maximum creativity, but also the archetype of unity and plurality. In the *Itinerarium,* after treating the Trinity as the mystery of the divine self-diffusion, Bonaventure points to the coincidence of "supreme consubstantiality with a plurality of hypostases."[32] As heir to Richard of St. Victor, Bonaventure studies how self-diffusive goodness demands a plurality of persons. In the first book of the *Commentary on the Sentences,* Bonaventure states:

Suppose there is in God supreme happiness. But wherever there is supreme happiness, there is supreme goodness, supreme charity and supreme enjoyment. But if there is supreme goodness, since it is characteristic of goodness to communicate itself supremely and this is especially in producing from itself an equal and giving its own being — therefore, etc. If there is supreme charity, since charity is not private love, but is directed to another, it therefore requires a plurality of persons. Likewise, if there is supreme enjoyment, since there is not enjoyable possession of a good without a companion, therefore for supreme enjoyment companionship is required and therefore a plurality of persons.[33]

Bonaventure continues by claiming that God's supreme perfection demands a plurality of persons. Since "it is characteristic of perfection to produce another similar to itself in nature," there must be a multiplication in God.[34] But this cannot be realized in the production of another divine essence; therefore it must be in terms of a production of persons. Bonaventure is following out the logic of the self-diffusion of the good. Maximum self-diffusion requires production on the level of the divinity; hence this means that there must be a plurality of persons, who are intimately united in several ways: (1) by their common source from the Father's *fontalis plenitudo*; (2) by their consubstantiality in that each shares the fullness of the divine nature; (3) by their mutual interpenetration of circuminsession. In this way the divine self-diffusion issues in the mystery of the divine unity and plurality.

The mystery of the Trinity, then, is like a precious gem which can be viewed from two sides: From one side it is the archetype of maximum productivity; from the other it is the archetype of the divine unity and plurality. The Greek East has viewed the mystery chiefly from the first perspective; and the Latin West, following Augustine, chiefly from the second. I believe that these perspectives are by no means incompatible but are related as complementary opposites. This is precisely the way in which Bonaventure has integrated them into his system. However, I believe that one must give a certain primacy to the dynamic Trinity, as Bonaventure does, following the Greek tradition. For it is the dynamism of the Father that is the source of the plurality of persons. In the West there has been a tendency to pose the Trinitarian question exclusively from the perspective of unity and plurality and to fail to take into account the entire problematic of the divine fecundity. This has caused not only an ignoring of problems that must be faced, but also a weakening of the doctrine of the Trinity. For the Trinity is not primarily a mystery that challenges the rational understanding of the divine simplicity; rather it is, as Bonaventure has so abundantly declared, primarily the mystery of the boundless creativity of God.

COINCIDENCE OF GOD AND THE WORLD

Bonaventure's doctrine of God emphasizes the divine transcendence. In view of his self-sufficiency, God does not need the world for his being; and in view of his intra-Trinitarian self-diffusion, he does not depend on the world for the activation of his creativity. Although God is transcendent in both poles of his being, he is immanent in the world. The coincidence of transcendence and immanence is achieved through the Son as *medium*. Just as the Son is the *persona media* of the Trinity, so he is the *medium* between God and the world. Through him is realized a coincidence of the infinite and the finite, the Creator and the creature, the eternal and the temporal, the beginning and the end.

When the Father generates the Son, he generates in the Son the archetypes of all he can make. As Bonaventure says: "The Father generated one similar to himself, namely the Word, co-eternal with himself; and he expressed his own likeness and as a consequence expressed all the things that he could make."[35] Thus the Father's fecundity which expresses itself in the Word also produces in the Word the *rationes aeternae* of all that can be made. Creation *ad extra*, then, is an overflow of this divine fecundity and remains deeply grounded in the Word. The Word, then, is the basis of Bonaventure's doctrine of exemplarism, for through their exemplaristic grounding in the Word, all creatures reflect God

Creation

and lead man to God. The world is like a mirror reflecting God,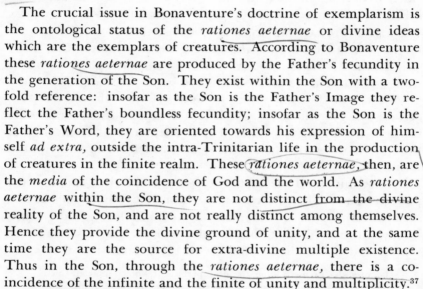
a stained glass window in which the divine light is reflected in
various colors, like a statue depicting God and a road leading to
God. With great precision, Bonaventure divides creatures into
various levels of representing God: shadow, vestige, image, and
similitude.[36]

The crucial issue in Bonaventure's doctrine of exemplarism is
the ontological status of the *rationes aeternae* or divine ideas
which are the exemplars of creatures. According to Bonaventure
these *rationes aeternae* are produced by the Father's fecundity in
the generation of the Son. They exist within the Son with a twofold reference: insofar as the Son is the Father's Image they reflect the Father's boundless fecundity; insofar as the Son is the
Father's Word, they are oriented towards his expression of himself *ad extra,* outside the intra-Trinitarian life in the production
of creatures in the finite realm. These *rationes aeternae,* then, are
the *media* of the coincidence of God and the world. As *rationes
aeternae* within the Son, they are not distinct from the divine
reality of the Son, and are not really distinct among themselves.
Hence they provide the divine ground of unity, and at the same
time they are the source for extra-divine multiple existence.
Thus in the Son, through the *rationes aeternae,* there is a coincidence of the infinite and the finite of unity and multiplicity.[37]

Note that we have here quite a different type of the coincidence
of opposites from those in the Trinity, where absolute consubstantiality is found in all cases. The Father's silence is consubstantial with his speech; his self-sufficiency with his self-diffusion.
Within the dynamic Trinity, the Father, Son, and Spirit are consubstantial, as are the two perspectives of the Trinitarian archetype: that of creativity and that of unity/plurality. In the case
of God and the world, however, consubstantiality is precisely
what is lacking. Since God and creation exist on radically different planes, this radical difference is at the core of the coincidence of opposites. God and the world are related as ontological
opposites and not as mere polar opposites within the realm of

dynamic spirit. Although it is true that the divine polarities are the source of all the polarities in the universe, we must not merely transpose the paradigms from the Trinity to the relation of God and the world without crucial modifications. Permeating the relation of God and the world, at every stage, is the coincidence of the ontological opposites of the Creator/creatures, infinite/finite, maximum/minimum, eternal/temporal.

Bonaventure's exemplarism can be described as involving three levels. The first contains the most general principle that there exist in the divine mind ideas which are the exemplars of created things. Bonaventure sees God as the great artist or maker who gives form to the things he produces. Hence "if he gives to a certain thing the form by which it is distinguished from another thing or the property by which it is distinguished from another thing, it is necessary that he have an ideal form or rather ideal forms."[38]

The second level of Bonaventure's exemplarism contains the position that in God there exist the ideas not only of generic and specific forms, but of singulars as well. Following Augustine, Bonaventure holds that the singular and the universal must be represented in the divine mind with the greatest actuality:

> Because the divine wisdom is most perfect, it knows most distinctly universal and singular things and represents all these things most distinctly and perfectly. Hence it is said to have the forms and ideas of singular things as the most perfectly expressive likenesses of things.[39]

The third level of Bonaventure's exemplarism draws us explicitly into his doctrine of truth. Not only do things exist actually in their divine exemplars, but they have their greatest reality there. Hence we know them most truly when we know them in the divine mind. Since God represents things preeminently, Bonaventure can say, "I will see myself better in God than in my very self."[40] In the disputed questions *De scientia Christi*, Bonaventure develops this point more in detail when he responds to an objection. Against his position that God knows things in their exemplars, the objection is posed that truth is found more in the thing itself than in its likeness. Hence God should know things better in themselves than in his eternal ideas of things.[41] Bonaventure answers by saying that truth can be looked upon in two ways: (1) "Truth is that which is," according to Augustine;[42] (2) or according to Anselm, "Truth is rectitude perceptible to the mind alone."[43] In relating these two aspects of truth, Bonaventure reveals his fundamental Platonism. For him the first type of truth — the way things are — is remote and removed from their ultimate reality. The second kind of truth touches the ultimate reality of things; for it grasps the rectitude of things, their ideal forms, the way they ought to be. Since the ultimate reality of things is found in their divine exemplars, their ultimate truth resides there as well:

> The exemplary likeness expresses the thing more perfectly than the caused thing itself expresses itself. On account of this, God knows things more perfectly through their likenesses than he would know them through their essences; and angels know things more perfectly in the Word than in their own reality.[44]

The full force of Bonaventure's exemplarism can be seen in this third level, where things have a preeminent existence in the Word. It is this preeminent existence that establishes the intimate coincidence between God and the world and which provides the central element in Bonaventure's speculative articulation of Francis' cosmic religious experience. We can attempt to reconstruct the essential elements in Francis' religious experience by searching through his own writings and the early biographies. From this evidence it would be safe to claim that Francis experienced each creature as a unique expression of God's fecundity. He rejoiced in the variety of creatures; he admired the grandeur of the sun and the simplicity of an earthworm. He reverenced each creature for its individuality, as expressing something unique about God.[45] We could say that for Francis each individual creature expressed something about God that no other creature could express. It is this profound sense of the interpenetration of the world and God that Bonaventure articulates in metaphysical-theological terms in his doctrine of exemplarism, whereby each individual creature has within the Word its own *ratio aeterna* and its preeminent existence. Thus echoing Francis, we can extend Bonaventure's statement, claiming that I will know *each thing* better in God than in its very self.

BONAVENTURE'S EPISTEMOLOGY

According to Bonaventure's exemplarism, all creatures are shadows reflecting God as their cause. All creatures are also vestiges of the Trinity, reflecting the divine power, wisdom, and goodness. Rational creatures reflect God in a special way for they are his image, having him as their object in the depths of their memory, understanding, and will. In his doctrine of man as image of God, Bonaventure's exemplarism coincides with his epistemology. In human knowledge, there is a coincidence of God and man, the unchangeable and the changeable, the infinite and the finite, the eternal and the temporal.[46]

According to Bonaventure, in all certain knowledge, God is present to us as the light that illumines our mind and the ground that supports the truth we discover. When man turns within himself and moves to God, he proceeds not through Aristotelian analogy but through Augustinian image. Man looks into his own subjectivity as into a mirror where the divine light shines. What he focuses on is the light that is reflected and not the mirror itself. God is both the light by which we see and the preeminent source of the forms we discern. He is, Bonaventure says, even more beautiful than the sun. While the sun has the power of radiating light, it does not contain within itself the forms of things, as God does. Hence God is more beautiful than the sun, since he not only radiates light, but has within himself the clear and brilliant forms of things. God, then, is the eternal exemplar, who represents things preeminently and in whom we read true reality.[47] Although we abstract the forms of things from sense objects, these very objects are ultimately grounded in the divine mind so that in some degree we attain in a shadowy way the

very archetypes of things in God. Thus our minds are bathed
in the divine light and in touch with the eternal forms. God is in
our mind and our mind is in God; all things are in God and
God in all things. Thus along with his metaphysics of exemplarism, his epistemology of illumination establishes profound
intimacy between God and creatures.

For a full exploration of Bonaventure's epistemology, we would
have to examine his positions on sense knowledge, abstraction,
and the agent and possible intellect; as well as his theory of
illumination and knowledge in the eternal reasons. Bonaventure's
epistemology is complex because it brings together both Aristotelian and Platonic elements; just how these elements are integrated in his system has been a matter of considerable discussion among his interpreters. Granted this complexity, the point I
wish to make here is that in his study of knowledge he takes a path
to God through human subjectivity — a path which implies a
coincidence of opposites in the human mind. We will examine
three series of texts where this is expressed: (1) his proofs for the
existence of God in the disputed questions *De mysterio Trinitatis*;
(2) his inner way in Chapter Three of the *Itinerarium*; (3) and
his classical text on knowledge through the eternal reasons in the
fourth question of the disputed questions *De scientia Christi*.[48]
In each case Bonaventure explores the coincidence of man and
God in the processes of human knowledge. I believe that it is
especially fruitful to approach Bonaventure's epistemology from
the standpoint of the coincidence of opposites; for it can, I believe, clear away some of the false presuppositions that have obscured this area of his thought.

An important series of texts on the coincidence of God and
man in knowledge appears in the first question of the disputed
questions *De mysterio Trinitatis*. He divides the question into
two articles, the first dealing with the certitude with which God's
existence is known and the second dealing with the faith by which
the Trinity is believed.[49] In the first article, he does not set out
to prove the existence of God in the way Thomas does in his

Summa theologiae.[50] Rather he follows a generic Augustinian approach, asking whether the existence of God is a truth which cannot be doubted. The very statement of the question situates the issue within the sphere of the mind with its subjective states of doubt and certitude. He will arrive at an Augustinian solution which involves a coincidence of opposites: Although the mind is changeable, it has within it infallible knowledge of unchangeable truth.

In order to establish his position, he moves in three directions: first within himself, then outside himself, and then above himself. Bonaventure claims that there is no rational basis for doubting God's existence, "Since if the intellect enters within itself or goes outside itself or gazes above itself, if it proceeds rationally, then it knows that God exists, with certitude and without doubt."[51] Although the posing of the question is from an Augustinian perspective, Bonaventure integrates into his perspective the Aristotelian proofs from act and potency based on the contingency of creatures. This is what he means by moving outside oneself. In the third division, in which the intellect gazes above itself, he integrates into the Augustinian perspective also Anselm's ontological argument. For when the intellect looks above itself to the notion of God as that than which no greater can be thought, it must realize that God necessarily exists.[52]

Although Bonaventure has subsumed all three approaches within an Augustinian perspective, it is the first approach which will command our attention here: namely, through our own subjectivity, since it involves a characteristically Augustinian coincidence of opposites in knowledge. Bonaventure begins this approach by stating that every truth impressed on all minds is a truth that cannot be doubted. But he contends: "Both by authorities and by reasons it is shown that God's existence is impressed on all rational minds."[53] He cites John Damascene as saying: "Knowledge of God's existence is naturally inserted in us." He next quotes from Hugh of St. Victor: "God so regulated knowledge of himself in man that just as what he is can never be totally

comprehended, so his existence can never be completely un-
known." Next he quotes Boethius: "There is inserted in the
minds of men a desire for truth and goodness." Bonaventure then
reasons that desire presupposes knowledge; hence there is impressed on the minds of men knowledge of truth and goodness
and the desire of what is most desirable. But, Bonaventure says,
this good is God. He then proceeds to draw from the *De Trinitate*
of Augustine the notion of the soul as image of God. According to
Augustine, the image consists in the mind, knowledge and love.
The soul, then, by its very nature is the image of God; hence it
has knowledge of God inserted within itself. "But what is first
known about God is that he exists; therefore this is naturally
inserted in the human mind." Then drawing certain principles
from Aristotle, Bonaventure interprets them in the same vein.
He concludes the section gathering other material from Augustine
and by reasoning on the soul's knowledge of itself. He brings his
exploration to a climax by saying: "God is most present to the
soul itself and through himself is knowable; therefore there is
inserted in the soul knowledge of God himself."[54]

In each of the ten paragraphs where he developed these themes,
Bonaventure has moved through the path of subjectivity to knowledge of God as a coincidence of opposites. Knowledge of God
is present in man's mind in such a way that he cannot logically
doubt God's existence. In the light of this Augustinian approach,
Bonaventure can even bring Aristotle into the path of the inner
way. The path through subjectivity is more clearly charted
in the *Itinerarium*, where the journey motif is made explicit as
the unifying theme of the entire work. Here, more clearly than
in the previous texts, the reader is led to see the coincidence of
opposites in the depths of man's faculties of memory, understanding, and will.

SUBJECTIVITY IN THE *Itinerarium*

In the *Itinerarium* the path of the journey is basically the same
as that outlined in the disputed question. Bonaventure contem-

plates God in the external world, within the soul and in God himself; however the Franciscan contemplation is interwoven with characteristic Augustinian speculation and dialectical self-reflection.

After contemplating the reflection of God in the external world, Bonaventure turns to the soul in the third chapter of the *Itinerarium*. He says that we are "to reenter into ourselves, that is, into our mind, where the divine image shines forth."[55] Using the image of entering into the tabernacle of Moses, he says that we are to leave the outer atrium, that is the external world, and enter into the inner realm of the tabernacle, that is into ourselves, where we will see God through a mirror, for the light of truth shines like a candelabrum in our minds. "Enter into yourself, therefore, and observe. . . ," Bonaventure bids us as he leads us on an inner journey into the depths of our memory, understanding and will, where we discover the reflection of God in the soul as image of the Trinity.[56]

Bonaventure first explores the memory, moving through its various levels until he comes to the reflection of God in its depths. On one level the memory retains and represents temporal things: "the past by remembrance, the present by reception and the future by foresight."[57] On another level it retains basic mathematical notions such as the point. On a deeper level it retains the principles and axioms of the sciences in such a way that it cannot forget them as long as one uses reason. For when he hears them again, he assents to them, not as though he were perceiving them anew, but rather recognizing them as innate and familiar. On this third level the memory has present in itself a changeless light in which it remembers changeless truths. Bonaventure then concludes:

> And thus it is clear from the activities of the memory that the soul itself is an image of God and a similitude so present to itself and having him so present to it that it actually grasps him and potentially 'is capable of possessing him and of becoming a partaker in him.'[58]

In a similar way Bonaventure explores the intellect, analyzing our knowledge of terms and definitions and our awareness of being. We can know limited being only in the light of unlimited being, since the mind knows negations only in the light of something positive. Therefore our intellect does not arrive at a full analysis of any single created being unless it is aided by a knowledge of the eternal and absolute Being. For, Bonaventure asks, how could we perceive something as defective if we had no knowledge of the Being that is free from all defect? Also the intellect grasps certain truths as changeless and necessary, but this knowledge can be had only in the divine unchangeable light.[59]

Bonaventure next examines the will or elective faculty. When it inquires of two things which is better, it does so in view of the notion of the highest Good which must necessarily be impressed upon the soul. Furthermore, when we judge that something is right, we do so in the light of the divine law that transcends our minds but nevertheless is stamped on the mind. Finally, when we desire something, we desire it in the light of the highest good, either because it leads to it or resembles it. After making this journey into the depths of subjectivity through the memory, understanding and will. Bonaventure concludes: "See, therefore, how close the soul is to God, and how, through their activity, the memory leads us to eternity, the intelligence to truth and the elective faculty to the highest good."[60]

KNOWLEDGE IN THE ETERNAL REASONS

In the fourth question of the disputed questions *De scientia Christi,* Bonaventure examines the epistemological issue from the standpoint of certain knowledge. He asks whether whatever we know with certitude is known in the eternal reasons. He answers affirmatively, but with certain precisions: "For certain intellectual knowledge even in this life, it is required that we attain in some way the eternal reason, as the regulating and motive reason, but not in all its clarity, but along with our own created reason and as in a glass darkly."[61]

For proof of his position, Bonaventure analyzes the ontological status of certain knowledge and of the knower. Certain knowledge requires immutability on the part of what is known and infallibility on the part of the knower. But created truth is not immutable and our minds are fallible. Therefore for certain knowledge, we must attain a truth which is immutable and which is known in an infallible light. Turning to his doctrine of exemplarism, Bonaventure observes that things have existence in themselves, in the mind of the knower and in the Eternal Art, that is, in the Word as the expression of the Father. Since created things are mutable in themselves and since man's mind is fallible, certain knowledge demands that we touch, in some way, things as they exist immutably in the Eternal Art.[62]

This leads Bonaventure to his doctrine of the soul. He distinguishes two portions of the soul: the lower (*portio inferior*), which is concerned with temporal things; and the higher (*portio superior*), which is turned to the eternal reasons. It is this higher portion that constitutes the soul as image of God, and it is this portion that inheres in the eternal norms (*aeternis regulis inhaerescit*).[63] These are the norms by which we search for truth and judge that what we have found is true; they are the norms of justice and charity, of fear and love of God — that are reflected even in the souls of evil men.[64] In certitude, Bonaventure says, we contact the eternal reason "as the normative and motive reason" (*ut ratio regulans et motiva*). This means that we contact the Word as the ultimate source and norm of all truth and goodness.[65]

How do we contact the Word? Certainly not in all his brightness, for Bonaventure is talking here about the lowest level of intellectual illumination. And even in mystical ecstasy, according to him, we do not experience God completely. In the experience of certitude we grasp the Word — in the midst of darkness and obscurity, without consciousness of his presence, precisely as the norm and motive of our certitude. The experience of the divine light is further bound up with our own created light of knowing (*propria ratio creata*) and the abstract concepts and impressions drawn from the sense world (*rerum similitudines abstractas a phantasmate*). Bonaventure says that the eternal reason is "contuited" (*contuita*), that it is known along with many other elements.[66]

"Contuition" is a basic concept for Bonaventure and touches the heart of his Franciscan experience. It means that we see God along with creation — not directly, nor in all his brightness, but in and through our experience: that is, in a Franciscan coincidence of opposites. This does not mean, however, that all of our knowledge is derived from sense data; on the contrary, Bonaventure says:

> The soul knows God and itself and what is in itself without the aid of the exterior senses. Hence if at some time the Philosopher says that nothing is in the intellect that was not previously in sense and that all knowledge has its origin from sense, this should be understood about those things which indeed have existence in the soul through an abstracted likeness. And these are said to be in the soul in the manner of writings. And therefore the Philosopher very pointedly says that there is nothing written in the soul, not because there is no knowledge in it, but because there is no picture or abstract likeness in it.[67]

Bonaventure sees the soul as a *tabula rasa* as far as abstract concepts are concerned, but not as far as knowledge of God, the ideals of the virtues, such as justice, charity, fear and love of God, or the norm of the true and the good. These are inborn in the soul, and by reflecting within himself man can come to an awareness of them. But even in our ethical striving, our desire for happiness, our thirst for knowledge, God is "contuited" — he is known along with our human experience, as the ground and the norm of our striving; he is not known directly in all his brightness, but in the coincidence of opposites whereby his light shines in our experience.

An example of "contuition" which includes the process of abstraction would be the first principle: The whole is greater than its part. We have no innate knowledge of this principle, since our mind is a blank tablet, having no pictures or concepts of whole and part. However, when we sense some material thing and abstract the concept of the whole and part, we immediately know that the whole is greater than its part. And we know this not as something new, but as if we always knew it, as something necessary and eternal.[68] In this knowledge we have touched the eternal; we know this in the eternal reason, in the divine light. The abstraction from sense data is necessary to give us the material, but in knowing this as a necessary principle, we "contuit" the eternal Word.

Through exemplarism, the epistemology of illumination, and contuition Bonaventure proposes a type of mysticism of knowledge. Through the coincidence of opposites, he draws into consciousness the religious depth that underlies everyday experience. He is typically Franciscan. What could be more ordinary than the statement: The whole is greater than its part? And yet God is present at the moment when we say, Aha! Bonaventure seeks to make God's presence known, to contemplate him in his reflection in our experience and to mount above through the successive stages of illumination he describes in the *Itinerarium*. Everyday experience leads to a philosophical insight that awakens religious consciousness that may, with God's grace, lead to mystical ecstasy. This is Bonaventure's journey, through the coincidence of opposites, into God.

THE FALLEN IMAGE

Through Bonaventure's epistemology man is seen as the image of the Trinity, reflecting through the coincidence of opposites the divine power, wisdom, and goodness. But to be an image of the Trinity is both man's glory and his tragedy, for he is a fallen image. The very coincidence of opposites that is the key to understanding man as image is also the key to understanding him as fallen image. Bonaventure uses vivid symbols to paint a picture of man in his tragic state: He speaks of man as having fallen *(ceciderit)* and lying on the ground, in need of someone to give him his hand to raise him up.[69] He describes a strange blindness of the intellect *(mira caecitas)* which prevents man from seeing the presence of God. Accustomed to darkness of sensation, man is like the bat in the daylight that sees nothing;[70] he is blinded *(excaecatus)* and bent over *(incurvatus)*, and he sits in darkness and does not see the light of heaven.[71] But man still has an appetite for the infinite; the coincidence of opposites still operates within his soul. But because he is not open to God, because he has fallen, the infinite pole of his being is thrust aimlessly into the prison of finitude. In his darkness and confusion he has entangled himself in infinite questions *(infinitis quaestionibus)*. He is filled with anxiety. He desires the infinite; he searches for it; he is never at rest.[72]

Being an image of God, then, is the cause of man's highest perfection and the reason for his present anxiety. It is also the source of his fall and the root of the suffering of the damned. Satan could tempt man with the premise that "a rational creature should desire to be like his Creator because he is his image — for this reason the punishment in the damned will be extreme, since to be an image is essential to the soul and such a desire will be essential in the damned."[73]

A major text on the fall of man is found in the preface of the second book of Bonaventure's *Commentary on the Sentences*.[74] In the plan of the *Commentary* the first book deals with God, the second with creation and the fall of man. In his preface, Bonaventure paints in vivid strokes a picture of the ideal from which man has fallen and his tragic groping for God. As Trinitarian image, his faculties of memory, understanding and will should in their depths be open to and rooted in the transcendent power, wisdom and goodness of the Trinity. Instead man is turned from his ultimate rootedness; in dizziness, darkness and uncontrolled desire, he is slave to his infinite desire in its endless and futile grasping after creatures.

Bonaventure begins his preface with a verse from Ecclesiastes (7:30): "Only this have I found, that God made man right and man has entangled himself in infinite questions." As the editors note, from this short text he draws the outlines of the entire second book of his *Commentary* and at the same time penetrates deeply into the tragedy of the human situation.[75] The text gives the two aspects of man: his right creation *(recta conditio)* and his miserable deviation *(miserabilis deviatio)*. God made man right by making him an image of God and turning him to God. "For man is right when his intelligence coincides with the supreme truth in knowing, his will conforms to the supreme loving and his power is united to the supreme power in acting. Now this is when man is turned to God in his total self."[76]

Bonaventure here is using his notion of man as image of Trinity as described above. When man turns to God as supreme truth, goodness and power, then he is right. Bonaventure draws the concept of rightness *(rectitudo)* from Anselm, who defines truth as "rightness perceptible to the mind alone."[77] Bonaventure observes that "when our intellect coincides with truth, it is necessarily made right."[78] He then integrates Anselm's definition with the medieval definition, attributed to Aristotle, that truth is the coinciding *(adaequatio)* of reality and the intellect. However, it must be noted here that Bonaventure means this not in the sense that the mind is like a blank tablet on which a true concept of an external sense object is delineated. Rather he means it in the sense of man as image of God, with supreme truth reflected in his soul. If man turns to this supreme truth, then he is made true: "Now when our intelligence is turned to truth, it is made true and as a result coincides with truth."[79] Bonaventure uses the same approach with goodness: "When the will is conformed to eternal goodness and equity, it is necessarily made right."[80]

In dealing with power, Bonaventure uses a different aspect of the Latin term *rectus*. The first meaning of *rectus* is straight, a meaning which is retained in the English derivative *rectilinear*. From this basic spatial meaning arises the moral and esthetic meaning of power: A thing is right when it has all that it ought to have. In the preface Bonaventure intends all these meanings. When dealing with man's being united to the supreme power, he begins with the spatial meaning of straight. Man is straight when he is in the straight line of moving without deviation from his first principle towards his ultimate end. God's action is always straight since everything is from God and on account of God; so when man unites himself to God's action or power, he will be made straight, since he will be rooted in his first principle and moving to his final end.

In being created right, man was turned above to God and subjected to him; he was also turned to creatures, but they were subjected to him. He had wisdom and knowledge about the world, and he could use all things for his purposes. "But man has entangled himself in infinite questions." Just as Bonaventure played on the meaning of *rectus,* so now he plays on the meaning of the Latin *quaestio.* The primary meaning of *quaestio* is a seeking or searching, hence an asking or questioning. When Bonaventure says that "man has entangled himself in infinite questions," he understands *quaestio* in its deepest level as searching and desiring. After the Fall, man is still an image of God; he has lost contact with God because he has turned from him, but he still bears his image stamped on his soul. He still has the desire for God, the appetite for the infinite; for this remains even in hell. He wanders about the world, never at rest, in an infinite search for the infinite good he has lost. He has fallen into the fragmented finite world, with a thousand desires, a thousand questions. "Man," Bonaventure says, "has been made anxious in his searching. And because nothing created can compensate for the good he has lost, since it is infinite, he desires it, he searches for it and he is never at rest."[81]

Bonaventure then describes man's infinite searching. "His intelligence, made ignorant by turning itself away from the supreme truth, entangled itself in infinite questions out of curiosity."[82] He is entangled in controversies and doubt, in disputes and wrangling. There is a touch of irony in Bonaventure's interpretation of man's fall as entangling him in infinite questions, for his preface introduces a commentary containing hundreds of scholastic questions *(quaestiones)* set in the argumentative form of the *disputatio.*

Man's will has been made poor by turning away from the supreme good. It is driven by concupiscence and infinite desires, and has become entangled in murder, theft, adultery. His power has become weak and unstable. He feels a kind of metaphysical dizziness, because he has lost his grounding in infinite power; he is like dust driven by the wind. "Since, therefore, dust cannot be at rest as long as there is a wind that whirls it around, so our power cannot remain stable. And therefore it searches and moves through an infinite number of places and begs support."[83]

This, then, is the state of infinite searching in which man, after having been created right, has become entangled and from which he has need to be redeemed. The coincidence of opposites at the base of his being has become distorted. He must be rescued, brought back from his fallen state by Christ, the greatest coincidence of opposites. As *persona media* of the Trinity and the *medium* in whom God and the world coincide, he takes upon himself in the Incarnation the depths of finitude and the burden of sin. Entering into the opposites of evil and death, he brings forth life and restores to its primitive rectitude the fallen image in man. As Incarnate Word, Christ re-establishes man as Trinitarian image and with the Spirit brings him back to the unity of the Father.

CHAPTER V

Christ the Center

N HIS doctrine of Christ the *medium,* or center, Bonaventure's theology of redemption coincides with his theology of creation. Christ the center reconciles man to God and brings creation to its fullness as expression of God. Thus in his notion of Christ the center, Bonaventure's Christology reaches its climax and his system attains its completion. Through this Christocentricity his vast theological edifice is capped with a second tower to balance that of his Trinitarian theology. The construction of this Christocentric tower proceeded gradually — from the sketchy designs found in his early writings, through the erection of the base structure in the *Itinerarium,* to its mature elaboration in the *Collationes in Hexaemeron,* delivered the year before his death. In this development of the doctrine of Christ the center, Bonaventure's understanding of the coincidence of opposites reaches its fullest realization. Not only is Christ seen as the greatest coincidence of opposites, as in the *Itinerarium;* but he is viewed as the center through whom all the opposites in reality are differentiated and held together. Thus all coincidences of opposites in the Trinity, in the world, and in the relation of God and the world are mediated through Christ the universal center.

Because Bonaventure's thought reaches such a point of integration and self-conscious expression in the doctrine of Christ the center, we can study this area both textually and systematically at the same time. Bonaventure has produced a single text, the first of the *Collationes in Hexaemeron,* which contains in a brilliantly graphic and synthetic form the mature elaboration of his

131

Christocentricity.[1] This piece sketches all the major dimensions of his theological-philosophical world view and studies each area analytically and systematically from the point of view of Christ the center. Furthermore, the coincidence of opposites permeates the entire selection, since Bonaventure's notion of *medium* or "center" involves a coming together of opposites in a midpoint. Our task, then, is clear: we will present an exposition of the first *collatio*, drawing into self-reflective consciousness the many types of coincidence of opposites therein contained. After completing this project, we will turn back and survey Christological themes from Bonaventure's other writings, seeing them in the light of the final development of his doctrine of Christ the center.

CHRIST IN THE *Itinerarium*

Before beginning our analysis of the first *Collatio in Hexaemeron,* it would be wise to recall Bonaventure's treatment of Christ as the coincidence of opposites in the *Itinerarium.*[2] For this latter work is the pivotal point in the emergence of his Christocentricity and of his consciousness of the coincidence of opposites. I believe that it is precisely the emergence into prominence of the image of Christ in the *Itinerarium* that makes Bonaventure aware of the coincidence of opposites in the Trinity and in God's relation to the world. In and through Christ, he eventually comes to see the coincidence of opposites everywhere. Struck by the coincidence of opposites in Christ, he becomes aware of the coincidence of opposites as the primordial structure of reality. It is not surprising, then, that when Bonaventure had his seminal insight into Francis' vision at La Verna, Christocentricity and a consciousness of the universal applicability of the coincidence of opposites begin to emerge simultaneously. It is not until fourteen years later, in the *Collationes in Hexaemeron* that the transition is made from Christ the greatest coincidence of opposites to Christ the center in whom all opposites coincide. But the germ of this full realization was, I believe, present in the Christ-image of the *Itinerarium.*

In the prologue of the *Itinerarium,* Bonaventure focuses on the image of Christ crucified, derived from the vision of the six-winged Seraph in the form of the crucified.[3] Immediately after sketching in a general way the symbolism of the six wings of the Seraph, he draws attention to Christ, who, he claims, is the road and the doorway into God. For Bonaventure there is no other road to God than through Christ crucified. Although Bonaventure gives primary place to Christ in his introduction, the mystery of Christ is not presented here according to the coincidence of opposites, nor does Christ become the pivotal point in the development of the first half of the *Itinerarium.* The first three chapters unfold according to the Trinitarian model of vestige and image, without any explicit systematic focus on Christ and without any heightened consciousness of the coincidence of opposites implicit in the Trinitarian model. It is only in Chapter Four that the image of Christ re-appears, this time as the one who lifts man up from his fallen state and restores his spiritual powers. The entire chapter is focused on Christ, the mediator and spouse of the soul. Finally at the climax of the chapter, the consciousness of the coincidence of opposites begins to emerge when Bonaventure speaks of Christ, "who is at one and the same time our Neighbor and our God, our Brother and our Lord, our King and our Friend, Word incarnate and uncreated Word, our Maker and our Re-maker, 'the Alpha and the Omega.' "[4]

Although the image of Christ as the coincidence of opposites surfaces here, it is not developed as the central theme. True, it ushers in the extended treatment of the coincidence of opposites in Chapters Five through Seven, which we analyzed above.[5] But Bonaventure does not re-introduce Christ as the coincidence of opposites until the middle of Chapter Six, after he has made an extended presentation of the coincidence of opposites in the divine nature and the Trinity. In Chapter Five, Bonaventure turns his gaze to contemplate God in his unity through his name which is Being. He bids the reader gaze in admiration on his divine being, which is the first and the last, eternal and yet the most present, most simple and the greatest, most actual and most changeless, most perfect and without measure, supremely one and yet possessing all aspects of the multiplicity.[6] Having been amazed at the coincidence of opposites in the divine essence, the reader turns his gaze to the Trinity and is overcome with wonder. For there he sees a remarkable coincidence of dynamic self-expression and intimate interpenetration: of supreme communicability with individuality of persons, supreme consubstantiality with plurality of hypostases, supreme similarity with distinct personality, supreme equality with ordered procession, supreme coeternity with emanation, supreme mutual intimacy with a sending forth.[7]

If we wondered at the coincidence of opposites in the divine nature and the Trinity, we will be struck with wonder when we turn our gaze to Christ and see in him the first principle joined with the last, God joined with man, the eternal joined with time-bound man, the most simple with the most composite, the most actual with the one who suffered and died, the most perfect and boundless one with the insignificant. If we wondered at the coincidence of plurality and unity in the Trinity, look at Christ in whom a personal unity exists with a trinity of substances and a duality of natures.[8] When we gaze at Christ, in whom are joined "the first and the last, the highest and the lowest, the circumference and the center, 'the Alpha and the Omega,' the caused and the cause, the Creator and the creature,"[9] we will be overcome with admiration and pass over to the stage of mystical contemplation which Bonaventure describes in his seventh chapter. Hence, the meditation on Christ as the coincidence of opposites is precisely the way to mystical elevation, because Christ is the way and the door, the ladder and the vehicle.[10]

Christ the coincidence of opposites plays a climactic role in the structure and dynamics of the *Itinerarium*. This dominant role is foreshadowed in the prologue, recalled in the middle of the treatise and rises into full prominence at the end. It is to be noted that the crescendo towards the climax mounts by way of our increased wonder at the coincidence of opposites in other spheres: namely, the divine nature and the Trinity. Although Bonaventure presents these other areas first, they are ordered to Christ as the coincidence of opposites. I believe that in the genesis of Bonaventure's thought the awareness of Christ as the coincidence of opposites has priority and is the source of the awareness of the coincidence of opposites in the other spheres. When Bonaventure does present Christ at the climax of the piece, he gazes upon him as the mystery of the greatest coincidence of opposites leading to the ecstasy of the seventh and final stage in the mind's ascent into God. Having arrived at the goal of the journey through Christ, Bonaventure does not retrace his steps and reexamine the early stages of the journey — the sense world and the soul — in the light of the mystery of Christ. The result is that, although in its beginning, middle, and end the *Itinerarium* is Christocentric, Christ the center is not the focal point around which all the successive stages are systematically ordered.

CHRIST THE CENTER IN *Collationes in Hexaemeron*

When we turn to the first *Collatio in Hexaemeron,* we find the very element that was missing from the *Itinerarium.* Through Christ the center Bonaventure organizes his entire world view, both in its general sweep and in all of its specific areas. Christ, who was depicted as the greatest coincidence of opposites in the *Itinerarium,* has become the universal center, uniting in himself as in a midpoint all the polarities of the divinity and the universe. This vision of Christ has a climactic position in Bonaventure's life and in the development of his thought; for it reaches expression the year before he died, when in the midst of intense philosophical-theological controversy, he delivered twenty-three lectures at the University of Paris. These lectures, under the title of *Collationes in Hexaemeron* or *Lectures on the Six Days of Creation,* contain Bonaventure's final statement of his vision. Covering the entire range of Christian belief, they express the mature synthesis of Bonaventure's thought, thus balancing the two syntheses, produced some twenty years earlier: the *Commen-*

tary on the Sentences and the *Breviloquium.* The first of the *Collationes in Hexaemeron* functions as an overture to the entire series so that the picture of Christ the center developed there is intended to be the organizing principle of the whole. Thus the notion of Christ the center expresses the full flowering of Bonaventure's Christology and reveals the final Christocentric development of his thought. This mystery of Christ the center, which was present in germ in his early writings and which began to emerge in the *Itinerarium,* now fourteen years after its appearance has reached such a remarkable self-consciousness and integration that he can present it as the single focal point for viewing the entire expanse of reality.

The title of the first *collatio* is: *Christus medium omnium scientiarum, Christ the Center of all the Sciences.* In the systematic development of the piece, Bonaventure studies Christ the center of seven sciences: metaphysics, physics, mathematics, logic, ethics, politics, and theology. Thus Christ is a sevenfold *medium: medium metaphysicum, physicum, mathematicum, logicum, ethicum, politicum, theologicum.* It would be more accurate to say that Christ is the center of those areas of reality studied by these sciences. The sciences study the entire sweep of reality: metaphysics studies God, the act of creation, and exemplarity; physics and mathematics study the material world; logic, the laws of argument; ethics, the sphere of moral conduct; politics, laws in society and juridical judgment made on their observance; theology, the goal of the Christian life, union with God. Bonaventure then correlates the mysteries of God and salvation history to each of these sciences, seeing Christ as the center of each. Christ is the metaphysical center in his eternal generation; the physical center in his incarnation; the mathematical center in his passion; the logical center in his resurrection; the ethical center in his ascension; the political center in the final judgment; and the theological center in the heavenly reward.[11]

Bonaventure uses the Latin term *medium,* which reflects a wide spectrum of meaning. It signifies basically the middle, the midst, between extremes, thus the midpoint of a line or the center of a circle, or the middle term of a syllogism. As the root of such terms as "mediation" and "mediator," it implies the action of joining or reconciling disparate parties. It is clear from the development of the text that Bonaventure intends this entire cluster of meanings.[12] As is typical of his use of supercharged images and words, he employs a term with a consistent basic meaning, allowing the distinct specifications to reveal themselves according to the changing context. In the light of Bonaventure's thought as a whole and of the first *collatio* in particular, it seems best in most cases to favor the single English translation of *medium* as center.

It is significant that Bonaventure uses the term *medium* in the *collatio* to express his most mature understanding of Christ as coincidence of opposites. The fact that he is the *medium,* the center, the midpoint means that opposites are reconciled in him. The notion of *medium* here emphasizes the fact that the specific type of coincidence of opposites that permeates Bonaventure's thought is that of the third major class we presented in the first chapter of this book, namely, the coincidence of mutually affirming complementarity.[13] As we will see graphically illustrated throughout the *collatio,* Christ stands at the midpoint reconciling in himself polar opposites. As eternal Word, he is the midpoint of the Trinity, the dynamic *medium* of the divine expressionism and the exemplarism of creation. As incarnate Word, he is the ontological midpoint between God and man — not, of course, a third being midway between God and man in a type of Arian subordinationism, but the point where the divine and the human are united and yet retain their identity. As mediator between God and man, he overcomes sin and reconciles mankind to God; and as the vehicle of our ascent to God, he draws us back to union with the Father. In Christ the *medium,* opposites are not absorbed into an all-encompassing unity, nor does one dominate and swallow up the other. Rather they remain as opposites precisely because of Christ the *medium,* sustaining their differentiation at the same time he effects their union. Since I believe this is of paramount importance for understanding Bonaventure's thought, we will return to it again when we make an extended systematic analysis of the types of coincidence of opposites in Bonaventure and when we compare him to others, especially in our comparison with Nicholas of Cusa.[14]

CHRIST THE METAPHYSICAL CENTER

In developing his theme in the first *collatio,* Bonaventure first considers Christ as the *medium metaphysicum* and grounds his consideration in the generation of the Son from the Father. As *medium metaphysicum* the Word embodies three types of the coincidence of opposites: The first is concerned with the Trinity itself; the second with the Trinitarian basis of creation; and the third with knowledge.

First, within the Trinity itself, Bonaventure considers the Son as the *persona media Trinitatis*:

> This must necessarily be the center of the persons: for if there is a person who produces and is not produced and a person who is produced and does not produce, there must necessarily be a central person who is produced and produces.[15]

This analysis views the Son as performing a mediating function within the Trinitarian life, linking the productive and receptive aspects of the deity. For the Father is the generating source, the *fontalis plenitudo,* the *principium originans.* At the opposite pole, the Holy Spirit is the person who is produced and does not produce, and hence can be called *spiratio passiva.* As Bonaventure observes, between these poles, there must be a *persona media,* who contains the opposites within himself and thus holds the poles in union. This *medium* is the Word, who is produced and produces. This type of coincidence is that of complementary opposites; the productive and receptive are complementary aspects of the divinity. Of course, the receptive does not imply limit or potency, but here refers to a pure perfection which is had in its absolute form in the divinity. In God are reconciled the opposites of absolute productivity and absolute receptivity. They are reconciled, but not merged. This is accomplished by the *persona media,* who acts as the unifying force of the opposites and the intensification of their differences. Hence one opposite does not resist the other, or absorb the other, or subordinate the other. They are held in absolute and eternal tension — eternally secure in their autonomy, yet nourished by their very differences. Thus by the union of opposites in the *persona media,* absolute unity and difference are achieved in the totality.

The view of the Word as *persona media,* uniting the polar aspects of the Father and the Spirit, may seem static. The coincidence of complementary opposites, like the coincidence of the *maximum* and the *minimum,* seems to have a static aspect. Yet Bonaventure's thought is alive with dynamism. As we saw above, his most profound view of the Trinity is that of the dynamic good which is infinitely self-diffusive. This diffusion takes place by the divine expressionism, in which the Father expresses himself in his perfect image the Son, who becomes the *medium* for the emanation of the Spirit, who completes the Trinity.[16] Thus the Word is the *medium,* not only the midpoint, but the dynamic means through which the Father objectifies himself and through which he returns to himself in the union of the Spirit. Thus there is with the Trinity a dynamism of emanation and return, which is mediated in the Son, who is the ground of both. This emanation and return in the Trinity becomes the archetypal ground for all emanation and return in the case of the created world. Thus within the Trinitarian life, the opposites of emanation and return are reconciled dynamically in the Word.

GOD AND THE WORLD

The Trinitarian life is viewed by Bonaventure as the ground for the second level of the coincidence of opposites. This level is concerned with the coincidence of God and creation: the infinite and the finite, the absolute and the relative, the unchanging and the changing, the eternal and the temporal, the one and the many. How are these opposites joined? Once again it is the Word as the *medium metaphysicum*. Just as he is the *medium* uniting the opposites in the Trinity, so he is the *medium* uniting the opposites of the Creator and the creature. It is precisely in his eternal generation from the Father, that the Son reconciles the opposites of the infinite and the finite. For in generating the Son, the Father produces in the Son all that he can create:

> For the Father from eternity generated the Son, similar to himself; and he expressed himself and his own likeness, similar to himself; and in so doing he expressed all his power. He expressed what he could do and especially what he willed to do; and he expressed all things in him, that is, in the Son or in that very center of his art.[17]

Bonaventure sums up his position in the compact statement: "Therefore the Word expresses the Father and the things that were made through him [the Word]."[18] As the eternal generation is the basis of expressionism in the Trinity, so it is the basis of exemplarism in creation. The eternal generation provides the theological foundation and philosophical articulation for Bonaventure's vision of the theophanic universe. His most basic religious experience is that of theophany. He is aware of the presence of God in all things, and he contemplates the reflection of God throughout the universe. This religious experience of theophany, or hierophany, is, as Eliade has indicated, precisely an awareness of the coincidence of opposites: the sacred and the profane, the eternal and the temporal.[19] Bonaventure's analysis of the metaphysical roots of hierophany leads him to the Word, in whom the opposites coincide. For all temporal things have an eternal existence in the eternal Word. In him the temporal and eternal are united; in him the opposites coincide. Hence both the religious experience of hierophany and its philosophical articulation reveal the logic of the coincidence of opposites.

As was the case in the Trinity, the coincidence of opposites does not produce a static balancing of the scales of being. Rather it inaugurates a dynamic process. In the eternal generation, in which the *rationes aeternae* are produced in the Word, the absolute and the relative coincide from the side of the absolute. However, in temporal creation, where the *rationes aeternae* are embodied in space and time, the relative and absolute coincide from the side of the relative. But the form created in time is so embedded in its *ratio aeterna* that it is swept up in a dynamic return to its source. Hence the entire universe is *en route*; the cosmos is pursuing an *itinerarium in Deum*. Since the Word is the *medium* uniting the eternal and the temporal, he embodies within himself another coincidence of opposites: namely the *Alpha* and the *Omega*. All things emanate from him; and since he is the eternal exemplar of the temporal, all things return through him to the unity of the Father; for, as Bonaventure says, "The Word . . . leads us to the unity of the Father, who draws all things together."[20]

Bonaventure quotes Christ's statement: "I came forth from the Father, and have come into the world. Again I leave the world and go to the Father."[21] Similarly, observes Bonaventure, each one should say:

> Lord, I have gone forth from you, who are supreme; I come to you, who are supreme, and through you, who are supreme. This is the metaphysical center that leads us back, and this is our whole metaphysics: emanation, exemplarity and consummation; that is, to be illumined by spiritual rays and to be led back to the supreme height. Thus you will be a true metaphysician.[22]

In the dynamic movement of creation, the opposites of emanation and return coincide in the Word, who is the *Alpha* and the *Omega*. Thus in the Word is had the reconciliation of motion and rest, of eternity and time, of the static and the dynamic, of the flux of history and the solidity of the eternal forms, of process and the eternal ground, of the way out and the way back, of the way down and the way up. *Emanatio* and *reditus* are united in the Word; for he is the *persona media Trinitatis,* who is the means of the Father's outgoing self-expression and the return in the unity of the Spirit. Thus through its reflection of the Word as its exemplar, the entire cosmos shares the dynamic interpenetration of opposites of its Trinitarian archetype.

CHRIST AND THE MIND

Although all the world shares in the coincidence of opposites, this is true of the human mind in a special way. First, the mind of man is turned as a mirror towards the external world, and in its knowing processes is related to the external world as subject to object, as microcosm to macrocosm. But man's mind is also a mirror turned upward to God. As image of God, man reflects God and is related to him with the polarity of subject to subject. In the realm of subjectivity there is a coincidence of interpenetration. God is more intimate to me than I am to myself. When I discover his presence in me, or my presence in the divine mind, I realize what is most real about me. The *medium* of both of these types of coincidence of opposites is the Word himself. For he is the ground of the conformity between the objective structures of the eternal world and my own mind. As archetype of creation, he is the single source from which flow both the objective world and subjective mind. Hence, when I know with certitude, I grasp the objective structures of the external world in their unifying ground in the eternal Word. Thus the Word becomes the *medium* uniting the microcosm of my mind and the macrocosm of the external world. The Word is the 'interior teacher', illumining all minds. He is the changeless light that flashes in my mind when I grasp truth. Hence Bonaventure calls the Word truth itself:

> Therefore that center is truth; and it is established according to Augustine and other saints that 'Christ, having his chair in heaven, teaches inwardly'; nor can any truth be known in any way except through that truth.[23]

In human knowledge the absolute and the relative, the changeable and the unchangeable, light and darkness coincide in a remarkable way. Only alluding to this in the first *Collatio in Hexaemeron*, Bonaventure had developed it at greater length in the disputed questions *De scientia Christi* and in the sermon *Christus unus omnium magister*.[24] The human mind is changeable and fallible; truth is unchangeable and infallible. In the act of certain knowledge, we grasp the eternal, unchangeable, infallible truth, although we ourselves remain finite. While we do grasp the eternal light we see now only in a glass darkly. What mediates this coincidence of opposites in knowledge? It is the uncreated Wisdom which is Christ: "Such a light is not the light of created intelligence but of uncreated Wisdom, which is Christ."[25] Thus Bonaventure's doctrine of illumination is seen to contain the logic of the coincidence of opposites. Perhaps more than any other position of Bonaventure, his epistemology of illumination has suffered from being approached through discordant models. Frequently it is viewed from the difference model, in which opposites do not coincide; and hence it is judged to lack an adequate foundation or logical coherence. We believe that by approaching Bonaventurian illumination through the model of the coincidence of opposites of complementarity, one can see how it is grounded in the metaphysics of exemplarism and how it contains within itself an impressive logical consistency.

The Word Incarnate

Having seen the types of coincidence of opposites in creation, we turn now to the coincidence of opposites in the Incarnation and Redemption. In his Incarnation, Christ is the *medium physicum,* uniting the polar opposites of being: the highest and the lowest, the divine and matter — united through the microcosm of human nature in the hypostatic union.[26] By uniting the lowest to the highest, he brings the cosmos to the heights.[27] He becomes a center of radiating energy. Like the sun in the macrocosm and the human heart in the microcosm, he is an energizing center — the head of the mystical body, diffusing the energies of the Spirit throughout his members who are united to him. Thus as *medium physicum,* Christ is seen in his positive cosmic role: he brings the cosmos to its fullness by uniting the *maximum* and the *minimum* through the hypostatic union and he brings about the coincidence of the one and the many through his dynamic activity, sending out spiritual energy and uniting his members to himself.[28]

Bonaventure considers Christ the *medium mathematicum* in his crucifixion. As the mathematician measures the earth, which for the medievalist stood at the lowest level of the universe, so Christ plumbed the depths of earthly existence. Bonaventure is here expressing the kenotic aspect of the Redemption, in which the divinity empties itself assuming the form of a slave.[29] The Son of God became lowly, poor, insignificant. He took up our clay and went not merely to the surface of the earth, but to the depths of its center; for after his crucifixion he descended into hell and restored the heavenly dwellings.[30] Thus Christ becomes the coincidence of opposites uniting the heights and the depths. From a dynamic point of view, the opposites coincide; for the way down becomes the way up. By going to the depths of the earth, Christ unites the depths to the heights. Man had lost his center. Although as a mathematician he could measure other things, he could not measure himself. He had lost his center of balance; he had no fulcrum. Clouded with pride, he worked his own destruction. But Christ plunged into suffering on the cross; he cut through human pride and worked out man's salvation in the ashes of humility. Through the cross, Christ locates man's lost center. As Bonaventure says: "For when the center of a circle has been lost, it can be found only by two lines intersecting at right angles."[31]

CHRIST AND SATAN

By going through the suffering of the cross, Christ reveals himself as the *medium logicum* in his resurrection. In the mystery of the cross, Christ confronts evil on its own grounds and comes away victorious. Bonaventure sees Christ confronting Satan in a type of cosmic *quaestio disputata*.[32] The opposites are joined, not in union but in combat. The two logics are opposed. Innocence confronts sin; good argues with evil. In the clash of good and evil, we see the most subtle and deceptive of the coincidence of opposites. For good and evil are related not as *maximum* and *minimum*, nor as microcosm-macrocosm, nor as complementaries — but rather as contraries: that is, evil is the negation of the good, but always retains an aspect of the good, although distorted, as its ontological foundation. Hence evil is the dark side of the good, or the shadow of the good. This is the basis for another coincidence of opposites: that of illusion and reality. Evil is deceptive; it appears to be good. It tempts one because it promises pleasure and benefits; but in reality, it brings the opposite — unhappiness and destruction. Hence Satan could use his deceptive logic on man. As his major premise he presupposed a true proposition: All men should desire to be like God because they are his image. But Satan's minor premise was false: If you eat, you will be like God. He promised life and gave death; he promised happiness and gave destruction. Man was overcome in his confrontation with Satan, for he was deceived by Satan's logic. Now Christ enters the debate; as ultimate reality and ultimate truth, Christ can deceive the deceiver and overcome the illusion of evil.

Christ becomes the middle term of a cosmic syllogism. Previously the extremes were not united; man and God were separated by sin. The Word unites the extremes in his person through the hypostatic union, but this means that he must take up suffering and death. He must be similar to man if he is to make man similar to God. As Son of the Father, he possessed the divine nature, equal power and immortality. Yet as man he took up their opposites: suffering, weakness and death. But since he is Life itself, he leads humanity through death to life. Satan used the coincidence of opposites, promising life and giving death; Christ also used the coincidence of opposites, taking up death and pushing it to its ultimate to draw from it newness of life. Bonaventure describes Christ's logic as follows:

> The major proposition was from eternity, the minor on the cross and the conclusion in the resurrection. The Jews believed they had confounded Christ, and they taunted him: "If you are the Son of God,

come down from the cross" (Mt. 27:40). Now Christ did not say:
Let me live. Rather he said: Let me assume death and be linked
with the other extreme, to suffer and to die. And then the conclusion
follows. And so he tricked the devil.[33]

Having shattered the hold of evil, Christ can lead man on his
return back to the Father. On the return Christ is first the
medium ethicum in his ascension. Bonaventure uses the symbol
of Moses' ascent of the mountain to illustrate the progress one
should make in the life of virtue.[34] Having climbed from the
foot of the mountain to its summit, man must stand before Christ
as the Judge. Here Christ is the *medium iudiciale* or *politicum*,
since he renders judgment and determines reward and punishment.[35] Finally, he is the *medium theologicum* in eternal happiness. For the Word is the *persona media* of the Trinity, and
from him is derived all happiness.[36] Having begun from the
Word as *persona media* in the Trinity, we return through this
medium, which is also our goal. Here at the end of the cosmic
process, we return to our source; the *Omega* is revealed as the
Alpha; the end is the beginning.

SUMMARY OF COINCIDENCE OF OPPOSITES

As we look back over the cosmic vision painted in this *collatio*,
we can see, first, several types of coincidence of opposites; secondly, that these are related in a dynamic way so as to become mo-
ments in an on-going process; thirdly, that Christ himself is the
greatest coincidence of opposites, who integrates in himself all
opposites and draws them to their completion and ultimate reconciliation.

In the Trinity we saw the coincidence of the static and dynamic: for the Word, as *persona media Trinitatis*, coincides
with the Word as dynamic expression of the Father, through
whom emanation and return are mediated in the Trinitarian
life. Again it is through the Word that the coincidence of opposites is mediated in the mystery of creation. In the Word, in whom
are produced the *rationes aeternae*, we have the ground for the
union of the eternal and the temporal, the *maximum* and the

minimum; and hence we have the metaphysical basis for Bonaventure's doctrine of exemplarism. Yet, from this point of view, exemplarism might appear static. However, the static aspect coincides with the dynamic, for the Word is also the *Alpha* and the *Omega* of the cosmic process. Just as the Trinitarian *emanatio* and *reditus* flowed through the Word, so the Word, as the *Ars Patris*, is the source of the emanation of temporal creation and, as divine Exemplar, he is the *Omega* drawing the cosmic process to its completion and return to the Father.

It is in the Word incarnate that creation reaches its highest perfection. For in Christ are united the polar opposites of divinity and matter in the microcosm of human nature. What appears as a union of static perfection becomes a cosmic force; for when Christ enters the cosmic process, he not only stands as the highest perfection on the scale of being, but also is a center of radiating energy drawing all things to himself. While, on the one hand, he brings the cosmos to its physical perfection, on the other, he has taken upon himself all the imperfections and suffering of a finite world burdened with sin. He has entered into the very depths of the universe, into the ashes of humility. But the way down paradoxically becomes the way up, for out of the destruction of death comes the glorified life of the resurrection. Since Christ has plunged into the depths of the struggle of the opposites of good and evil and emerged victorious, he can draw the cosmic process to its completion and bring man through a virtuous life and final judgment to eternal happiness.

Christological Opposites

Having seen Bonaventure's Christocentric vision in its mature expression in the first *Collatio in Hexaemeron,* we will now analyze in greater detail the chief types of the coincidence of opposites in his Christology. We will isolate the different types and study systematically their inner structure and interrelation. Taking our point of departure from Bonaventure's mature vision in the *collatio,* we will range back over his earlier writings drawing material that will clarify the development of the coincidence of opposites in his thought and that will indicate how his mature vision was foreshadowed in the earlier periods. We will focus here on the specifically incarnational coincidence of opposites since we dealt systematically with the Trinitarian coincidence in the previous chapter. We must bear in mind, however, that since the incarnate Word is also the eternal Word, the coincidence of opposites in the mystery of the Incarnation is rooted in the Word as the *persona media* of the Trinity, the Art of the Father and the eternal Exemplar of creation.

Bonaventure's treatment of Christ as incarnate Word embodies three major types of the coincidence of opposites: (1) cosmological, (2) soteriological, and (3) mystical. In the cosmological, Christ unites in his being the polar spheres of reality: the uncreated and the created, the eternal and the temporal, the highest and the lowest. In the soteriological, he frees man from the power of evil; by entering into its logic of evil, he transforms destruction into creativity, bringing life out of death. The redemptive process leads to the mystical coincidence of opposites. As mediator and redeemer Christ leads the soul in its mystical ascent into God. This cosmological-soteriological-mystical coincidence of opposites can be studied through two basic religious symbols found throughout the world, both among primitive peoples and in developed cultures: the *axis mundi* and the *mandala*. The *axis mundi* is a cosmic pillar linking together heaven, earth, and the underworld. The mandala is a geometric design with a center, a circle or square and cross, which is used in ritual and meditation as a symbol of total integration. Drawing from the research of Mircea Eliade, in this section we will use the *axis mundi* as a way of understanding Bonaventure's Christological coincidence of opposites. In the following chapter, we will study Christ as the center of the mandala, basing ourselves on the research of Jung, Eliade, and Tucci.[37]

Eliade describes the *axis mundi* as follows:

This communication [between levels] is sometimes expressed through
the image of a universal pillar, *axis mundi,* which at once connects
and supports heaven and earth and whose base is fixed in the world
below (the infernal regions) . . . around this cosmic axis lies the
world (our world), hence the axis is located 'in the middle,' at the
'navel of the earth'; it is the Center of the World.[38]

In the first *Collatio in Hexaemeron,* we have a graphic example of Christ as *axis mundi.* As *medium physicum,* Christ
stands at the center, linking God and creation; as *medium mathematicum* and *medium logicum,* Christ goes not only to the earth,
but to the underworld. He encounters evil and Satan. In the
cosmic struggle between good and evil, he emerges victorious.
He has entered into the depths of evil, has unmasked its deception, has transformed death to life and so restores the heavenly
dwellings. Christ is seen as the great mathematician who restores
the cosmic order — not by a simple external measurement, but
by entering into the very depths of the cosmos to right its axes
and to bring the human spirit to its center. Although Christ as
axis mundi has restored the cosmic harmony and has provided
a center for the integration of the universe, each soul must go
through the cosmic process on its return to the Father. As
medium ethicum, politicum and *theologicum,* Christ leads the
soul through death and resurrection into union with the Father.
As *axis mundi,* Christ is the road, the doorway, the vehicle of
our ascent from the depths of fallenness to the heights of glory.

The notion of Christ as *axis mundi* — along with all of the
forms of the coincidence of opposites therein contained — is
based on the hypostatic union. The union of the human and the
divine natures in the person of the Word is a first principle
supporting the coincidence of opposites structure of Bonaventure's Christology. He studied the mystery of the hypostatic
union at great length in his *Commentary on the Sentences* and in
a highly condensed way in the *Breviloquium.*[39] Although the hypostatic union is the base of the coincidence of opposites, Bonaventure does not treat it systematically from that perspective in
his early writings; yet foreshadowings of the later perspective are

not lacking. The essence of his understanding of the hypostatic union is expressed in the following passage from the *Breviloquium*:

> The Incarnation was brought about by the Trinity, through whom the Godhead assumed flesh, and a union was accomplished between Godhead and flesh in such a way that the assuming was not only of the material flesh, but also of the rational spirit in its three functions, vegetative, sensitive, and intellective; and that the union occurred through oneness, not of nature, but of person; not of a human person, but of a divine; not of any [divine] Person indifferently, but of the Word alone, in whom the oneness is so absolute that whatever may be said of the Son of God may be said of the Son of Man, and vice versa; excepting, however, such matters as designate the union itself or imply some contradiction.[40]

THREE TYPES OF COSMOLOGICAL OPPOSITES

As the union of God and man, the incarnation involves three types of the cosmological coincidence of opposites: (1) *maximum-minimum*, (2) microcosm-macrocosm, and (3) Alpha-Omega. The first is based on ontological hierarchy, with the highest joined to the lowest; the second is based on similarity of structure: e.g., man is the microcosm who recapitulates or contains within himself the elements of the universe as a whole. The third is based on time or origin, and implies that the beginning is the end. In Christ all three types interpenetrate in such a way that they embody the highest form of the coincidence of opposites.

In the incarnate Christ the *maximum* is joined with the *minimum*, for the hypostatic union unites the person of the Word with human nature, which includes within itself material nature. Thus the *maximum* in the realm of being — that is, the divinity — is joined in an intimate union with the least substance. This union of the divinity and matter in Christ then becomes a microcosm reflecting the macrocosm of the entire universe, for God is present in the entire universe, even in the least particle of matter. According to Bonaventure, man is a microcosm reflecting all the levels of creation; hence he is a type of the coincidence of opposites, since matter and spirit are joined in him. Thus

in the incarnate Christ two types of the coincidence of opposites
converge: the *maximum-minimum* of creator-creature and the
microcosm-macrocosm of human nature itself. This produces
a new microcosm-macrocosm in Christ, who is the greatest reflection of all the levels of reality, because in him there is a hypostatic expression not only of the union of matter and spirit,
but of the divinity as well. This union of the *maximum-minimum*
with the microcosm-macrocosm produces the third type of the
coincidence of opposites, Alpha-Omega; for Christ is the primary and ultimate reality in the universe, the beginning and
the end, the Exemplar from which all things are derived and the
goal to which they are striving.

The theme of microcosm-macrocosm is developed by Bonaventure in the third book of the *Commentary on the Sentences*.[41] He
considers the question whether it was more appropriate for the
hypostatic union to take place in man than in the universe as a
whole or in an angel. He concludes that it was more appropriate
in man because man is the microcosm, or as Bonaventure says,
the *minor mundus,* a little world summing up in himself the
larger world. It is precisely the fact that man is the microcosm
that gives the Incarnation its special value as representing the
universe, for in man there is a greater representation of the universe than in the angels. Bonaventure writes:

> For the rational soul represents God not only as it is considered in
> itself, but insofar as it is united to the body, which it rules and in
> the totality of which it dwells, just as God does in the larger world;
> and Augustine says this many times. By reason of this greater simi-
> larity, there is a greater basis for union . . . Because man is com-
> posed of bodily and spiritual nature, and in a certain fashion has
> something in common with every creature, as Gregory says, it follows
> that when human nature is assumed and deified, in a certain fashion
> every nature is exalted in it when it is united to the Deity in what is
> similar to it.[42]

Since man is the center of the world of creatures, in whom
matter and spirit are united, when the eternal Word assumes flesh
in human nature, he joins the *maximum* and the *minimum* at the

midpoint of creation. He thus enters into the microcosm-macro-cosm structure of the universe and transforms it into a more striking coincidence of opposites and more profound centering. The incarnation thus brings the Trinitarian expressionism and exemplarism to its ultimate realization: the hypostatic expres-sion of the divine in matter through man the microcosm. As theophany in matter Christ reveals the theophanic nature of the created world, even in its lowest and most insignificant stratum of matter. The incarnate Christ manifests the mystery of the coinci-dence of opposites that is found in the very depths of the material world. Thus by contemplating Christ as the *Verbum incarnatum,* we are brought to make a *reductio* by which we are led back to the *Verbum increatum,* where once again we find the world of the many mysteriously united to the Godhead in the divine ideas.

By reason of his discreteness, Christ is the microcosm in com-parison with the entire universe. Yet by reason of intensifica-tion, he is the macrocosm — the greatest of all realities, the maxi-mum manifestation of the divinity. By this reversal of opposites through the concept of intensity, Christ becomes the Alpha and Omega. By uniting the *maximum* and the *minimum* and the microcosm-macrocosm in the intensity of the hypostatic union, Christ is seen as the model in which the universe has been made, the goal of divinization to which it is going and the vehicle by which it will make its passover. By this reversal of opposites we arrive at the metaphysical ground in Bonaventure's exemplarity where he approximates the Scotist position on the primacy of Christ in creation. Since Christ is the Alpha and Omega, all of material creation points to Christ and tends to Christ.[43] In the *De reductione artium ad theologiam,* Bonaventure writes:

> Again, the natural tendency in matter is so ordained toward intel-lectual causes that the generation is in no way perfect unless the rational soul be united to the material body. By similar reasoning, therefore, we come to the conclusion that the highest and noblest perfection can exist in this world only if a nature in which there are seminal causes, and a nature in which there are intellectual causes, and a nature in which there are the ideal causes are simultaneously

combined in the unity of one person, as was done in the Incarnation of the Son of God. Therefore all natural philosophy, by reason of the relation of proportion, predicates the Word of God begotten and become incarnate so that he is the Alpha and the Omega, that is, he was begotten in the beginning and before all time but became Incarnate in the fullness of time.[44]

All of the universe is hierarchical, pointing and moving towards Christ, the maximum coincidence of opposites. Bonaventure calls Christ the supreme Hierarch, the Alpha and the Omega, who leads us to perfection:

> . . . Jesus, who is at one and the same time our Neighbor and our God, our Brother and our Lord, our King and our Friend, Word incarnate and uncreated Word, our Maker and our Re-maker, "the Alpha and the Omega," who is also the supreme Hierarch, who purifies, enlightens, and perfects his spouse, that is, the whole Church and every sanctified soul.[45]

The combination, then, of these three types of coincidence of opposites produces the notion of Christ the center. The logic proceeds as follows: Christ as *maximum-minimum* is united with human nature, which itself is a microcosm, and thus there is produced a supreme microcosm-macrocosm as Alpha-Omega. By adding the dimension of divinity to human nature as microcosm through the hypostatic union, Christ reverses the relation to macrocosm-microcosm, becoming the Alpha and the Omega of all the universe. Thus every creature is related to the incarnate Word — not merely to the eternal Word — as Alpha and Omega. This means, then, that Christ is the universal cosmic center. In this way, Christ as *axis mundi,* uniting the polar zones of the universe through the hypostatic union, becomes through the coincidence and reversal of the microcosm-macrocosm the cosmic center to which all things are related. In the emergence of Christ as center there appears a new form of the coincidence of the universal and the particular. Through the hypostatic union, the universal is joined to the particular, for the eternal Word is united to individualized human nature. Yet because Christ is the supreme microcosm, this particularized humanity is not merely one point among many in the universe, but the unique center of the whole to which all the other points are related. Thus in Christ the particularizing element is universalized through its very particularity by becoming the universal cosmic center.

The basic elements of this cosmological aspect of Bonaventure's Christology were present as early as the *Commentary on the Sentences,* in his treatment of the hypostatic union and the appropriateness of the Incarnation in human nature as microcosm. The awareness of Christ as *maximum-minimum* emerged to prominence in the mid-period in the *Itinerarium.* Finally in the *Collationes in Hexaemeron,* these elements combined through their inner logic to produce Bonaventure's crowning Christological notion of Christ the center, in which all the other forms of coincidence of opposites are drawn together.

SOTERIOLOGICAL OPPOSITES

A similar evolution can be discerned in Bonaventure's treatment of the soteriological coincidence of opposites. As in the case of the cosmological opposites, the doctrine of redemption is founded on the hypostatic union as a first principle. Bonaventure sums up his position in the *Breviloquium*:

> The most excellent Restorer could be none but God, the most friendly Mediator, none but a man, and the most superabundant Satisfier, none but him who was both God and man: therefore, it was absolutely the most fitting thing for our restoration that the Word become incarnate. For as the human race came into being through the Word Not Made, and as it sinned because it failed to heed the Word Inspired, so it would rise from sin through the Word Made Flesh.[46]

In Christ's work of redemption the most intricate forms of the coincidence of opposites are found, for in Christ the cosmological opposites confront the opposites of evil and their destructive logic. Out of this encounter a new logic of death and resurrection emerges: Christ reverses the entire logic of the sphere of evil and brings life out of death rather than death from life. I believe that the coincidence of opposites is the proper logic for understanding Anselm's satisfaction theory of redemption, which Bonaventure and the medieval theological tradition in general incorporated into their synthesis.[47] For the entire satisfaction theory is founded on the coincidence of opposites: Because finite man's sin produces an infinite offense against God, it is required — at least for condign or proportionate satisfaction — that reparation be made by the God-man. But this means that the God-man, who embodies the cosmological coincidence of opposites, must enter into the destructive opposites produced by evil: into humiliation, suffering and death. By taking this logic to its ultimate on the cross, Christ transforms it to its opposite by resurrection.

This comprehensive grasp of the dynamics of evil and redemption reaches full flowering in Bonaventure's notion of Christ as *medium mathematicum* and *medium logicum* in the first *Collatio in Hexaemeron,* but its elements are present throughout his extensive treatment of redemption in the *Commentary on the Sentences* and are studied often from the standpoint of the coincidence of opposites in the *Breviloquium.*[48] For example, in the latter treatise, Bonaventure says: "The work of restoration must respect the harmonious functioning of the universe. Wherefore it was achieved by means wholly consonant to that end, for it is most fitting that evils should be healed through their opposites."[49] He goes on to show how man's pride should be overcome by humility, man's lust by physical suffering.

Christ's confrontation with the logic of evil draws him to the very depths of the cosmos so that he can restore the cosmic harmony on all levels. Thus in the soteriological aspect Christ becomes the complete *axis mundi,* linking the underworld, the earth, and heaven. In the *Breviloquium,* Bonaventure develops this theme, which he will repeat later in the first *Collatio in Hexaemeron*:

> The means used for man's redemption was utterly sufficient, for it embraced heaven, earth and the nether world. Through Christ, the souls in the lower regions were recovered, those on earth restored and the heavenly ranks replenished . . . . After the passion, the soul of Christ descended into hell in order to release the souls detained there; then he rose from the dead in order to restore life

to those dead in sin; he ascended into heaven and led captivity cap-
tive in order to fill the ranks of the heavenly Jerusalem.[50]

The relation of the two spheres of opposites — the cosmological
and the soteriological — is seen clearly in the mature vision of the
first *Collatio in Hexaemeron*. With the clarification that comes
with the notion of Christ the center, Bonaventure is able to reveal
the logic of the opposites in the sphere of evil and the way in
which they are transformed by the cosmological opposites of the
hypostatic union. Having explored the cosmological opposites in
Christ as *medium metaphysicum* and *physicum,* he takes up the
soteriological opposites in his treatment of Christ as *medium
mathematicum* and *logicum*.[51] We will recall here, in this more
systematic context, some of the points we explored above in our
exposition of the *collatio*.[52]

For Bonaventure, Christ is the *medium mathematicum*. Mathematics measures the earth and studies the movements of the
heavenly bodies as they influence the lower bodies. In the cosmology of the Middle Ages, the earth was at the center and at the
lowest level of the structure of the universe. In the incarnation,
Christ came to the depth of the universe. "The Son of God —
lowly, poor, insignificant — came not only to the surface of the
earth, but even to the depths of its center,"[53] since after his crucifixion, he descended into hell. In the incarnation, and crucifixion,
he emptied himself and plunged into the depths. Christ, then,
is the *medium mathematicum* in his crucifixion, because he
plumbed the very depths of humility. We are tempted to pride,
but Christ worked our salvation in the ashes of humility on the
cross. "For when the center of a circle has been lost, it can be
found only by two lines intersecting at right angles."[54]

Bonaventure next calls Christ the *medium logicum* and depicts
a confrontation of Christ and Satan in the form of a scholastic
debate. He transforms the universe into a medieval debate hall,
where in a type of cosmic *quaestio disputata* Christ argues with
Satan over the fate of man. Satan with his false logic has tricked

man into sin. Christ with the subtle logic of suffering destroys Satan's logic and saves man from hell.

Bonaventure sees Christ as the *medium* or middle term of a cosmic syllogism. Prior to redemption through Christ, the extremes of the syllogism were not united. They did not harmonize since man and God were separated by sin. But through the middle term which is Christ, the extremes are united in the conclusion. Satan had tricked Adam with his sophistry, using a true major premise: All men should desire to be like God since they are his image. But Satan's minor premise was false: If you eat, you will be like God. Christ's argument is true; it saves man from evil and makes him truly like God, and it destroys the logic of Satan. To unite the extremes, Christ had to be both God and man; and he had to assume human nature in all of its suffering, poverty, and death. Christ's "major proposition was from eternity, the minor on the cross and the conclusion in the resurrection."[55] From all eternity he was God; he assumed human nature in time, and in all of its suffering, on the cross; and he led man to the glory of his resurrection. "Now, Christ did not say: Let me live. Rather he said: Let me assume death and be linked with the other extreme, to suffer and to die. And then the conclusion follows. And so he tricked the devil."[56] For the devil considered Christ's argument worthless when he saw him suffering. Bonaventure exhorts us to use the logic of Christ: "This is our logic, this is our reasoning which we have against the devil who constantly disputes against us."[57] Like Christ, we must assume the minor premise of suffering, even though it is against the grain. "In assuming the minor, we must exercise our full force, since we do not want to suffer, we do not want to be crucified."[58]

MYSTICAL OPPOSITES

By entering into the depths of the mystery of evil, Christ has transformed the entire sphere to its opposite. Thus through the complex logic of the coincidence of opposites redemption is effected on all levels. It is here that the cosmological-soteriological aspects of Bonaventure's Christology reach their climax in the mystical. Through the coincidence of opposites on the cross, the estranged opposites of God and man are united through the God-man. Although the cosmic harmony is restored, each soul must make the ascent to the Father, which according to Bonaventure is accomplished through Christ as *medium ethicum, politicum* and *theologicum*. These latter three points encompass the mystical dimension of Bonaventure's Christology. Although the return of the soul is sketched from the standpoint of Christ the center in the *collatio,* it is more thoroughly developed in the *Itinerarium* and in the mystical writings of the middle period.[59]

The mystical aspects of Bonaventure's Christology are ground-ed in the cosmological-soteriological aspects, on the one hand, and in the notion of the soul as image of God, on the other. The soul as image is itself a form of the coincidence of opposites; for in the soul, the infinite is reflected in the finite. However by sin the image has been turned away from its Exemplar and is in need of restoration. In the mystical perspective this means a turning back to the Word and a growth as image of the Word. These themes are developed systematically in the fourth chapter of the *Itinerarium* and are completed in the treatment of mystical ecstasy in chapter seven. The specifically Christological function of Bona-venture's mysticism is spelled out in chapters six and seven, where the contemplation of Christ as the greatest coincidence of op-posites becomes the doorway and vehicle of our passage into the ecstasy of union with the Father. As Bonaventure says: "With Christ crucified, let us pass 'out of this world to the Father,' so that, when the Father is shown to us, we may say with Philip: 'It is enough for us.' "[60] In Bonaventure's doctrine of mystical union, the soul is not absorbed into the oneness of the divinity. Rather precisely through Christ as *medium,* the individuality of the soul is preserved in the union of the soul with God as lover and beloved.

From the point of view of the mystical ascent, all the forms of the coincidence of opposites in Bonaventure's Christology reach

their culmination. In Christ the center — as the road, the doorway, the passage to the Father — all forms of opposites in the
cosmological-soteriological spheres are focused. Through Christ
as *maximum-minimum*, microcosm-macrocosm and Alpha-Omega,
evil is overcome and death transformed into life. As *axis mundi*
Christ has linked the cosmic zones, overcoming evil, restoring
cosmic harmony and uniting earth and heaven. As the center of
the cosmos and the center of our soul, he leads us to union with
the Father. In the next chapter we will see these themes graphically expressed in Bonaventure's symbolism, particularly in the notion of Christ as the center of the mandala.

CHAPTER VI

MANDALA SYMBOLISM

AVING explored the coincidence of opposites in Bonaventure's texts and in the systematic structure of his thought, we now turn to symbolism, which plays such an important role in his writings and in medieval culture as a whole. Although in the previous sections we have used Bonaventure's symbols as a way into the coincidence of opposites, we concentrate here on his symbolism itself, studying both his generic theory and the function of specific symbols in his writings. In this study the coincidence of opposites can be both illuminating and illuminated. On the one hand, it throws considerable light on Bonaventure's symbolism; and on the other, it finds powerful expression in Bonaventure's use of integrative symbols.

Throughout his writing Bonaventure expresses himself on two levels simultaneously: (1) the theological-philosophical level, and (2) the level of religious symbols. One might look upon Bonaventure's use of symbols as mere literary devices to adorn his style, but such a judgment would not take into account the depth and power of his symbolic imagination and the intricate interrelations of his symbols as they form a coherent pattern of their own and give structure and support to the theological-philosophical level. Thus for Bonaventure the symbol embodies a twofold coincidence of opposites. If we view the religious symbol on its own level, we see that it performs the function of theophany, for it attempts to manifest the divine in matter — through the coincidence of the infinite and the finite, the *maximum* and the *minimum*. Seen within Bonaventure's total thought, the symbol also unites matter and spirit, for it expresses on its own concrete level the theophanic vision that Bonaventure's theological and philosophical formulations are attempting to express. Thus the religious symbol becomes a microcosm for viewing the entire theological-philosophical structure of his thought. It is here that we see the Christological significance of religious symbols. The religious symbol is a microcosm pointing to Christ the macrocosm — who unites within himself the greatest possible coincidence of opposites.

SYMBOLISM IN THE MIDDLE AGES

In the Middle Ages symbolism reached one of its richest flowerings in the history of Western culture. Too often the logic of the schoolmen, their metaphysical speculations and their scholastic disputations have distracted twentieth century scholars from the importance of symbols in the fabric of medieval life. Medieval man lived in a world that was alive with symbols. All about he saw graphic representations of Biblical themes: on frescoes on chapel walls, on the capitals of Romanesque columns, on the facade of Gothic cathedrals, on the pages of illuminated manuscripts. Each year in his liturgical cycle he re-enacted the great events of his religious past: the Exodus, the Last Supper, the Crucifixion and Resurrection. Knighthood and courtly love provided him with new variations to ancient mythic themes. Allegory flourished in all genres of literature: in the romances, the songs of the troubadours, the miracle and morality plays. Political and military life were ablaze with color and embellished with symbols of power, courage, and fidelity.

Medieval symbols were decidedly Christian and were molded by the political and economic forces of the times. Yet they were deeply grounded in the past. Their roots plunged back into the Roman and Greek era and to the more primitive mythic substructure of the Indo-European world. They were ultimately grounded in the most basic mythic level of mankind. In many respects, the symbolic world of the Middle Ages was like the cathedral of Chartres. In ancient times the area of Chartres was an important Druid center, where ceremonies were held around a well which has been discovered under the cathedral crypt. In the Gallo-Roman era there were venerated at such sacred areas statues of the mother goddess, at times depicted seated with an infant on her knees. Christian legend claimed that before the birth of the Virgin Mary a pagan king of the region of Chartres, under mysterious inspiration, had a statue sculptured of a woman holding an infant and containing the inscription: *Virgini pariturae.*[1] On the site of the ancient pagan place of worship, Christians built a series of churches where devotion to Mary flourished. Through the centuries the structures became more elaborate until in the twelfth and thirteenth centuries there rose the great cathedral Notre Dame de Chartres, with its intricate Gothic-Romanesque design, its elaborate stained glass windows, and its delicate sculpture. Like the cathedral of Chartres, the symbols of the Middle Ages emerged from primitive levels and evolved through succeeding stages until they flowered in the elaborate synthesis of the high Middle Ages.

Symbols not only played a major role in medieval life, but they were reflected upon with considerable self-consciousness. The architects of the great cathedrals employed a type of symbolic geometry in developing their intricate structures. Theologians explored religious symbols systematically according to the fourfold sense of Scripture. Philosophers developed a metaphysics that was so profoundly in touch with symbols that it not only provided a philosophical explanation of symbolic thinking, but affirmed that the symbol was the key to understand the deepest level of reality. All of reality — the inner life of God and the created world — is to be understood according to the metaphysics of expression and representation. The divine life is self-expressive; for the Father begets his Son, who is his Image. The Son contains the archetypes of all possible creation; hence the created world — as a whole and in all of its parts — is the expression of the divinity; for it participates in and reflects the divine Image or Word. Thus the world is seen as a mirror reflecting God.

Consequently it is not enough that one understand the internal intelligible structure of finite beings or see them as created by the power of God. One must also see them as reflections of God, for this is their deepest reality.

This metaphysics of expressionism and exemplarism was derived from Platonism and Neo-Platonism but was developed with distinctly Christian and medieval dimensions. It was Augustine who formulated Christian Platonism for the West, and from him the tradition flowed into the Middle Ages. He situated the Platonic ideas in the divine mind, thus laying the basis for Christian exemplarism. The Pseudo-Dionysius underscored the dynamic aspect of God, whose self-diffusive goodness overflows into the entire created cosmos. Anselm highlighted the expressive aspect of the generation of the Son, and the Victorines explored a wide spectrum of religious symbols. To the earlier Augustinian and Victorine traditions Bonaventure brought specifically Franciscan elements: Francis's love of nature, an interest in individual material objects, and a sense of the coincidence of opposites. This exemplaristic tradition, which reaches a certain climax in the early Franciscan school, is of paramount importance for understanding symbolism in medieval culture. Unfortunately, the predominance of Aristotelian logic throughout the Middle Ages and of Aristotelian metaphysics in the late thirteenth century — with its emphasis on efficient, formal, and final causality — has tended to obscure the strong current of exemplarism that permeated the earlier Middle Ages and provided a philosophical and theological basis for the rich symbolic life of the period.

SYMBOLISM IN BONAVENTURE

These two strands — the rich symbolic life of the Middle Ages and its philosophical-theological theory of symbol — converge in a remarkable way in Bonaventure. His theory of symbol is highly developed and integrates systematically the richness of the long exemplaristic tradition. On the other hand, in keeping with the medieval ethos, Bonaventure's writings abound in symbols: Biblical images such as the tree of life, the Exodus, the journey, the tabernacle, the mountain; philosophical images such as the sun, light, and darkness used to express basic epistemology; geometrical images such as the circle, the center and lines intersecting in the form of a cross. These images are not used as mere ornaments overlaid on a philosophical or theological treatise; rather they form part of an organic whole. They are intimately connected with the grasp and expression of his metaphysics and theology. Bonaventure's chief images emerge from the deepest strata of the psyche and provide a comprehensive vision; yet they manifest a cultivated and not a primitive aspect. They are to a large extent present to conscious reflection and are integrated into his abstract philosophical and theological speculation.

Bonaventure belongs to the tradition of medieval writers who use symbols to convey their theological vision. In an age when scholastic logic had been developed into a precision instrument for the theologian, Bonaventure did not abandon the language of symbols for that of abstraction. He used the logic of the schools with great skill, especially in his *Commentary on the Sentences,* the *Breviloquium,* and the disputed questions, but even here symbols play a role. Submerged under the logical structure, they appear obliquely and offer the alert reader a clue to Bonaventure's meaning. In his spiritual treatises such as *The Tree of Life,* as well as in many of his sermons, symbols provide the central structural elements. In the third group of writings — the shorter treatises such as the *Itinerarium* and the later *collationes* — symbols combine with abstractions to form an organic matrix. Often the fusion is so effective that the reader cannot disengage the symbols from the abstractions without destroying the texture of the whole.

In this last body of writings, symbols constitute an entire structural level. They convey in their own way the philosophical and theological vision that Bonaventure also formulates in abstract terms. For example, in the *Itinerarium* he works out a network of the following symbols: the journey, the mirror, the ladder, the tabernacle, light, darkness, the six-winged Seraph and the two

Cherubim.[2] This pattern of symbols is interwoven with his meta-physical analyses of exemplarism, his epistemology, a dialectic of being and non-being, and his analysis of the Trinity under the aspect of the self-diffusive good. These two strata — the symbolic and the abstract — mutually clarify and re-enforce each other. The abstract element brings the meaning of the symbol to re-flexive consciousness; and the symbol gives vivid, concrete ex-pression to metaphysical and theological speculation. Bonaven-ture has a rare gift for blending the abstract and the concrete, the philosophical and the symbolic. This is the secret of his effec-tiveness as a literary artist: he combines imaginative power with philosophical penetration. Not only is he sensitive to his heritage of cultural symbols, but he has the creative power to present a symbol with vividness and the rhetorical skill to shape it into the structure of his work.

BONAVENTURE'S THEORY OF SYMBOLISM

It is not surprising that beneath this powerful and intricate use of symbols Bonaventure has developed a most articulate meta-physics of symbol. As Gilson says:

> Far from being an accident or an adventitious element, St. Bonaven-ture's symbolism has its roots deep in the very heart of his doctrine; it finds its whole rational justification in his fundamental metaphysical principles, and it is itself rigorously demanded by them as the only means of applying them to the real.[3]

What are these metaphysical principles? They are two: the prin-ciple of expressionism and that of exemplarism. That these two principles are at the core of Bonaventure's metaphysics is suc-cinctly stated at a key point in his most mature work:

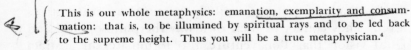

> This is our whole metaphysics: emanation, exemplarity and consum-mation: that is, to be illumined by spiritual rays and to be led back to the supreme height. Thus you will be a true metaphysician.[4]

For Bonaventure the true metaphysician is the one who traces all created things back to their source — through exemplarity to the divine emanation or expressionism. Through the principle of exemplarity one is led to the principle of expressionism at the core of the divine life itself. It is here at the center of the divine life — in the principle of expressionism — that we find Bonaventure's ultimate basis of symbolism. For Bonaventure all symbolic thinking and all symbolic reflection within creation are grounded in the expression of the Word by the Father.

Since we have presented Bonaventure's Trinitarian theology and his doctrine of exemplarism at some length in previous chapters,[5] we will merely summarize them as a backdrop for understanding his theory of symbolism. Bonaventure has a dynamic notion of the divinity. He views the inner life of God as consisting of self-communication, self-diffusion, self-expression. In the *Commentary on the Sentences,* he describes the Father as *fontalis plenitudo* — fountain-fullness, or the one who as source is pre-eminently fecund.[6] He applies to the Father a principle derived from the *Liber de causis*: the more primary a thing is the more fecund it is.[7] Since the Father is most primary, he is most fecund. In his fecundity he eternally generates his Son, who is his perfect Image. The Son, then, is both the Image of the Father and his Word through whom he expresses himself in creation.

In the *Itinerarium* Bonaventure applies a principle derived from Anselm to the Pseudo-Dionysian notion of God as self-diffusive good:

> Behold, therefore, and observe that the highest good is unqualifiedly that in comparison with which a greater cannot be thought. And this good is such that it cannot rightly be thought of as non-existing, since to be is absolutely better than not to be. And this good exists in such a way that it cannot rightly be thought of unless it is thought of as triune and one. For good is said to be self-diffusive, and therefore the highest good is most self-diffusive.[8]

The absolute self-diffusive nature of God requires that there be a diffusion that is absolute, actual, and eternal. Could creation satisfy this demand? Bonaventure answers in the negative; for creation is limited, like a mere speck before the vastness of the divine fecundity. Hence we must look within the divinity itself.

Through revelation we learn that the demands of the divine fecundity are met by the mystery of the Trinity, in the generation of the Son and the procession of the Spirit.[9]

In Bonaventure's view of the relation of philosophy and theology, revelation can bring to greater consciousness a principle that is grasped only vaguely prior to revelation. Hence the revelation of the dynamic self-expressive nature of the divinity in the Trinitarian processions brings to greater realization the principle of the absolute self-diffusiveness of the good. The significance of this expressionism for a metaphysics of symbol is profound. It means that at its deepest level — within the dynamics of the divine life itself — reality is self-expressive and symbolic. The Son is the expression of the Father; the Father is not knowable in himself, but only through the Son, his Image and Word. As Logos the Son is the principle of intelligibility; however as Image and Word he is not merely a self-contained principle of intelligibility, but the expression and manifestation of the Father, who is silent ground and generative power. With this expressive base within the divinity, the symbolic nature of creation and the function of symbolic thinking are solidly grounded. Since all created things share in the Son, they are symbolic expressions of the Father. Hence symbolic thinking, in its most authentic form, is not a second-best mode of grasping reality, but a penetration of its most profound metaphysical structure and dynamics.

From this divine expressionism flows the principle of exemplarity. In expressing the Son, the Father produces in the Son the archetypes of all that he can create. Bonaventure states: "The Father generated one similar to himself, namely the Word, co-eternal with himself; and he expressed his own likeness and as a consequence expressed all things that he could make."[10] Hence it is through the Word that creation takes place, and creation — grounded in the expressiveness of the Word — reflects back to the Word and ultimately to the Father. This theme runs through Bonaventure's writings and is expressed in both technical philosophical terms and in images such as the book, the mirror, and light shining through a window. For example, Bonaventure states:

> . . . the entire world is a shadow, a road, a vestige, and it is also "a
> book written without." [Ez. 2:9; Ap. 5:1]. For in every creature there
> is a shining forth of the divine exemplar, but mixed with darkness.
> Hence creatures are a kind of darkness mixed with light. Also they
> are a road leading to the exemplar. Just as you see that a ray of
> light entering through a window is colored in different ways according
> to the different colors of the various parts, so the divine ray shines
> forth in each and every creature in different ways and in different
> properties; it is said in Wisdom: "In her ways she shows herself."
> [Wis. 6:17]. Also creatures are a vestige of the wisdom of God.
> Hence creatures are like a kind of representation and statue of the
> wisdom of God. And in view of all of this, they are a kind of book
> written without.[11]

Bonaventure divides creatures according to their degree of representing God and classifies them in a descending scale: similitude, image, vestige, and shadow. Shadow refers to a general reflection of God; vestige indicates the reflection of God's power,
wisdom, and goodness; image refers to rational creatures and indicates the presence of God reflected within subjectivity in the
memory, understanding, and will; similitude refers to the rational
creature transformed by grace.[12] Of special interest here is Bonaventure's notion of vestige, since he applies vestige most extensively to the material world and it is the material world that has most
direct bearing on symbol. In the *Itinerarium* Bonaventure contemplates the material world as vestige. After a general consideration that visible things reflect the power, wisdom, and goodness
of God, he embarks on a detailed study of the sevenfold properties
of creatures: their origin, greatness, multitude, beauty, plenitude,
activity, and order. In each case he sees the reflection of the
power, wisdom, and goodness of God.[13]

Although Bonaventure's analysis is detailed and profound, I
believe that it leaves untouched a major aspect of his own symbolism. It does not uncover the specific nature of the very symbols he uses throughout his writing. Are his own literary and
mythic symbols — such as light, darkness, the tabernacle, and the
mountain — vestiges? From one point of view, they are; but in

my opinion this point of view does not exhaust or pinpoint their most significant function. If we bring to bear on Bonaventure's symbolism the research of Mircea Eliade and C. G. Jung, we may be able to complete the picture. Both Jung and Eliade have studied extensively the type of symbol that Bonaventure uses in his writings. For example, Eliade has studied, especially in primitive peoples, the symbolic meaning of sacred space, and specifically of the holy building or temple. By taking into account a vast array of data, Eliade can isolate the common elements and indicate that the temple and its holy precincts are an elaborated form of the more primitive and universal symbol of the center.[14] In the same vein, but dealing within the psyche, Jung can describe the function of symbols for interior life and the process of individuation. Jung indicates that there are certain basic patterns or archetypes such that certain symbols seem to have the same meaning for men throughout time and space. Hence the inner way and the center of the soul are often described by the symbol of entering into a holy building or temple and discovering the center which is simultaneously the center of the soul.[15]

The data studied by Eliade and Jung have a common presupposition: that material objects and their varied configuration have a direct bearing on one's spiritual awareness and development. Independently of the rational analysis that Bonaventure does of material objects, certain objects — such as light, water, temples, mountains — have an immediate, nonreflexive meaning for man's spirit. This meaning follows certain patterns and dynamics, such as those explored by Jung and Eliade. The goal of this is man's spiritual self-realization, or from a religious perspective his journey to God. If this is the case, then the material world provides resources for spiritual development that are enormously powerful and fruitful. This seems to indicate a much closer interpenetration of matter and spirit in the area of symbolism than Bonaventure articulates. Yet this interpenetration of matter and spirit is quite in harmony with the major structure of Bonaventure's metaphysics and theology.

Two Types of Symbolism

I claim, then, that there are two types of symbolism in Bonaventure. Corresponding to the two poles of Bonaventure's theology studied in Chapter Two,[16] these can best be designated in theological terms as Trinitarian and Christological symbolism. The Trinitarian symbolism is grounded in the expressionism of the Trinity and has for its philosophical and theological matrix Bonaventure's doctrine of exemplarism. This symbolism is universal, applying to all creatures: to angels, men, and material beings. All creatures are symbols of the divinity since all are grounded in the Word and reflect the divine power, wisdom, and goodness. All creatures are shadows reflecting God as their cause and all are vestiges of the Trinity. This symbolism is not rooted in materiality as such, as is the case of the symbols studied by Jung and Eliade; rather it applies uniformly to all created beings, whether rational spirits or material objects. However, there are degrees of symbolic representation, as distinguished by Bonaventure: All creatures are shadows just as all are also vestiges; but only rational creatures are images, and only those rational creatures adorned with grace are similitudes. This type of symbolism is based on the form of the being, seen in its most general mode, not in its unique materiality. For example, all material objects are vestiges in so far as they reflect the divine power, wisdom, and goodness. But in the case of the other type of symbol, such objects as light and fire, the temple and the center function as archetypal symbols with special power and significance.

This second type of symbol can be called Christological because it mediates the divine through its very materiality. Such symbols as water, fire, the temple, and the mountain do not act merely as vestiges in a general Trinitarian symbolism, but exercise a specific effect in the process of spiritual growth: They divinize the spirit of man precisely through their materiality. As material symbols they have a power to divinize the human spirit in a way that reflects the power of Christ in his materiality to divinize the spirit of mankind. Because they mediate human spirit and divinity through their materiality, and not merely through their grounding in the Word, they contain a Christological model of the coincidence of opposites in addition to the Trinitarian model through exemplarism. They are a microcosm pointing to Christ, the macrocosm of the coincidence of opposites.

Bonaventure's Trinitarian symbolism has its roots in Platonism and Neo-Platonism and in the theology of the Greek Fathers, which Bonaventure inherited as an elaborated tradition and which he built into his synthesis in the earliest stage of his writing. Having been thoroughly developed in the very beginning, it does not undergo an evolution in his later writing. However, from the time of the *Itinerarium* onward, this Trinitarian level of symbolism is expressed and supported also by the Christological level of symbols, by material symbols functioning precisely in their materiality. Although Bonaventure's Christocentricity evolves during this period, there is no evolution of a theory of Christological symbols that would compare with his theory of Trinitarian symbolism. In spite of the fact that Bonaventure is extraordinarily gifted in expressing his vision in archetypal religious symbols, he develops no theory of these symbols nor any consciousness of them as a distinct class.

MANDALA SYMBOLISM

This lack in Bonaventure's system can be supplied by tapping the extensive research done in the twentieth century in this area of symbols. In the remainder of this chapter, I will explore the Christological level of Bonaventure's symbolism in the light of this research. Making no attempt to be comprehensive, I will concentrate on a group of symbols that play a central role in his work. These symbols are the circle, the center, the cross, and the journey. Appearing at key points in his theological writing, these symbols convey themes relating to his doctrine of the Trinity, creation, Christology, and spiritual growth. As my analysis proceeds, I will make the claim that this group of symbols and the corresponding themes can be coherently understood from the perspective of the mandala, as it has been explored by C. G. Jung, Mircea Eliade, and Giuseppe Tucci.[17] Described briefly, the mandala is a symbol of total integration, usually in the geometric form of a circle with a center, along with a square or cross. To view Bonaventure's work from the perspective of the mandala can bring to light a deep level of dynamic unity both in his symbols and in his thought as a whole. This will have the effect not only of illumining Bonaventure's system, but of completing the development of the Christocentric pole of his theology; for I believe that Bonaventure's Christocentricity reaches its culmination in the symbol of Christ the center of the mandala. Finally since in the history of religions the mandala is the most basic and most elaborate symbol of the coincidence of opposites, it will reveal the most highly developed form of the coincidence of opposites in Bonaventure's thought.

I will concentrate on three instances of this group of symbols in Bonaventure's text: the circle, the center, and the cross in the first of the *Collationes in Hexaemeron,* where he develops the theme of Christ the center;[18] the six-winged Seraph in the form of the crucified, on which he meditates as a symbol of the mind's journey into God in the *Itinerarium;*[19] and the symbol of the tabernacle, in the latter part of the *Itinerarium,* where he leads the reader into the various sacred zones, as a symbol of the inner way, until he encounters Christ at the center of the Holy of Holies.[20] After analyzing the structure and function of these symbols in their literary context, I will view them as instances of mandala symbols and draw certain conclusions relative to the interpretation of Bonaventure's thought.

The image of the circle or sphere appears throughout Bonaventure's writing, often with a reference to the center. For example, borrowing from Alanus de Insulis, he refers to God as an "intelligible sphere, whose center is everywhere and whose circumference is nowhere."[21] He also speaks of the "circle of eternity," in which the temporal process terminates.[22] He sees the life of the Trinity as a circular process and describes the emanation of creation and its return as participating in this great circular dynamism. For example, he says that rational creatures return to their source in the Trinity "by way of an intelligible circle":

> Hence this alone is eternal life: that the rational spirit, which flows from the most blessed Trinity and is an image of the Trinity, return by way of an intelligible circle by memory, understanding and will, through divine likeness of glory to the most blessed Trinity.[23]

Bonaventure is here referring to the great circle of emanation and return that forms the foundation of medieval theological syntheses. All things emanate from God and all things return to God. He links the emanation and return of creatures with the inner life of the Trinity. Hence the great circle begins with the Father in the Trinity — with the generation of the Son and the completion of the Trinity in the Spirit. This circular movement is the basis of the emanation of creatures *ad extra* and the return of rational creatures "by way of an intelligible circle" to their Trinitarian source.[24] In this circular process, Christ is the center. As eternal Logos, he is the *medium* of the emanation of creatures; and as incarnate Logos, he is the *medium* of their return. Perhaps more than any other medieval theologian, Bonaventure emphasizes the fact that Christ is the center, or *medium*, of this circular process.

As we saw in the previous chapter, the theme of Christ the center is developed by Bonaventure with striking vividness in the first of the *Collationes in Hexaemeron.* Bonaventure calls Christ the *medium* or center of all the sciences. For Bonaventure, Christ is the *medium metaphysicum, physicum, mathematicum, logicum, ethicum, politicum, theologicum.*[25] Christ is the center of the divine life, the center of creation, and the center of man's return to God. First, as eternal Word, he is the center of the Trinitarian life, the *media persona* of the Trinity.[26] As expressive Word, he is the dynamic center of creation; for he is the *medium* through which creation takes place.[27] As incarnate Word, he is the center of the universe; like the sun in the heavens and the heart in the body, Christ is the center of radiating energy.[28] Finally, he is the center of man's return to God: In the suffering of the cross, Christ locates man's lost center; and through his resurrection and ascension, he leads man back to the unity of the Father.[29]

This latter point is graphically depicted in the *collatio* through the geometrical figure of the circle whose center is found by two lines intersecting in the form of a cross.[30] Bonaventure claims that Christ is the mathematical center in his crucifixion. By his cross he was able to locate man's lost center and restore the structure of order that was lost through pride and sin. Bonaventure says: "For when the center of a circle has been lost, it can be found only by two lines intersecting at right angles."[31] Bonaventure sees the cross leading to resurrection, death to life, sin to redemption, humility to glory. Thus in Christ and in his cross the opposites are reconciled.

This *collatio* is more than an isolated statement of Bonaventure's ideas. Rather it presents in concentrated and graphic fashion the essential lines of his vision. It is not only a microcosm of the entire series of *collationes* of which it is the introduction, but it is the full flowering of the vision that had taken shape in his youth and whose major lines had clarified and deepened through the years. In this context the symbols of the circle, the cross, and, above all, the center take on added significance.

A second example of Bonaventure's symbolism is the six-winged Seraph in the form of the crucified, the major structural symbol of the *Itinerarium*. As we saw above, this image is derived from the vision Francis of Assisi had on Mount La Verna in 1224 at the time he received the stigmata.[32] Thirty-five years after Francis' vision, Bonaventure retired for a period of time to the same mountain, as he tells us, in order to seek peace.[33] While he meditated there on the vision, the thought occurred to him that the six-winged Seraph indicated the height of contemplation Francis had attained and at the same time symbolized the stages by which this goal could be reached. "The figure of the six wings of the

Seraph, therefore," Bonaventure writes, "brings to mind the six steps of illumination which begin with creatures and lead up to God, whom no one rightly enters save through the crucified."[34] The entire structure of the *Itinerarium* is based on Bonaventure's interpretation of the wings of the Seraph. The six stages symbolized by the six wings are the subject matter of the six chapters of the *Itinerarium*, leading to the seventh and final chapter, which deals with mystical ecstasy. The first two stages deal with the material world, the next two with the soul of man, and the last two with the contemplation of God. Bonaventure believes that by contemplating the material universe as a vestige of God, by gazing within the soul as image of God, and by meditating on God as Being and the Good, man rises through progressive stages toward the height of contemplation Francis reached at the climax of his life. By the fact that the Seraph has at its center the figure of the crucified man, Bonaventure sees that Christ and his cross are at the center of the passage into God. Thus from the standpoint of the literary structure of the *Itinerarium*, the Seraph is the master symbol providing the skeletal pattern of the whole. From the standpoint of a cosmic vision, the Seraph symbolizes the structure of the cosmos, which as vestige and image reflects God and provides man with an ascending path into the divine. From the standpoint of the soul's journey along this path, the Seraph symbolizes the progressive stages, the passage by way of the cross and the goal of the ascent.

The six-winged Seraph leads to the third symbol under consideration, that of the tabernacle in the latter half of the *Itinerarium*. As we observed above, when Bonaventure reaches the third stage of the mind's journey, he introduces the symbol of the tabernacle to depict the entrance of the soul into its own depths.[35] The symbol is drawn from Exodus, where a detailed description is given of the tabernacle or tent that Moses prescribed to be built to house the ark of the covenant.[36] As described in Exodus, the tabernacle had an outer court; an inner area or sanctuary, in which a golden candelabra was placed; and finally, a most sacred innermost chamber, the Holy of Holies, in which the ark was housed. Upon the ark between two golden Cherubim was placed the propitiatory or Mercy Seat, from which God was to communicate to men. All of these elements enter into Bonaventure's symbol. After contemplating the material world as a vestige of God, he bids the reader to enter into himself. Leaving the outer court of the external world, we now enter into the sanctuary of the tabernacle, that is into our own souls, where "the light of truth, as from a candelabra, will shine upon the face of our mind, in which the image of the most Blessed Trinity appears in splendor."[37] After contemplating this reflection of God, we move deeper into ourselves, into the Holy of Holies, that is, into the contemplation of God himself. The Cherubim symbolizes two different modes of contemplating God: as Being and as the Good. In each case Bonaventure contemplates God as a coincidence of opposites. Finally, he turns his gaze to the Mercy Seat, which he appropriately sees as a symbol of Christ. If we wondered at the union of opposites in the divinity itself, we will be amazed at Christ, the God-man, who embodies the most extraordinary *coincidentia oppositorum*. Contemplating Christ as "the first and the last, the highest and the lowest, the circumference and the center, 'the Alpha and the Omega', the caused and the cause, the Creator and the creature,"[38] the mind passes over into the mystical silence of the seventh stage.

Like the Seraph, the tabernacle provides a symbolic matrix for the stages of the mind's journey into God and hence for the literary structure of the *Itinerarium*. In most respects the symbols of the Seraph and the tabernacle are related as opposites. The Seraph is an exterior image; the tabernacle symbolizes the interior of the soul. The Seraph suggests height and ascent, for the Seraph is a heavenly messenger appearing on a mountain top. The tabernacle suggests depth, for we enter into the inner chambers and into the depths of our souls. Yet they have a common center in Christ. In the wings of the Seraph is the form of the crucified; and at the center of the Holy of Holies is the Mercy Seat, which is Christ. As center of each symbol, Christ is the way to union with God.

MANDALA IN RELIGION AND PSYCHOLOGY

Although we have explored these symbols previously by analyzing their function in their literary context, we can now understand them on a deeper level in the light of contemporary research on the mandala. The term *mandala* is a Sanscrit word which is translated as "circle" or "center" or "that which surrounds."[39] It denotes "the ritual or magic circle used in Lamaism and also in Tantric yoga as a *yantra* or aid to contemplation."[40] By meditating on the mandala symbol or by participating in a mandala ritual, the Oriental seeks to effect an inner transformation and to advance towards the goal of the spiritual journey. In his book *The Theory and Practice of the Mandala*, Giuseppe Tucci observes that "the theories of the *mandala* took their origin in India and then penetrated into Tibet and these theories, expressed in symbols, allegories and connotations, have, as it were, the colour of the spiritual world in which they developed."[41] However, Tucci does not believe that the mandala is confined to the Orient or that its meaning is limited to an external design or ritual pattern. Rather the mandala symbol reflects a basic dynamic structure — or archetype — of the human psyche. Tucci observes that his study of the Oriental mandala will reveal "some striking analogies with comparable ideas expressed by currents of thought in other countries and in other ages."[42]

Jung has explored the mandala in terms of the structure and dynamics of the psyche. He believes that mandala symbols "signify nothing less than a psychic center of the personality not to be identified with the ego."[43] This psychic center Jung calls the "self," which he describes as "not only the center but also the whole circumference which embraces both conscious and unconscious; it is the center of this totality, just as the ego is the center of the conscious mind."[44] In the process of psychic growth, the self is both the beginning and the end, the source and the goal. The

process of growth — or in Jung's term, the process of individuation — consists in a differentiation and integration of psychic
forces leading to the realization of one's full potential, or a realization of the self. From a dynamic point of view, the self is the
alpha and the *omega* of the spiritual journey; from a structural
point of view, it is both the center of the psyche and its organized
totality.

If the nature of the self be granted, its symbol — the mandala
— contains a focus on the center, an encompassing circle, an ordered pattern of four and an interrelation of elements forming
a *coincidentia oppositorum*. Jung's follower Jolande Jacobi describes the structure of the mandala symbol as follows:

> The mandalas all show the same typical arrangement and symmetry of
> the pictorial elements. Their basic design is a circle or square (most
> often a square) symbolizing wholeness, and in all of them the relation
> to a center is accentuated. Many have the form of a flower, a cross,
> or a wheel, and there is a distinct inclination toward the number
> four.[45]

Since from Jung's point of view the mandala is the symbol of
a universal psychic archetype, it is to be expected that mandalas
should have a wide diffusion. Hence they are found not only
in Hinduism and Buddhism, but in Western religions as well.
They are not confined to religious settings, but appear in works
of art and literature and in the dreams and fantasies of individuals.
Granted differences due to diverse cultures, the basic pattern of
the mandala is found throughout the world and across history
since prehistoric times in both primitive peoples and advanced
cultures.[46]

The mandala plays an important role in primitive rituals, in
the architecture of temples and churches, and even in the development of a cosmological vision. Mircea Eliade has studied the
mandala in the context of extensive research on the symbolism
of the center.[47] Since primitive times man has sought a center
around which to organize his universe and through which to enter into the divine sphere. He has located this center in a sacred

mountain, a sanctuary, a temple, a palace, a city. He has expressed the significance of this center through the symbol of the center of the world: the point where the three cosmic cones — heaven, earth, and the underworld — are put in communication. This communication is effected through the universal pillar, the *axis mundi,* which appears at times as a ladder, a mountain, a vine, or the Cosmic Tree with roots in hell and branches in heaven. Here, Eliade notes, "we have a sequence of religious conceptions and cosmological images that are inseparably connected and form a system that may be called the 'system of the world' prevalent in traditional societies."[48] Basic to this system is the organization of a cosmos around a center, the integration of opposites through the center, and access through the center into the divine sphere. Thus the same forces that shape the mandala symbol in Lamaism and Tantric yoga are at work in shaping a cosmological vision.

Cosmic Mandala

If we view Bonaventure's symbols in the light of contemporary research into the mandala, we can discern that the three examples of symbols we have studied are, in fact, three different types of mandalas. The first of the *Collationes in Hexaemeron* presents a cosmic mandala. By depicting Christ as the center, Bonaventure has developed a vision of the universe according to the mandala structure, a vision closely associated with the research of Eliade into the symbolism of the center and its relation to the construction of a cosmological scheme. In the *collatio* Bonaventure constructs his cosmic vision around Christ. As eternal Logos, Christ is the source of order and form within the cosmos; as incarnate Logos, he performs the function of the *axis mundi* linking the zones of the universe; through his cross he restores the lost center of the circle; and through his passage to the Father he is the gateway of man's return to the Trinity.

Bonaventure develops his theme by seeing Christ as the center of all the sciences that study the various aspects of the universe. As metaphysical center Christ is the source of the exemplaristic structure of the world; as physical center he is a source of radiating energy in the cosmos; as mathematical center he functions as the *axis mundi,* for he links the cosmic extremes: heaven, earth, and the underworld. Bonaventure says of Christ: "In taking up our clay, he came not only to the surface of our earth, but to the depths of its center . . . For after his crucifixion his soul descended into hell and restored the heavenly dwellings."[49] As logical center Christ overcame Satan and sin and re-established cosmic order. As ethical, political, and theological center, Christ leads mankind to the Father. At the midpoint of his presentation, Bonaventure introduces the geometrical figure of the circle whose center is rediscovered by lines intersecting in a cross. This figure, which has the elements of the classical geometrical mandala, reflects the mandala structure of Bonaventure's cosmic vision as a whole: Christ is the center of the world, the *axis mundi,* the *coincidentia oppositorum,* the center of the great cosmic circle of emanation and return. From this perspective, the mandala is a key not only to unlock the meaning of particular symbols in Bonaventure's writing, but to reveal the structure of his entire cosmic vision.

SPIRITUAL JOURNEY

While the first *collatio* presents a cosmic mandala, the *Itinerarium* contains two mandalas relating to the spiritual journey. Both the six-winged Seraph and the tabernacle symbolize the progressive movement of the soul towards God. Although both reflect a cosmic structure, their chief function is to direct the soul on its spiritual path. The six-winged Seraph gives evidence of being a mandala from a variety of perspectives. In terms of its geometrical structure, there is a cross, a center, and the number four — all contained in the figure of the crucified. Whether the symbol also contains a circle is not clear, since Bonaventure's description gives no indication. The six wings may be arranged in the form of a circle, as is the case in certain representations of the vision in medieval art. Other representations show a circle formed by rays of light or a glowing aureole around the Seraph.[50] Such a conception may be suggested by Bonaventure's account of the vision in the *Legenda major,* which speaks of the "Seraph, with six wings that were fiery and shining."[51] Other representations give no suggestion of a circle, but depict the wings in different configurations and without a circle of light. On the other hand, the six wings themselves may symbolize a circle; for Jung indicates that the numbers twelve and six are known to constitute symbolic circles and hence may be found in mandalas.[52] Whether or not a circle is present does not seem to be crucial here since the other geometrical elements combine with the function of the symbol to indicate its mandala character.

The six-winged Seraph functions as a symbol of organized totality. First, it is a symbol unifying the entire literary piece. Secondly, it is a microcosm of the universe, since the three pairs of wings reflect the material world, man, and God. It is also a symbol of the soul, since it reflects the successive stages of the soul's journey to God. The six wings, then, symbolize the organized totality of the universe and of man's inner world and his spiritual progress. It is this total organization of the inner world according to a cosmic scheme as depicted in a symbol or image that is characteristic of the mandala. It is interesting to note, further, that in Bonaventure's meditation, the Seraph plays a role similar to that played by the Oriental *yantra,* or geometrical aid to contemplation. In the prologue to the *Itinerarium,* Bonaventure describes how he had retired to Mount La Verna and meditated on "that miracle which in this very place had happened to the blessed Francis—the vision he received of the winged Seraph in the form of the crucified."[53] In a flash Bonaventure grasped how the Seraph symbolized both the goal of the spiritual journey and the stages of the process. It is this combination of goal and stages of the journey that constitutes the very essence of the mandala design. Thus the personal vision of Francis is seen as a universal symbol of the goal and the stages of the spiritual ascent. It was precisely Bonaventure's reading of the geometrical configuration of the six wings that was the key to rendering the personal vision of Francis a universal psychic and cosmic symbol. The remainder of the *Itinerarium* can be seen as a continuation of this meditation on the Seraph as a mandala, leading ultimately to penetration into the divine realm in the seventh chapter.

ARCHITECTURAL-RITUALISTIC MANDALA

On reaching the third stage of the journey, Bonaventure introduces the tabernacle, another mandala symbol. Not only does the tabernacle have a different configuration from the Seraph, but it belongs to a different class: that of the architectural-ritualistic mandalas. The Seraph functioned as an image for contemplation, like the Oriental *yantra*. In the description of the tabernacle, however, the reader is bid to enter a sacred structure and to move from zone to zone in a type of ritual of penetration. In terms of geometrical structure, the tabernacle follows the mandala pattern, since it consists of a square or rectangle, with various sacred zones leading to a center, namely Christ symbolized by the Mercy Seat. From a functional point of view, the tabernacle symbol is a mandala since it leads to a centering of the self on Christ and a passage into the divine sphere. The contemplation of Christ as the coincidence of opposites suggests the integration of opposites around the center of the mandala.

Bonaventure's use of the tabernacle as a mandala recapitulates a long history of architecture and ritual. Since primitive times, as Eliade's research has shown, man has sought a center for contact with the divine. These centers have been natural objects such as stones, mountains, springs, trees. However, man has also established a center in his buildings, especially in temples and churches. Since ancient times temples were built according to a mandala pattern. In addition to the basic center point, the walls and chambers were designed as a labyrinth or in successive stages to allow for gradual entrance into the sacred center. This architectural pattern provided the context for a ritual of entrance that would lead by successive stages to the point of contact with the divine sphere.[54] In the tabernacle in the *Itinerarium*, Bonaventure has used a mandala design from temple architecture as a symbol of the structure of the psyche; and he has employed the ritualistic entrance as a symbol of the inner way.

Seen in interrelationship, the three types of mandalas we have studied — the cosmic, the *yantra,* and the architectural-ritualistic — represent three diverse forms of the mandala structure. Every mandala is simultaneously a picture of the cosmos, of the inner world, and of the spiritual journey. Each of these forms is related to the other by way of microcosm-macrocosm. The soul reflects the cosmic structure, and the spiritual journey follows the pattern of both the cosmos and the soul. Each form, then, contains the other according to the specific coincidence of opposites that is realized in the microcosm-macrocosm relationship. The single point through which the opposites pass and unite is the center. In each of Bonaventure's three mandalas, the center is Christ. It is Christ who unifies the cosmos, the soul, and the journey. In studying the three types of mandalas in Bonaventure, we are viewing three different facets of the intricate structure of his thought — each facet itself structured according to the mandala design and each focusing on the single center: Christ.

Other Mandala Symbols

In this study we have confined ourselves to three major mandala symbols used by Bonaventure: the cosmic vision of the first *collatio in Hexaemeron,* with Christ as the center, the six-winged Seraph and the tabernacle of the *Itinerarium.* We can add to this group the image of Christ in the treatise *The Tree of Life.*[55] In this work, written shortly after the *Itinerarium,* Bonaventure presents the life of Christ through the symbol of the tree of life, on whose branches blossom the fruits of virtue to nourish the soul. Bonaventure describes the image as follows:

> Picture in your imagination a tree. Suppose its roots to be watered by an eternally gushing fountain that becomes a great and living river, a river which spreads out in four channels to irrigate the whole garden of the Church. Suppose next that from the trunk of this tree there spring forth twelve branches, adorned with leaves, flowers and fruits.[56]

Since Bonaventure identifies the life of Christ with the tree of life, artists through the ages have depicted Christ crucified on the trunk of the tree with his arms outstretched on two of the branches. On the twelve branches of the tree are often painted the scenes from Christ's life that Bonaventure describes in the treatise and from which the reader is to draw nourishment for his spiritual life.[57] The image is in the form of a mandala since Christ is clearly at the center and the tree is in the form of a cross. In some reproductions the foliage produces the effects of a circle, although the circle design is not always present. On the other hand, the twelve branches may constitute a symbolic circle, according to the observations of Jung, cited above, on the symbolic meaning of the numbers six and twelve.[58] The configuration of four is present in the cross and in the river which waters the tree's roots and branches into four channels to irrigate the entire garden of the Church.

Bonaventure clearly intends the tree of life to be an image of total integration: Christ's life is presented in its entirety as the ideal for the Christian moral and spiritual life. By meditating on the individual incidents in Christ's life, we identify ourselves with him as our center and are thus transformed into him. *The Tree of Life*, then, is situated in the great tradition of spirituality which affirms that one reaches spiritual maturity by identifying with Christ. Yet Bonaventure's treatise reflects the specific emphasis of Francis, since he meditates on the concrete particulars of Christ's life, seeking to imitate the virtues there manifested. As a mandala, the tree of life is comparable to the six-winged Seraph, in that it functions as a *yantra*, an image for contemplation, providing in Christ's life an ideal to be emulated and in the progressive meditation on his virtues the stages in the spiritual journey towards that ideal.

CONFIGURATION OF FOUR

The mandalas studied above embody the geometrical form of the center, the cross, the circle, and the journey. There is, however, another type of mandala which is also found in Bonaventure. This is the mandala in which the configuration of four predominates. Of course, the configuration of four is found in the cross as an element in the above mandalas; but at times it provides the very basic structure of the mandala design. Jung has pointed out how the configuration four appears in dreams and in culture as an archetype of total integration.[59] This can be seen, for example, in the four directions, the four seasons, the four elements, the four causes, the four moral virtues, the four senses of Scripture. In religious art this configuration is found in the mandala of the four evangelists, with Christ as a center. Two striking uses of the fourfold mandala design occur in the introductions to Bonaventure's two versions of his scholastic synthesis: the *Commentary on the Sentences* and the *Breviloquium*.

In the *prooemium* to the first book of his *Commentary on the Sentences,* Bonaventure proposes as an introduction to his work a consideration of the four causes of the book of *The Sentences* by Peter Lombard: the material, formal, efficient, and final causes.[60] The *prooemium* begins like a medieval sermon, taking its point of departure from a Biblical text and proceeding by way of the interpretation of symbols and complex divisions. Bonaventure chooses the following text from Job: "He searched into the depths of the rivers and brought hidden things to light" (28:11). According to Bonaventure, this text provides us with a key to understand the four causes of *The Sentences*: for in the river we see symbolized the material cause; in searching the depths, the formal cause; in bringing to light hidden things, the final cause; and in the one who searches and brings to light, the efficient cause.

Bonaventure then explores the material cause according to another configuration of four. The subject matter, or material cause, is like a river, and the four books of *The Sentence* can be correlated to the four properties observed in a river; for a river flows constantly, it is extensive, it circulates, and it washes. The first book of *The Sentences* correlates with the constant flow of the river, since it deals with the eternal Trinitarian processions.

The second book correlates with the vastness of the river, since it treats the vast expanse of creation. The third correlates with the circulation of the river since it deals with the Incarnation. "Just as in a circle the end is joined to the beginning, so in the Incarnation the highest is joined to the lowest, since God is joined to clay, and the first is joined to the last, since the eternal Son of God is joined to man created on the sixth day."[61] The fourth book correlates with the fact that a river washes, since it deals with the sacraments, which without being polluted themselves cleanse us from the stains of sin.

Bonaventure then compares the four books of *The Sentences* to the four branches of the river which watered the garden of Eden: "A river flowed out of Eden to water the garden; and from there it divided into four branches" (Gen. 2:10). Since there are four rivers, there are four distinct depths, which the four books of *The Sentences* search into: the depth of the eternal emanation, the depth of creation, the depth of the Incarnation, and the depth of the sacraments. This searching into the depths is the formal cause; and the bringing to light of the hidden things is the final cause, which itself is divided into a configuration of four according to the four types of hidden things brought to light: the greatness of the divine substance, the order of divine wisdom, the strength of the divine power, and the sweetness of the divine mercy. Pointing, then, to Master Peter Lombard, the author and efficient cause of *The Sentences,* Bonaventure completes his original configuration of four according to the four causes.

Does this configuration of four have a center? There is reason to detect at least the beginnings of the Christocentricity which years later will blossom into the image of Christ the center of the *Collationes in Hexaemeron.* Immediately following the treatment of the symbol of the river, Bonaventure devotes four scholastic *quaestiones* to the four causes of *The Sentences.* In contrast with the earlier rhetoric, this section is cast in the scholastic form of reasons, counter-reasons, the resolution of the question, followed by answers to objections. In the *quaestio* on the material cause, or subject matter, Bonaventure considers Christ the "integral subject" of *The Sentences*. Christ is the "integral subject" because all things treated in the work are led back (*reducuntur*) to him as to an integral whole (*totum integrale*):

> The subject to which all things treated in this book are led back, as to an integral whole, is Christ, in so far as he encompasses the divine and human nature or the created and uncreated, which the first two books are about. He also encompasses the head and the members, which the two following books are about. I am taking the term "integral whole" in the sense that it embraces many things not only by composition, but by union and by ordering.[62]

In this passage, Bonaventure formulates the two modes of Christocentricity that will unfold throughout his life. As God-man, Christ is the mediating center between God and the world; he is the microcosm in which all of reality is reflected. As the head of the members and the universe, he is the focal center through which all things are ordered. As "integral subject," he is also the midpoint between the two other types of subject matter which Bonaventure distinguishes in this *quaestio*. The "root subject" (*subjectum radicale*) is God, since all things are led back to him as to their source; the "universal subject" (*subjectum universale*) consists of the things and signs (*res et signa*) or the objects of belief as understood by reason.[63] As microcosm and organizing center, Christ draws together in an integral whole these other two subjects.

This configuration of four, with Christ as its center, is by no means as thoroughly developed a mandala structure as those found later in the *Itinerarium* and the *Collationes in Hexaemeron*; for here the element of Christ the center has not emerged into prominence. However, it is significant in that it is present at the very beginning of his writing career, and secondly, because it appears as the microcosmic design of his most extensive and comprehensive work, his *Commentary on the Sentences*. This means, in effect, that at the early stage of the formulation of his vision, the mandala was its controlling design.

Several years after the *Commentary* when Bonaventure composed the *Breviloquium,* the abbreviated version of his scholastic
synthesis, he introduced it with a symbolic interpretation of the
configuration four.[64] Once again taking his departure from a
Biblical text, he quotes from the letter to the Ephesians: ". . . so
that being rooted and grounded in love, you may be able to com-
prehend with all the saints what is the breadth and length and
height and depth and to know Christ's love which surpasses knowledge" (Eph. 3:17-19). This pattern of four is then developed in
two ways. Basing himself on Scripture rather than *The Sentences*
of Peter Lombard, he views the breadth, length, height, and depth
of the universe as it is described in Scripture; and then he studies
the same four dimensions of Scripture itself. Speaking of the first
perspective, he says:

> Using, therefore, a language sometimes literal and sometimes figura-
> tive, it [Scripture] sums up, as it were, the content of the entire uni-
> verse, and so covers the BREADTH; it describes the whole course of
> history, thereby comprehending the LENGTH; it displays the glory
> of those finally to be saved, thus showing the HEIGHT; it recounts
> the misery of the reprobate, and thus reveals the DEPTH, not only
> of the universe, but also of God's judgment.[65]

Looking at Scripture itself, Bonaventure studies its breadth in
the various books that make up the Old and the New Testament.
Once again he sees a configuration of four: in the legal, historical,
sapiential, and prophetical books of the Old Testament, which
have their counterpart in the New Testament. He sees the correspondence of the two Testaments prefigured in the vision of
Ezechiel, "who saw the wheels of the four faces, each wheel being,
as it were, within another."[66] Bonaventure makes a further correspondence between the books and the four faces of the vision:
the lion, the ox, the man, and the eagle. He proceeds to sketch
another pattern of four in the ways that Scripture draws us toward
good and away from evil.

Bonaventure studies the length of Scripture in the entire span
of history that it describes; he explores its height in its description
of the hierarchies and their ordered ranks; and he studies its depth

in its fourfold interpretation: the literal, allegorical, moral, and anagogical. Further on, in dealing with the explanation of Scripture, he correlates the fourfold interpretation with a fourfold division of the content of Scripture. He concludes his prologue with the following image:

> Scripture, then, deals with the whole universe, the high and the low, the first and the last, and all things in between. It is, in a sense, an intelligible cross in which the whole organism of the universe is described and made to be seen in the light of the mind.[67]

The pattern of the prologue to the *Breviloquium* is very similar to that of the *prooemium* of the *Commentary on the Sentences.* Just as there are complex patterns of four in each, so there is only a hint of Christocentricity. In the *Breviloquium* Christ the center is merely suggested in the image of Scripture as an intelligible cross manifesting the universe. Although Christ is not mentioned explicitly, the image of the cross in Bonaventure's writing naturally suggests Christ crucified. There are further hints in the text, such as the following: "By knowing and loving Christ . . . , we can know the breadth, length, height and depth of Scripture."[68] As in the case of the *Commentary,* the Christocentric element of the mandala design is not yet prominent; yet the general outlines of the mandala design are present, some of them in a high degree of development. Thus we see foreshadowed even in the early period the highly developed Christocentric mandala design that will emerge progressively throughout his writings.

CLARIFICATION THROUGH MANDALA

To study Bonaventure's work from the standpoint of the mandala throws light on many aspects of his thought. First, the mandala, as a symbol of total integration, reflects the distinctive quality of Bonaventure's synthesis. Even in an age of synthesis, Bonaventure stands out for the synthetic nature of his vision. For he integrates Aristotelianism and Platonism, mysticism and scholasticism, affectivity and abstraction, the simplicity of Francis and the subtlety of the schools. Perhaps more than any other

thirteenth-century writer, Bonaventure represents the differentiation and integration of major strands of medieval culture. Given
this integral quality of his thought and the prominence of mandala symbolism therein, it is not surprising that his integrated
cosmic vision should take the pattern of the mandala.

The mandala symbol is the ultimate revelation of the coincidence of opposites in Bonaventure's thought. Both in the history
of religions and in psychology, the mandala is the most profound,
the most complex, and the most comprehensive expression of the
coincidentia oppositorum. By its very nature the mandala is constituted by the coincidence of opposites. The integration of polarities is not accidental to the mandala or of secondary importance;
it is of its very essence. Furthermore, mandalas are comprehensive
symbols, integrating an entire cosmos, the totality of psychic forces
and the entire sweep of the spiritual journey. Thus the mandala
symbols in Bonaventure reveal the depth, complexity, and comprehensiveness of the coincidence of opposites in his thought. The
constant recurrence of mandala symbols at key points in his
writings — in the introduction to the *Commentary on the Sentences* and the *Breviloquium,* in the *Itinerarium* and *The Tree
of Life,* and finally in the *Collationes in Hexaemeron* — indicates
that the coincidence of opposites is the foundational and overarching architectonic pattern in his thought.

Furthermore, the mandala provides a perspective for clarifying
elements within Bonaventure's synthesis. Basic to his vision is
the role of Christ as *medium* or center. In the three examples
studied, Christ is the center of the cosmos, the center of the self,
and the goal and path of the spiritual journey. From a hermeneutical point of view, it is difficult to give a philosophical and theological account of his notion of Christ as center. He is clearly
assigning to Christ a pre-eminent significance in creation, redemption, and spiritual growth; but the precise nature of this significance has to be spelled out. The theologian needs a set of
hermeneutical categories that will clarify this significance and
account for the power of Christ in the synthesis. The mandala

provides such a set of categories. When we scan the history of man's religious experience and observe — with Jung, Eliade, and Tucci — the significance of the 'center' as an organizing point for the psyche and the cosmos and if we see the power of the 'center' to integrate opposites and lead to union with the divine, we can glimpse some of the power of Christ in forming the center of Bonaventure's Christian mandala.

In the light of this, we can appreciate Bonaventure's opposition to Aristotle. We will touch this only briefly here, but will return to it in the next chapter.[69] Each generation of scholars attempts to re-interpret the great controversy of the thirteenth century and specifically Bonaventure's role as spokesman of the opposition to the new Aristotelianism at the University of Paris. Research into the mandala can throw new light on this controversy. In view of this research, Bonaventure's objection could be epitomized in the following way: Because the Aristotelians do not know Christ its center, they have shattered the Christian mandala. Without Christ as center, the divinity is separated from the universe, the world is eternal and history has no direction. For without Christ as eternal Word, there is no exemplarism and the world ceases to be expression of the divinity.[70] The world is thus uprooted from its ground in the divine life and stands apart, separated from the divinity by an infinite abyss. Without the incarnate Christ history has no center, and time is merely the endless repetition of events without meaningful direction. Hence there is no circle of emanation and return.

Another important point is that Bonaventure integrates history into his mandala. This may show a major difference between Christian mandalas and those of the Orient. The circle of Bonaventure's mandala is not merely the "intelligible sphere" of Alanus de Insulis that symbolizes the fact that God is eternal and without limits.[71] Bonaventure's is a dynamic circle because his doctrine of God is dynamic. His mandala circle symbolizes the dynamic life of the Trinitarian processions. This Trinitarian dynamism stands behind the circle of emanation and return in the universe. It is here that Bonaventure finds his metaphysical grounding for his notion of history. For him, history has a positive value, since it is involved in the emanation and return of creatures from the fecundity of the Trinity. Bonaventure's notion of center makes possible the emanation and return, and this notion likewise gives history meaning.

In a study of Bonaventure's theology of history, Joseph Ratzinger indicates how his notion of Christ as center emerges to shape his notion of history. Jesus Christ, the middle person of the Trinity and the mediator between God and man, gradually becomes the synthesis of all that is expressed in the notion of the center. "And as a consequence of this general interpretation of Christ from the notion of center, he becomes also the 'center of time.' "[72] Ratzinger shows how Bonaventure's notion of time differs radically from the Aristotelian notion. "For Aristotle and Thomas, time was the neutral measure of duration, 'an accident of movement.' "[73] But for Bonaventure it was much more. He considered time a positive reality involved in the emanation and return of things from the creative power of God. "It is integrated right from the start into the great Bonaventurian vision of the world, for whenever we speak of *egressio,* we affirm a *regressio* together with it."[74] In such a context the thought of an infinite duration of time is nonsensical.

THE MANDALA: FRANCIS AND BONAVENTURE

In addition to clarifying philosophical-theological issues, the mandala can throw light on the lives of Francis and Bonaventure. Does the vision of the Seraph function as a mandala in the life of Francis? There is much reason to think that it does. It comes at the climax of his life, as an extraordinary spiritual gift, as the sum and expression of his entire spiritual past. Yet it lifts him to a new level of incorporation into Christ, for he bears in his body the sign of Christ crucified. It would be of special interest to explore the stigmata as an incorporated mandala, that is, a mandala realized within the body. One of the forms of the mandala studied by Tucci is that of the mandala in the human body.[75] From this perspective, the mandala revealed by the vision of the Seraph was so incorporated into Francis' person that his body expressed the identity through the wounds of Christ crucified. It may be that the highest stage of incarnating the Christian mandala within the body is precisely in the stigmata which Francis received.

Does the Seraph also function as a mandala in the life of Bonaventure? At times of crisis or transition in one's life, the archetype of the self — and its symbol the mandala — may emerge to bring about an integration of psychic forces and to give a new direction to one's life. Such seems to have been the case for Bonaventure. Whereas the Seraph functioned as a goal-mandala for Francis, it seems to have brought Bonaventure to a new level of integration at a stage along the journey. The period of the composition of the *Itinerarium* was a troubled time both for Bonaventure and the Franciscan Order. The year was 1259, just two and a half years after he had been chosen Minister General of the Friars. The young General had inherited a host of problems. The Order was torn by dissension with the Spirituals, who were armed with the ideology of Joachim of Fiora. In this controversy, Bonaventure would have to preside over the trial of John of Parma, his predecessor as General and his personal friend. Throughout these years Bonaventure had to deal with the tension between the Franciscan ideal of poverty and the demands of practical life, between the simplicity of the early friars and the learning of the universities, between the spontaneity of Francis' spirit and the need for institutional structures in an expanding order. It was in this context that Bonaventure withdrew to Mount La Verna to seek peace. He describes his mood as follows:

> It happened that, thirty-three years after the death of the Saint [Francis], about the time of his passing, moved by a divine impulse, I withdrew to Mount La Verna as to a place of quiet, there to satisfy the yearning of my soul for peace.[76]

Bonaventure sought this peace, he tells us, "with yearning soul."[77] He had come to his spiritual source: to the holy mountain where Francis had received his greatest spiritual gift. In this setting, while meditating on the vision of the stigmata, Bonaventure saw in a sudden insight its symbolic meaning: "the uplifting of Saint Francis in contemplation" and "the way by which that state of contemplation can be reached."[78] The six wings symbolize the six stages of the journey and the form of the crucified suggests that the road "is through nothing else than a most ardent love of the crucified."[79] This love so absorbed Francis that "his spirit shone through his flesh the last two years of his life when he bore the most holy marks of the Passion in his body."[80]

The setting, Bonaventure's description of his psychological mood, his meditation on the image, the insight, its immediate yielding of meaning, and its elaborate unfolding in the text of the *Itinerarium* all indicate that the image of the Seraph functioned as a mandala in Bonaventure's personal life. The *Itinerarium* shows a new integration of Franciscan elements and his own cosmic vision.[81]

From the standpoint of the mandala, this would not mean something radically new in Bonaventure's life. Rather it would indicate a new level of integration of elements that had operated from his early years. From this point onward the scholasticism of the University of Paris is more integrated with his Christocentric and Francis-centered vision. This trend can be traced in a growing fashion into the *Collationes in Hexaemeron*. Thus we can observe that not only does Christ become ever more sharply focused as the center of Bonaventure's cosmic mandala, but that Francis becomes more clearly centered with Christ. For Bonaventure, the Franciscan General and architect of the developing Order, this meant that both he and the friars would enter the Christian mandala through the personality of Francis.

CONCLUSIONS

By applying to Bonaventure the twentieth century research into the mandala, we can clearly discern the two levels of his symbolism: (1) the universal level on which all creatures are sym-

bols of the divinity in so far as they reflect the Trinity; (2) the
more particularized level on which certain material symbols, such
as the tree and the tabernacle, divinize the human spirit through
their materiality. Although particularized in being a specific
symbol, in the mandala they take on a universal function since
they integrate through themselves as through a center the totality
of reality; in a cosmic structure or a spiritual journey. In this
they reflect the mystery of Christ the center, who as the greatest
coincidence of opposites unites all the polar aspects of reality.
Having established these two classes of symbolism, I do not wish
to give the impression that they are so diverse in Bonaventure
that they are not integrated. On the contrary, Christ the center
draws them together. As divine Word and archetype of creation,
he is the center of all Trinitarian symbolism; and as incarnate
Word, he is the center of all material symbolism. Thus in the total
mystery of Christ as eternal Word and incarnate Word, we have
the integration of these two forms of symbolism in Bonaventure's
thought — in the all-embracing mandala of which Christ is the
center.

Seen against the background of the twentieth century research
into the mandala, then, Bonaventure's thought reveals its enormous depth and richness. On the one hand, Eliade, Jung, and
Tucci aid in our understanding of Bonaventure; but on the other,
Bonaventure provides a concrete case of religious symbolism which
brings to a high point of expression the very principles they
propound. Bonaventure was a religious genius, whose creative
powers were in close touch with the archetypal religious symbols which are the heritage of men throughout the world. In this
context, we can see the universal value of Bonaventure's thought
and his relevance to our present age. For he not only draws richly
upon universal religious symbols, but he provides an example of
that fully developed and integral consciousness which is the goal
of mankind. It is not by chance that mandala symbols abound
in his writings, for he embodies in his own person a high degree
of differentiated opposites which are at the same time integrated

into a multi-dimensional totality. And he points the way to others, at their own position in space and time in the cosmic process, to join with him in the return to the Father. For it is by the integration of all the opposites: of matter and spirit, of the eternal and the temporal, of the divine and the human, of death and life, of the resolution of the struggle of good and evil, that one reaches the height of the mountain and enters into the fullness of union.

CHAPTER VII

TYPES AND IMPLICATIONS OF THE COINCIDENCE OF OPPOSITES

N THE notion of Christ the center the coincidence of opposites in Bonaventure's thought reaches its climax. From the perspective of Christ the center, then, we can draw together the various types of the coincidence of opposites which we have studied in different texts and from different points of view; we can see their variety and at the same time discern how they participate in a complex unity. With this clarification, we can relate Bonaventure's vision to the three classes of unity and difference which we presented in the first chapter. From the vantage point of this overarching hermeneutical framework, we can explore the implications of Bonaventure's coincidence of opposites for situating him within the history of thought. If, as I have claimed, the coincidence of opposites is the key for understanding Bonaventure's thought, then it would also be the key for relating him to his predecessors and contemporaries, for clarifying his position in the controversies of the thirteenth century and for relating him to the subsequent history of thought.

In drawing together the various types of the coincidence of opposites, we will review the evidence for my basic claim in this book: namely, that the coincidence of opposites is the indigenous logic of Bonaventure's system in its entirety and in all of its major parts. I hope that by this time this claim is substantiated both by an analysis of key texts and by the systematic study of Bonaventure's thought. In the course of our analysis, we studied Bonaventure's thought both structurally and genetically. From the beginning of his writing career, the coincidence of opposites was implicit in the structure of his thought, especially in its Trinitarian and exemplaristic pole. In his Christological pole the

basic elements of the coincidence of opposites were present at
the outset, but only gradually emerged into prominence and
self-consciousness in the course of his writings. The pivotal work
is the *Itinerarium,* in which Christocentricity comes to the fore
along with a consciousness of the coincidence of opposites in the
spheres of the divine nature, its relation to creation, the Trinity,
Christology, and the spiritual ascent. However, the full realization of Christocentricity, in the notion of Christ the *medium* in
which all opposites coincide, does not emerge until the final
period in the *Collationes in Hexaemeron.* Yet even here the coincidence of opposites does not reach the full abstract self-consciousness as a specific logic in the way it did in Nicholas of
Cusa. It is this self-consciousness of the coincidence of opposites
that I have tried to draw out of Bonaventure's system.

FIVE CLASSES OF THE COINCIDENCE OF OPPOSITES

In the process of bringing Bonaventure's coincidence of opposites to self-reflective consciousness, we discovered that there is
not one uniform type of the coincidence of opposites that permeates his thought. Quite the contrary! Each area of his thought
contains a specific type of the coincidence of opposites based on
the specific metaphysical status of that area. For example, within
the Godhead, there is a coincidence of the non-manifesting and
the manifesting aspects of the divinity. Within the manifesting
aspect of the divinity, there is the coincidence of the dynamic opposites of the Trinity: in the Father's self-expression in the Son
and the return through the Son in the unity of the Spirit. The
dynamic emanation within the Trinity provides the basis for the
coincidence of unity and plurality, for the persons of the Trinity
coexist in the unity of the divine nature.

These opposites within the Godhead are eternal and necessary,
since they are part of the very being of God. This means that
within the divinity, there is the coincidence of silence and speech,
of darkness and light, of simplicity and fecundity, of the ground
and of emanation, of self-sufficiency and self-communication,

of unity and plurality. This differentiation and polarity within the divinity is not based on creatures: on either a necessary emanation of creatures from the divine nature or on God's free-will decision to create. Even if there were no creatures, this polarity would exist, for it is bound up with the divine mystery itself. It follows, then, that it is of paramount importance to be conscious of the coincidence of opposites within the divinity, for the Christian mystery of the Trinity implies that there is a coincidence of opposites in God, independently of creatures. Because of what has been revealed to the Christian community, God cannot be seen merely as the timeless Absolute, the undivided One, or Pure Act. Of course, God is all of these — but also more! For he is the self-diffusive Good, the dynamic Trinity: the one divine nature in three divine persons.

The next class of the coincidence of opposites involves God and creation. Here we find the coincidence of the creator and the creature, the infinite and the finite, the eternal and the temporal, the beginning and the end. This necessarily involves another generic class because the elements here constitute a different metaphysical configuration from those of the first class, mentioned immediately above. In the first class, we dealt exclusively with the divinity and found there, independently of creation, several specific types of the coincidence of opposites. In this second class, we add to the divinity the realm of creation, which stands on a different metaphysical level; and in so doing, we constitute a different generic class of the coincidence of opposites.

In Bonaventure the same *medium* that links the divinity and creation also links the two classes of the coincidence of opposites: namely, Christ as *medium metaphysicum* and the *persona media* of the Trinity. For Bonaventure, Christ is the *medium metaphysicum* in his eternal generation. When the Father generates the Son, he produces in the Son the *rationes aeternae* of all that he can make; thus all creatures have an eternal existence in the Son as the Art of the Father. The two metaphysical spheres — the divinity and creation, the infinite and the finite, the eternal and the temporal — are united in and through Christ the *medium metaphysicum* in his eternal generation as the Son and Word of the Father. Not only does Christ link the two metaphysical spheres, but he also links the specific types of the coincidence of opposites within each class. In the divinity Christ is the *persona media* of the Trinity because as Word he is the center of the dynamic opposites of the Trinity. Yet precisely because he is the *persona media* in the divine sphere, he is the *medium metaphysicum* linking the divine sphere with the sphere of creation. Through Christ as *medium metaphysicum* this second class is constituted as the class of exemplarism, in which creatures reflect their divine Exemplar in various types of the coincidence of opposites graded in a hierarchical pattern: as shadow, vestige, image, and similitude. Based on exemplarism, Bonaventure's epistemology of illumination involves a coincidence of opposites in all certain knowledge through the "contuition" of the changeable, concrete finite particular and the unchangeable *rationes aeternae*.

The third class of the coincidence of opposites is constituted by Christ as *medium physicum* in his incarnation. As in the second class, we have here the coincidence of the creator and the creature, the infinite and the finite, the eternal and the temporal, the beginning and the end. But what constitutes the difference is the Incarnation. Whereas in exemplarism all creation is united to the divinity through the Word, in the Incarnation the Word is hypostatically united to human nature in such a way as to constitute a single person. This establishes a much more intimate and complex union of the divinity and creation than was realized in universal exemplarism. It also introduces a new cluster of the coincidence of opposites which can be called the specifically Christological or Incarnational opposites to distinguish them from the coincidence of opposites in exemplarism.

In Chapter Five we saw that the Christological opposites are based on the hypostatic union and involve three types of the coincidence of opposites which I have termed cosmological since they deal with dimensions and aspects of the cosmos. This first is the *maximum-minimum* because in Christ the highest is joined to the lowest, the divinity with creation, even with matter. The second is the microcosm-macrocosm; for the Incarnation takes place in man who is the microcosm reflecting the macrocosm of all creation, since he combines within his nature both matter and spirit, thus reflecting all the grades of material creation and the angels as well. The combination of the *maximum-minimum* and microcosm-macrocosm constitutes the third type of cosmological coincidence of opposites: namely, Alpha-Omega. The union of the *maximum* (divine nature) in the microcosm (human nature) establishes in Christ the greatest intensity of perfection in the universe, recapitulating in himself all creation and at the same time bringing it into a new and more intimate union with the divinity. Thus Christ is the pinnacle of creation, the Alpha and Omega of the entire cosmos, the firstborn of all creatures and the goal towards which all are striving. Together these three types of the coincidence of opposites form the complex notion of Christ the center, which is the culmination of all Bonaventure's forms of the coincidence of opposites. As *maximum-minimum*, microcosm-macrocosm and Alpha-Omega, Christ stands at the center of the universe, uniting the opposites of matter and divinity through human nature the microcosm. Thus Christ is established as the center to which all the universe is related and through which it will realize its goal. In this way Christ becomes the center of the Christian mandala, which is at the same time a cosmogram, a psychogram, and an itinerary of the return of all things to the Father.

The fourth class of the coincidence of opposites is based on the metaphysical difference between good and evil and is concerned with sin and redemption. In my study of Bonaventure's Christology, I have called these soteriological opposites and have explored them from the standpoint of Bonaventure's notion of Christ the *medium mathematicum* and *medium logicum*. Sin introduces into the world an entirely new sphere of the coincidence of opposites: with its own power, structure, and logic. Instead of being related in a harmonious balance of complementarity, like the cosmological opposites, good and evil are contraries, constantly at war one with the other. Evil is the negation of good; it distorts good, deludes, seduces, and deceives. It promises life and brings death; it offers fulfillment and ends in destruction. In fact, it inverts and upturns all the creative power and inner logic of the good. Evil turns the creativity of the good into destruction, the truth of the good into deception. When man sinned, he upset the order of the good with its creative power and harmony and turned these to their opposite: creativity to destruction, truth to deception, reward to punishment, the positive logic of the good to the negative logic of evil.

Into this sinful world, with its distortion of the good, the God-man came to redeem man from the destructive opposites of evil. Within Bonaventure's Christology, the cosmological opposites in the God-man effect the soteriological opposites. The positive opposites of the God-man confront the negative opposites of evil and transform them into their opposites; namely the good. As *medium mathematicum* Christ enters into the depths of the universe and as *medium logicum* he transforms the logic of evil into its opposite; out of death he brings life, deceiving the deceiver to re-establish truth. Bonaventure incorporates Anselm's satisfaction theory into his soteriology and throws new light on its meaning through his logic of the coincidence of opposites. Anselm's entire theory of the redemption can be seen as an application of the logic of opposites: sin involves an infinite offense effected by finite man. This infinite offense establishes a debt which man cannot remove; it is necessary for a new coincidence of opposites to enter the universe — the God-man who by accepting the punishment for sin can unite the shattered poles and restore harmony in the universe. This is done, according to Bonaventure, by Christ's accepting the logic of evil. Christ enters into a dispute with Satan, taking upon himself the destructive logic of evil. Because he is the God-man, containing within himself all the opposites of the incarnational class — *maximum-minimum*, microcosm-macrocosm, Alpha-Omega, and universal center — he is able to win a victory over Satan and his destructive logic. By following the logic of evil through suffering and death, he is able to transform death into life through his resurrection. Thus he is the *medium logicum* in his resurrection, transforming the entire sphere of evil, along with its logic of destruction, into its opposite.

The fifth class of the coincidence of opposites concerns the return of all things to the Father and deals with Bonaventure's mystical theology and his theology of history. Bonaventure treats this return through the notion of Christ the *medium ethicum, politicum,* and *theologicum,* and through Christ the spouse of the soul and the greatest coincidence of opposites who leads to the passage of the soul into mystical ecstasy. The return of the soul is based on the fact that the soul is the image of God: a coincidence of the finite and the infinite. Through sin the soul is turned away from its Archetype, but is restored by the incarnate Word and his work of redemption. As *medium mathematicum* Christ restores the lost center of the soul through two perpendicular lines intersecting in the form of a cross. Once the soteriological opposites of evil have been transformed by the cosmological opposites of the Word incarnate, the soul with Christ as its center can grow as image of God in the moral and theological virtues and through infused contemplation to mystical ecstasy. Even in ecstasy and in the beatific vision, the soul is not absorbed into an undifferentiated unity with the divinity. The coincidence of opposites remains to the end of time and through eternity; for the more intimate the union of the soul with God, the more its uniqueness is intensified.

Not only does the soul return to its Archetype, but all of creation and history are on a journey back to their divine source. As *medium metaphysicum,* the eternal Word is both the Alpha and the Omega of the *exitus* and *reditus* of creatures. All things emanate through him in the act of creation, and all things refer back to him through exemplarism. In him all creatures find the coincidence of their beginning and their end. As we indicated, the incarnate Christ is also the Alpha and the Omega of creation, because he is the universal center of the cosmos through the complex interrelation of the *maximum-minimum* and the microcosm-macrocosm. In a special way Christ is the center of history and its final consummation. Through the notion of Christ the center of history Bonaventure combines the two poles of his theology — the Trinitarian and the Christocentric — thus avoiding the heresy of the Joachites, whereby the age of the Spirit supersedes that of the Son to the point of challenging the centrality of Christ in salvation history. Since Christ is the *persona media* of the Trinity, he remains the center of the historical process. Just as the totality of creation as vestige reflects the total Trinity, with the Word as *persona media,* so does salvation history reflect the integral Trinity, with the Word incarnate at its center. Thus the opposites of the eternal Trinity and the temporal process are linked in the single *persona media,* with the culmination of the historical process partaking of the coincidence of opposites that is at the heart of the Trinitarian life.

CHRIST THE 'MEDIUM' LINKS THE FIVE CLASSES

These five classes of the coincidence of opposites, which are differentiated by the different metaphysical elements in each class, have a single unifying factor in the notion of Christ the *medium,* or center. As we have pointed out, the notion of Christ the *medium* functions differently in each class according to the metaphysical differences involved. For example, in the Trinity he is the *persona media,* at the center of the dynamic Trinitarian life. As incarnate Word he is the *medium physicum,* summing up in himself the opposite poles of reality. Thus the notion of Christ the center unifies the classes of opposites while maintaining their differences. Throughout this book I have claimed that although the coincidence of opposites is the universal logic of Bonaventure's system, each major area of his thought has its own specific form of the coincidence of opposites based on the metaphysical structure of that area. The notion of Christ the center, then, accounts for the common logic at the same time that it sustains the specific difference of each class.

The notion of Christ the *medium* not only provides a unifying thread running through the five classes of opposites; it also designates the specific form of the coincidence of opposites that operates in all of the classes. In the first chapter I sketched three architectonic models of the coincidence of opposites, indicating that only one of these merits the full meaning of the coincidence of opposites: namely, the model of unity and difference, in which opposites coincide through mutually affirming complementarity.[1] In this model the opposites are differentiated and united in such a way that their very coincidence intensifies their differences. Bonaventure's notion of Christ the *medium* implies that Christ is the center in which opposites converge and are maintained. For example, in the Trinity he is the *persona media,* eternally the center of the Father and the Spirit. In the Incarnation, the divine and the human natures are united in the person of the Word in such a way that the identity of each is maintained. The divinity does not swallow up the humanity, nor does the humanity contract the divinity to the point of losing itself in finitude. Yet both are genuinely united, not merely juxtaposed. In each of the above cases there is a coincidence of mutually affirming complementarity. In neither case does Bonaventure's coincidence of opposites slide into an all-consuming unity nor polarize itself into a radical separation. Thus through his notion of Christ the *medium* each class of Bonaventure's system is clearly situated within the architectonic model of complementarity and avoids being drawn into the other two architectonic models: either the model of non-differentiated unity in which opposites coincide to the point of losing their opposition, or the model of polarized differentiation in which no genuine coincidence occurs. Thus in each of the five classes unity and difference are maintained in mutually affirming complementarity through the notion of Christ the *medium,* applied consistently to each class according to the metaphysical differences of that class.

It is necessary to make certain precisions in the case of the fourth class, which is based on the metaphysical differences between good and evil. Good and evil are not related according to the coincidence of complementarity. They are contraries and uniquely related, embodying aspects of all three architectonic models. From one point of view good and evil are related as radical opposites since they struggle against each other. On the other hand, evil disguises itself as good and attempts to slip into the architectonic model of undifferentiated unity. From another perspective, good and evil are related by way of unity and difference, since evil is the negation of the good, its negative image retaining some of the power and attractiveness of the good. However, what evil lacks is the positive aspect required to enter into a creative coincidence of complementarity with the good. This raises the interesting suggestion that what makes evil evil is precisely the fact that it is a false coincidence of opposites. Hence the redemption from evil is brought about by the God-man, who is the greatest realization of the true coincidence of opposites. By entering into the false logic of evil, Christ can plunge to the roots of its distortion of the coincidence of opposites and overcome the distortion precisely by transforming it into its opposite. Even in this fourth class, then, the notion of Christ as model of the coincidence of complementarity still holds; for it is precisely because he is the *persona media* of the Trinity and the God-man that he can effectively enter into the false logic of evil and transform it into good.

BONAVENTURE AND THE HISTORY OF THOUGHT

Having clarified the five classes of the coincidence of opposites in Bonaventure and having related them by way of the notion of Christ the *medium* to the architectonic model of complementarity, we can now use this interpretation to relate Bonaventure to the history of thought. In the first chapter I made the claim that Bonaventure does not stand alone but belongs to a major current of Western thought which can be called the Christian Neo-

Platonic tradition. This current flowed through the Greek Fathers, the Pseudo-Dionysius, Anselm, the Victorines, Alexander of Hales, and Bonaventure. Although eclipsed by the rediscovery of Aristotle, it continued in Nicholas of Cusa and the Platonists of the Renaissance. It emerged again in German romanticism and has manifested itself in a number of currents in the twentieth century. Although this is not a uniform tradition and is often unaware of its historical continuity, I believe that there are sufficient grounds for considering it in a generic way a unified current. I further claimed that, just as in Bonaventure's case, this entire current belongs to the architectonic model of unity and difference of complementarity and that its indigenous logic is that of the coincidence of opposites. In the light of this interpretation and in the light of the coincidence of opposites we have just studied, I will attempt to relate Bonaventure to the history of thought, chiefly to thinkers within this current. To do this adequately would be a monumental task since I would have to establish these points in the case of many thinkers with the same painstaking analysis of texts I have attempted with Bonaventure. Then I would have to do a detailed comparison of each thinker with Bonaventure in all major areas. Realizing, then, the limitation of what will follow, I will simply attempt to give some indications of the implications of our study of the coincidence of opposites for the history of thought. Perhaps at a later date I will have the opportunity to deal with some of the specific thinkers more adequately through a critical textual analysis which hopefully would substantiate my general theory.

In relating Bonaventure to the history of thought, the first strategic move is to read his system on its own terms, with its own internal optic and logic. This we have attempted to do through the coincidence of opposites. The next strategic move is to retain this perspective in relating him to the history of thought, both to his own tradition and to other traditions. It is this that we will attempt to do in the remainder of the book. I believe that considerable clarification can result from this procedure, since for many reasons the distinctive elements in Bonaventure's tradition have been obscured both in the Middle Ages and in the twentieth century. I realize that if we relate Bonaventure to the history of thought from his own perspective, we have not said the last word and closed the case. The history of thought is multidimensional and must be interpreted from many different perspectives. We cannot merely assume that Bonaventure's system is valid or that it is the most adequate that has been achieved or that can be achieved by the human mind. In brief, we cannot assume that Bonaventure, or his tradition for that matter, has said the last word. Bonaventure must be seen and judged also from the perspective of other thinkers and other traditions. And he must be drawn as an active participant into that great dialogue which through the centuries has engaged thinkers to test and establish the validity of their positions. We cannot here enter completely into that total enterprise. Ours must necessarily be a more modest task, but one which is a necessary stage in the total process. For if we effectively clarify Bonaventure's relation to other thinkers from his own perspective, we can more fruitfully enter into the larger dialogue among different traditions.

BONAVENTURE AND THOMAS

The first step in situating Bonaventure in the history of thought is to relate him to Thomas Aquinas. This is necessary since Thomas' thought has been made the focal point for interpreting medieval philosophy and theology. In the era of the neo-scholastic revival, Thomas' thought not only was adopted by many as their own philosophical system, but became the context in which most of the history of medieval thought was explored. Many philosophers and historians saw earlier medieval thought — in Augustine, Anselm, and Bonaventure — as stages leading up to the Aristotelian synthesis of Thomas, who inherited, corrected, and transformed this tradition through his own metaphysical genius and his use of Aristotle. This position implies that Thomas'

thought should serve as a norm for judging other medieval thinkers. I do not wish to deal directly with this normative question
here, since my task is one rather of description and interpretation on the level of internal structure. I wish simply to indicate
that this position has caused the distinctive dimensions of Bonaventure and his tradition to be obscured. For some it meant that
the earlier tradition was in continuity with Thomas, but not cor-
rectly and adequately developed; for others it meant that the
earlier tradition was distinctly different, but since Thomas' position was superior, there was no compelling reason to enter within
the inner structure of the other. Since I believe that Thomas'
synthesis is considerably different from Bonaventure's and, in
fact, represents another tradition, I believe that both of the above
readings of the Middle Ages tended to obscure the indigenous
structure and logic of Bonaventure's synthesis.[2] The result was
that only those aspects of Bonaventure's thought were seriously
studied that converged on the main concerns of Thomas. The
chief thrust of my present study can be seen as an attempt to
bring to light the obscured dimensions of Bonaventure's thought.

In the light of our study of the coincidence of opposites, we
can now compare Bonaventure and Thomas. To do this adequately would require a book. I can deal with the relation only
schematically here, without giving the detailed sources from
Thomas or the reasons that might substantiate my interpretation
of his thought. Realizing that my statements will seem like sweeping generalization, I hope that they will at least raise issues for
more detailed investigation and discussion. Seen against our
analysis of the coincidence of opposites in Bonaventure, the
thought of Thomas reveals itself as containing a different structure and logic. In Bonaventure the overarching model is the coincidence of opposites of complementarity, which has two major
specifications: the dynamic Trinitarian model and the cosmological model of Christ the center. Both of these involve a threefold
structure with two opposites coinciding in a midpoint or *medium*.
These models do not exist in the same way in Thomas' system,

which is built in a binary structure with such twofold patterns as follows: act/potency; existence/essence; necessary/contingent; form/matter; substance/accident. Further there is a concerted analysis of reality from the standpoint of the four causes: efficient, final, formal, and material. All of these notions are drawn by abstraction from the world of physical nature, which is conceived as the realm where reason can operate effectively and from which it can draw concepts and principles for reasoning to the existence and attributes of God. When divine revelation is given to man, he can further extend these categories analogously to study the mysteries of Christ, redemption, and the Trinity.[3]

Thomas' thought falls into the architectonic model of difference and not into the model of unity and difference of complementarity. Since the various polarities in his system are related as act and potency, there is a subordination of one to the other, with potency being subordinated to act. This is not the *medium* model of Bonaventure, in which the *medium* sustains the opposites. In Thomas the result of this subordinated bi-polarity is that it establishes a difference model between God and creation. In Thomas God and creation are viewed primarily from the standpoint of their difference, whereas in Bonaventure they are seen primarily from the standpoint of their coincidence. In Thomas God is seen as Pure Act and creation as contingent, dependent on God's power for its participation in the act of existence. Bonaventure, of course, also sees creation dependent on God and hence employs the act/potency model as well. But in his case, it is subordinated to the coincidence of opposites model of complementarity. While Thomas emphasizes the participated dependence of creatures on God, Bonaventure emphasizes their coincidence with God as mediated by the eternal Word in exemplarism.

In Thomas there is a further and more intimate involvement of God in the world through revelation, the Incarnation, and salvation history. This, however, is not interpreted according to the coincidence of opposites, but through God's freewill choice to communicate himself to men.[4] As in the case of the contingency of creation, Bonaventure also maintains the freedom of God's grace, but this aspect of his thought is always integrated into the *medium* model of the coincidence of opposites. On the supernatural level, Thomas moves into the architectonic model of complementarity through the revelation of the mysteries of Christ and the Trinity. However, when he explores these mysteries theologically, he applies the categories drawn from nature — namely, the binary notions and the four causes — and does not draw his categories from the mysteries themselves as Bonaventure does.[5]

This indicates that Thomas and Bonaventure have radically different ways of conceiving the relation between philosophy and theology. Bonaventure draws his primary models from the Trinity and from Christ and applies them comprehensively to creation. Thomas draws his primary models from the realm of nature — seen through binary categories — and applies these, with the appropriate alterations, to the mysteries of revelation.[6] Does this mean that Bonaventure has overstepped the bounds of reason? Not at all — at least, not within his system. For within the comprehensive extension of the architectonic model of complementarity, the Trinitarian and Christological models apply not only to the sphere of the mysteries themselves, but permeate the cosmos and its dynamics. I believe that the difference in the systems is not rooted in where Bonaventure and Thomas derive their Trinitarian models. Both derive them from revelation. The basic question is whether the Trinitarian models apply also to nature and can be discerned at least partially in nature, perhaps only after revelation. If so, then they establish a comprehensive Trinitarian logic to which binary logic is subordinated. That, I think, is Bonaventure's position. In contrast, Thomas conceives nature according to the binary model and reserves the Trinitarian model to revelation.[7] From this statement of the question, the debate could proceed to whether it is more accurate to use Trinitarian or binary models in reading nature — or some combination of these or other models. If one holds that philosophy deals with nature and that nature has a binary structure, then one would come to Thomas's position on the relation of philosophy and theology. If, however, nature also has a Trinitarian structure, as well as a binary structure, then one could hold Bonaventure's position.

BONAVENTURE AND HIS PREDECESSORS

In the light of this understanding of the relation of philosophy and theology, it is possible to clarify the theological method found in Bonaventure's tradition, especially in Augustine, Anselm, and the Victorines. This tradition regularly uses models drawn from the Trinity to interpret the physical world as vestige and man as image. Furthermore, the Pseudo-Dionysius sees the self-diffusion of the good applying both to the Trinity and to creation. Bonaventure employs his notion of Christ the center to understand the dynamic orientation of space and time. This theological method has been described in general terms as faith seeking understanding *(fides quaerens intellectum)* and more specifically in Anselm, Richard of St. Victor, and Bonaventure as seeking for necessary reasons *(rationes necessariae)* for the mysteries of faith.[8] Although both Thomas himself and contemporary Thomists have severely criticized this method of seeking *rationes necessariae,* I believe that it can be seen as a logically consistent method within the architectonic model of the tradition.[9] This tradition believes that the mysteries of faith have their own *ratio* and logic which can be ascertained by reason's reflection on the mysteries revealed without using analogies drawn from the sense world. These mysteries can, in a partial way at least, yield their inner logic, which then is discerned as not merely limited to the mysteries but as forming an important dimension of the cosmos and of human experience and history. In this approach there is a Platonic element of descent from the archetype which is quite the reverse of the traditional Aristotelian ascent through analogy. In the Platonic perspective, for example, the Trinity is an archetype, whose traces are found throughout the universe and whose image is found in man. The fullness of the archetype is not known except through the Incarnation and the revelation of Jesus as the Son of the Father. But when that mystery is known, then the entire universe can be seen in its light. When one grasps the inner logic of the divine archetype — the *ratio necessaria* — then one can see more clearly relative realizations of this throughout creation. I believe that the logic of the archetype manifested in revelation and explored by this tradition is precisely the logic of the coincidence of opposites which we have studied in Bonaventure.

In the light of this analysis, it is apparent why the Trinity plays such a foundational role in the systems developed by Bonaventure's tradition. As we saw in Bonaventure's theology, there are two major models of the coincidence of opposites in the doctrine of the Trinity: the dynamic opposites of emanation and the opposites of unity and plurality. For Bonaventure's tradition these models operate in an absolute way in the Trinity and in a relative way in creation. In Bonaventure's tradition the notion of the One God — or the divine nature or Pure Act — plays a subordinate role to the Trinity. Because the Trinity does not have so important a function in the total structuring of Thomas' system, the place of the Trinity in medieval thought has not been adequately appreciated or investigated in the twentieth century.[10] During the neo-scholastic revival, much more attention was given to the One-God and to man's knowledge of the One-God, in response to the Kantian critique.[11]

Even when Thomas' doctrine of the Trinity was studied, it was not usually related to Bonaventure's tradition. The reason for this is complex. In his Trinitarian theology Thomas is distinctly Augustinian — developing to a point of technical refinement the basic Trinitarian theology laid out by Augustine in Books V-VII of the *De Trinitate*.[12] Here Augustine began with the common divine nature and saw the persons as mutual relations. In a similar way, in the *Summa theologiae*, Thomas begins with the divine nature and then proceeds to discuss the persons as subsistent relations.[13] In this approach the unity of the divine nature is correlated with the plurality of persons, thus embodying the model of the coincidence of unity and plurality. For Bonaventure this model is subordinated to the emanation model, which is the foundation of his entire system. This emanation model came to him from the Greek Fathers through John Scotus Erigena's translations of the Pseudo-Dionysius, passing through the Victorines and Alexander of Hales. This tradition did not flow in the same way to Thomas, whose Trinitarian theology remained basically Augustinian. It is important to note that the emanation model of the Trinity is not thematized in a major way in Thomas's system. Against the background of the neo-scholastic period, this means that the significance of the Trinitarian emanation model in the Middle Ages has been obscured in the twentieth century. Although this is true of a general climate, nevertheless there has been important historical scholarship, beginning with the work of de Régnon, that can support a reassessment of the Trinitarian emanation model in the Middle Ages.[14] Such a reassessment would, I believe, lead to an interesting reclassification of Bonaventure and Thomas. In general, the neo-scholastic revival has designated Bonaventure as Augustinian to distinguish him from Thomas the Aristotelian, especially in epistemology, where Bonaventure is more classically in the Augustinian illumination tradition than Thomas. However, in the area of Trinitarian theology, Thomas is the Augustinian and Bonaventure the heir of the Greek Fathers.

Once we strip away the Thomistic framework for interpreting the Middle Ages, we can more clearly discern Bonaventure's relation to his predecessors. In the light of our analysis of the coincidence of opposites, we can see more clearly the continuity of the tradition and Bonaventure's specific relation to it as a thirteenth century synthesizer. In control of its deepest structure and sensitive to its logic, he brought its elements to a new synthesis and a heightened self-consciousness. I personally believe that his greatest contribution to this tradition was to integrate its rich Trinitarian models with the emerging Franciscan sense of Christocentricity. In Bonaventure, we find more emphasis on the concrete humanity of Jesus than we do in his great predecessors, such as Augustine and the Pseudo-Dionysius. A significant change begins to appear in Anselm, although it is strongly focused on soteriology. In Bonaventure this trend blossoms into a cosmic Christo-centricity, which incorporates the cosmological, soteriological and mystical dimensions of the mystery of Christ. Richly differentiated and developed, this Christological pole is integrated into the Trinitarian pole through Bonaventure's notion of Christ the *medium*, with its complex structures of the coincidence of opposites.

CONTROVERSY OVER ARISTOTLE

The coincidence of opposites can not only throw light on Bonaventure's relation to his predecessors and to Thomas, but can also clarify the stand that he took in the controversies of the thirteenth century. In addition to the dispute between the mendicants and the seculars, the two major controversies that involved Bonaventure were over Aristotle and Joachim of Fiore. Bonaventure's mature opinions on these controversies are stated in the *Collationes in Hexaemeron,* which also contain his most mature statement of the coincidence of opposites.[15]

Although Bonaventure incorporated much of Aristotle's thought into his own system, he severely criticized Aristotle on certain points. These issues were drawn into sharp focus by the development of a form of heterodox Aristotelianism in the faculty of arts at the University of Paris in the late 1260's and early 1270's. It is against this Aristotelianism that his polemic attacks are aimed in his three series of *collationes,* delivered in 1267, 1268, and 1273.[16] In the sixth lecture of the series, the *Collationes in Hexaemeron,* Bonaventure summarizes his objections to various positions of Aristotle, relating them all to a single principle: exemplarism.[17] Because Aristotle rejected the ideas of Plato, he fell into a series of errors. Bonaventure's strong feelings on this matter are expressed in the term he uses, saying that Aristotle "cursed" the ideas of Plato.[18] Hence Aristotle claims that God knows only himself, that he has no need of the knowledge of anything else and that he moves creatures in so far as he is desired and loved. It follows, then, that God knows no particular thing.

From this fundamental error two others follow: that God exercises no providence nor judgment over the world. First, from the rejection of exemplarism, there follows another error, "that is, that God has neither foreknowledge nor providence, since he does not have within himself the reasons *(rationes)* of things through which he could know them." Since there are no truths about the future except what is necessary, it follows that all things come about by chance or by necessity. Because they reject chance, the Arabs "conclude to the necessity of fate, that is, that these substances that move the world are the necessary causes of all things." If all things are determined, there is no basis for reward and punishment in the afterlife.[19]

Bonaventure's attack goes right to the heart of the central issue as he sees it. Aristotle has radically separated God and the world by eliminating the *medium* between the two. Aristotle's model of difference is incompatible with Bonaventure's model of complementarity. As Bonaventure asserted in his introductory *collatio*, Christ is the *medium metaphysicum,* in whose eternal generation from the Father are produced the archetypes or ideas of all that can be created.[20] These archetypes are the *medium* between God and the world. Without them the world is severed from God and paradoxically made the slave of rigid necessity. For Aristotle there can be only difference, no coincidence of opposites.

From Aristotle's basic cluster of errors there follows, Bonaventure claims, a threefold blindness or darkness; namely, that the world is eternal, that there is a single intellect, and that there is no personal immortality. Bonaventure presents the reasoning as follows:

> For if the world is supposed to be eternal, one of the following propositions necessarily follows: that souls are infinite in number since there would be an infinite number of men; or that the soul is corruptible; or that it is transmitted from body to body; or that there

is a single intellect in all [rational beings], an error attributed to Aristotle by his commentator.

From these two propositions it follows that after this life there is neither happiness nor punishment.[21]

Because Aristotle has fallen into error by rejecting exemplarism, he was blind to the issues involved in the eternity of the world and the consequent loss of radical personal identity. As Bonaventure sees it, the plurality involved in an eternal world contradicts genuine personal individuality. This atomistic plurality leads to an undifferentiated union of all in the single intellect which ultimately absorbs all men. In this view, there is no coincidence of opposites which grounds individuality in complementarity such as we see in Bonaventure's notion of the soul as image, similitude, and spouse of Christ.

Throughout his writings Bonaventure engaged in a polemic against Aristotle's doctrine of the eternity of the world, which he considered impossible, unlike Thomas, who thought it a philosophical possibility but not a fact since we know by revelation that the world was created in time.[22] I believe that the ultimate root of Bonaventure's rejection of Aristotle's eternal world lies in the architectonic model which controls his system. In the model of complementarity with its coincidence of opposites, Bonaventure has integrated the Hebrew notion of time with the Greek notion of the self-diffusion of the good. For Bonaventure God is related to time not as Pure Act, but as self-diffusive Trinity. From this perspective God is not the Unmoved Mover of an eternal temporal flux in which individuals in infinite number merely repeat themselves endlessly. Rather he is the dynamic Trinity whose inner life involves an *exitus* and *reditus* in which the Son is the *persona media*. If time flows out of this dynamism, then it too must share in the same model: it must move out from God as Alpha and return to God as Omega. If we add to this Trinitarian model of the temporal process the mystery of the Incarnation with its implications of Christ the center of history, then we see that the Trinitarian model of the process is intensified by the Christocentric model. A Trinitized, Christocentric process cannot be devoid of centering and stripped of personality and immortality like the aimless flux that Bonaventure saw in Aristotle's eternal world.

JOACHIM OF FIORE AND RADICAL ESCHATOLOGY

One can interpret Bonaventure as steering a middle course between the eternal world of Aristotle and the radical eschatology of Joachim of Fiore. By holding the doctrine of Christ the *medium* Bonaventure was able to affirm what was politically a moderate position within the Franciscan Order and theoretically a mid-position between the endless process of Aristotle and the radically negating process of Joachim. From Bonaventure's perspective, Aristotle's temporal process was not Trinitized and Joachim's was Trinitized according to a faulty model, which ultimately negated the Trinity and Christocentricity.

The problems associated with Joachim of Fiore were interwoven into the early history of the Franciscan Order and the events of Bonaventure's life.[23] The roots of the issues go back to the tensions between three groups within the Order: (1) the Spirituals, who espoused exclusively the simplicity of Francis' ideals; (2) the relaxed, who were willing to depart substantially from these ideals; and (3) the moderates, who wished to remain faithful to the ideals but admitted adaptation and evolution. Some of the Spirituals drew from the eschatology of the twelfth century Calabrian monk Joachim of Fiore to support their position. They claimed that a new age of the Spirit had been ushered in by Francis and that the institutionalization proposed by the moderates had been radically superseded by this new age. While Bonaventure was embroiled in the disputes at the University of Paris between the seculars and the mendicants, Joachite elements were introduced into the controversy by the *Liber introductorius in evangelium aeternum* of Friar Gerard of Borgo San Donnino.[24] Not long after this Joachite problems precipitated Bonaventure's election as General when John of Parma was forced to resign be-

cause of his Joachite leanings. Throughout Bonaventure's life
Joachite tensions continued within the Order, reaching a climax
in the fourteenth century with the suppression of the radical group
called the Fraticelli.[25]

Joachim proposed a theory that there are three ages of history
corresponding to the three persons of the Trinity.[26] The age of
the Father extends from Adam to Christ and is characterized by
the married state. This is followed by the age of the Son, which
is characterized by the clerical state and which will be superseded by the age of the Spirit, characterized by the monastic
state. This third period, which began with Benedict, was to reach
its flowering in a spiritual age that was to be ushered in, according
to Joachim's prediction, in the imminent future. What makes
his thought radical is that he saw in the age of the Spirit the triumph of the spiritual and the charismatic over the institutional
forms of the previous age.

Bonaventure's relation to the Joachite tradition is complex. On
the practical level, he emerged as a leader of the moderates against
the radical Spirituals, a position which he maintained through
his life. But one can trace in his thought a growing eschatological
consciousness and a tendency to interpret Francis in this context.
As Ratzinger has pointed out, Bonaventure has incorporated
some Joachite elements into his thought, or one could say that
he developed his own position in ways that approximate certain
Joachite positions.[27] However, there always remained a basic incompatibility between the architectonic models of Bonaventure's
thought and those of Joachim. Bonaventure's integral Trinitarian
model, in which Christ is the *persona media,* prevents him from
adopting the divisive Trinitarian model of Joachim, in which the
age of the Spirit radically negates the age of the Son. Furthermore,
the full development of his notion of Christ the *medium* in the
first *Collatio in Hexaemeron* intensifies his position against Joachim. In the context of his integral Trinitarianism and his Christocentricity, we can see that Bonaventure's view was politically
moderate because it was theoretically integral. For Bonaventure

the processes of history move forward towards an eschatological spiritualization, which has a radical dimension, true; but this goal is always achieved through an integral Trinitarian dynamism and a Christocentricity. It is precisely because Bonaventure holds the coincidence of opposites — in all five classes we studied above — that he can be true to the radical side of Francis and to the conservative side of the tradition, and so be properly characterized as a moderate.

BONAVENTURE AND NICHOLAS OF CUSA

Bonaventure's synthesis of his tradition not only represents a high point of development; it also represents the end of an era. The new Aristotelianism triumphed in the thirteenth century with the result that subsequent formulation of theological and philosophical problems was done within an Aristotelian context. Bonaventure's tradition was transmitted by the mystical currents of the later Middle Ages but emerged later at certain periods within the areas of philosophy and theology. One of the most significant representatives of this tradition in subsequent thought was Nicholas of Cusa.[28] Our study of the coincidence of opposites makes it possible to explore some of the similarities and differences between his thought and Bonaventure's.

In a special way our present study calls for a comparison between Bonaventure and Nicholas of Cusa, for the latter immediately comes to mind when one hears the term the *coincidentia oppositorum*. It was Nicholas, who in the history of Western thought consecrated the term and brought the coincidence of opposites to a level of self-reflective consciousness. It becomes for Nicholas a self-reflective logic based on a metaphysics, and it was used methodologically in his study of the Trinity, God and creation, and the doctrine of Christ. This means, of course, that Nicholas brought his understanding of the coincidence of opposites to a greater level of self-reflection than Bonaventure did. This leads us to two questions: how are Nicholas and Bonaventure related historically? And how similar are the two thinkers on the coincidence of opposites?

It is abundantly clear that both writers are in the same large current of Western thought which I previously called the Christian Neo-Platonic tradition. Both writers were significantly influenced by the Pseudo-Dionysius and hence by the theology of the Greek Fathers. Bonaventure's Trinitarian theology and his mystical writings are profoundly shaped by the Pseudo-Dionysius; the *docta ignorantia* of Nicholas can be interpreted as a way of incorporating the negative theology of the Pseudo-Dionysius into his system.[29] It is interesting to note that in addition to this Greek influence on their thought, both men played significant roles to effect the reunion of the Greek East and the Latin West: Bonaventure at the Council of Lyons and Nicholas at the Council of Florence.

Granted that their thought has affinity because it belongs to a common tradition, the further question arises: Did Bonaventure have a direct influence on Nicholas, and specifically did he have a direct influence in shaping Nicholas's understanding of the coincidence of opposites? Certainly Nicholas read Bonaventure, especially the *Itinerarium,* the *Breviloquium,* and the *Collationes in Hexaemeron.* There is reason to think that Nicholas first came upon the term *docta ignorantia* in the *Breviloquium* of Bonaventure: there is also reason to think that Nicholas was influenced by the passages in Bonaventure's *Itinerarium* and *Collationes in Hexaemeron* which contain an almost explicit treatment of the coincidence of opposites.[30]

This brings us to the second question: How similar is the coincidence of opposites in these thinkers? In dealing with this question, I will follow the methodology employed throughout the book: namely, to analyze whatever types of coincidence of opposites found in a man's thought, without taking any particular form as the norm. I will conclude that there are both similarities and differences in the two thinkers and that, in a certain sense, they had different understandings of the coincidence of opposites. This means that I am not taking Nicholas' version as the sole possible form, merely because he is the first to have made it self-reflective; nor am I taking his version as the norm.

Since I will use it systematically to relate Bonaventure and Nicholas, it might be wise to recall the scheme of three architectonic models of the coincidence of opposites which I presented in the first chapter: (1) unity; (2) difference; and (3) unity and difference.[31] In the first, opposites coincide so much that they become one. In this monistic view, opposites are swallowed up in an undifferentiated union. In the second model, there is a radical dualism, in which the opposites persist to such an extent that they repel each other, preventing any genuine union. In the third model, there is both difference and unity. While remaining opposites, they coincide in a union that intensifies their difference. This is a union of mutually affirming complementarity. As I have stated throughout, I believe that Bonaventure's coincidence of opposites falls consistently within this third model, through his notion of Christ the *medium*. In the case of Nicholas, I believe that there is a tension between the first and the third: that is, between a monistic coincidence and one of mutual complementarity.

When we compare Nicholas' system with that of Bonaventure, we find the same structural elements but with different emphases and, I believe, with certain differences in the coincidence of opposites. Since Nicholas is in the same generic tradition as Bonaventure, we find the following common themes: the non-manifesting and manifesting poles of the divinity; the dynamic Trinity, expressed chiefly by Nicholas through the Father as unity, the Son as equality, and the Spirit as connection; this dynamic level leads to the coincidence of unity and plurality in the divinity; exemplarism, although this is much more developed in Bonaventure than in Nicholas; and a doctrine of Christ as center.[32]

Although these elements are present in Nicholas' thought, they do not have the same function in his system that they have in Bonaventure's. For example, in Bonaventure the emanation model of the Trinity is central. Derived from the Greek Fathers through the Pseudo-Dionysius, this emanation model emphasizes the fecundity and dynamism of the Father in the Trinitarian processions. In contrast, Nicholas is much more in the Augustinian tradition — not merely because he uses the Augustinian terms of unity, equality, and connection, but because, like Augustine, he is much more interested in the Trinity as a mystery of unity and diversity than as a mystery of the divine emanation. This produces a significant difference in the coincidence of opposites. In Bonaventure the dynamic coincidence of opposites predominates, that is, the coincidence of emanation and return; however in Nicholas the more static coincidence of unity and plurality predominates.[33]

Perhaps the greatest difference lies in the area of God's relation to the world. As a disciple and interpreter of Francis of Assisi, Bonaventure is primarily concerned with God's presence in the universe. This leads him to find the highest in the lowest, the most significant reality in the least. This paradox — embodied in the personality of the *poverello* and in Franciscan humility and poverty — Bonaventure sees as the universal structure of reality, rooted in Trinitarian exemplarism. Through contemplation of the world, Bonaventure leads us back to the Exemplar of all things, the Trinitarian Word, who is the *medium* through whom opposites coincide.

Nicholas, on the other hand, is primarily interested in mathematical and philosophical problems dealing with infinity and in the coincidence of the *maximum* and the *minimum*. He moves from the world of multiplicity, of contradictions and contraries to God, where opposites coincide in the divine unity; for in God the *maximum* and the *minimum* coincide. God is the *maximum* who cannot be greater, and he is the *minimum* since he cannot be less; therefore the *maximum* and the *minimum* coincide in him.[34] From one point of view, this type of coincidence of opposites can be interpreted in a monistic sense, since the polarities in the world are transcended in the undifferentiated unity of God. From another point of view, this coincidence can be considered a mathematical route into the classic doctrine of exemplarism, shared by Bonaventure, and hence would reflect the coincidence of the third class, namely, of mutual complementarity. In any case, this much can be said: Nicholas emphasized the coincidence of the *maximum* and the *minimum,* and Bonaventure a coincidence through the *medium,* who is Christ. This coincidence through *medium* is much more clearly in the third class than is Nicholas's coincidence of the *maximum* and *minimum.*

The area where Bonaventure and Nicholas are closest is Christology. The following passage from Nicholas' *De docta ignorantia* presents a vision of Christ very similar to Bonaventure's conception of Christ the *medium.* However, in characteristic fashion, Nicholas analyzes the mystery of Christ from the standpoint of the *maximum* and the *minimum,* although here his approach converges with Bonaventure's analysis through the notion of *medium.*

> In him [Christ] the smallest things of nature, the greatest and all between, would so coincide in a nature united with the absolute maximum, as to form in him the perfection of all things; and all things, in their limitation, would repose in him as in their perfection. . . . By him who is the maximum in limitation, all things are to come forth into their limited being from the Absolute Maximum, and by means of him revert to the maximum. For he is the first beginning of their setting forth and the last end of their return.[35]

On the level of architectonic structure the vision of Bonaventure and that of Nicholas are very similar since they are in the same generic tradition. In all major areas, this architectonic structure contains the logic of the coincidence of opposites: in the doctrine of God, of God's relation to the world, and in Christology. Moreover, this coincidence of opposites is clearly of the class of unity and difference, or mutual complementarity. Bonaventure's treatment of this type of coincidence through the notion of *medium* brings its distinctive nature to light, even though he does not use the term *coincidentia oppositorum* nor bring the pattern to self-consciousness as an abstract model. Although Nicholas brings the coincidence of opposites to an abstract self-consciousness, there is a tension in his thought between a monistic coincidence and one of mutual complementarity. In his later writings, however, he moves closer to Bonaventure — more clearly and consistently within the framework of mutual complementarity.[36]

As Bonaventure's tradition moves through the subsequent centuries, it diversifies considerably, partially because of the major cultural revolutions it encounters and expresses, partially because it lacks the self-consciousness of its own continuity that it possessed in the Middle Ages. As it flows into the contemporary scene, it becomes the vehicle through which modern man becomes aware of some of his major problems and possibilities in the twentieth century. Through the coincidence of opposites we can identify the threads of this tradition and their relatedness to Bonaventure; and we can bring Bonaventure into dialogue with contemporary thinkers as they attempt to chart man's journey into the future. This will be the task of our next chapter.

CHAPTER VIII

Bonaventure and Twentieth Century Thought

HROUGHOUT the central chapters of this book, I have attempted to establish my major claim: that the coincidence of opposites is the key to understanding the structure of Bonaventure's thought. For the coincidence of opposites reveals the logic of his theological metaphysics, which brings his philosophical metaphysics to a culmination and which provides the architechtonic pattern to his thought as a whole. Thus the coincidence of opposites provides a hermeneutical key for interpreting all the elements of his system. We have studied the evidence for this claim, both textually and systematically, in the Trinitarian and Christological poles of Bonaventure's thought; and we have seen its bearing on his doctrine of God's relation to the world, the epistemology of illumination, and the dynamics of history. This major claim involves two subordinate claims: (1) By clarifying Bonaventure's thought through the coincidence of opposites, we can better situate him within the history of thought. (2) Through the coincidence of opposites, we can find a gateway into the universal philosophical and theological issues which overarch the centuries and constitute the substance of the Great Dialogue in Western culture.

In the light of our major claim, we will explore in this chapter the two subordinate claims as these touch contemporary thought, especially twentieth century Christian theology. As we have indicated in the previous chapter, Bonaventure belongs to a tradition of Western thought which was by no means circumscribed to the Middle Ages. Through the coincidence of opposites we have already seen Bonaventure's relation to the subsequent development of this tradition as it unfolded in Nicholas of Cusa. In the present chapter we will observe how this tradition has flowed into the twentieth century and how it attempts to deal with problems which Bonaventure himself confronted. At this point Bonaventure can enter into the Great Dialogue, for in his era he penetrated so deeply into the universal issues that he has something creative to say in dialogue with twentieth century thinkers as they confront the same issues in our own time. Here the coincidence of opposites can clarify the universal issues and highlight Bonaventure's distinctive contribution to the dialogue.

In this chapter our approach will be more issue-oriented than in the last, where we focused on the structural relationship of Bonaventure to Nicholas of Cusa. It would be illuminating to embark on a detailed comparative study of the structure of Bonaventure's thought and that of such twentieth century theologians as Rahner and Tillich. But such an enterprise is beyond the scope of the present chapter, where we will show structural similarities and differences chiefly as these have bearing on the universal issues. In this way we hope to reveal the vitality of Bonaventure's thought and to give an impetus to more systematic studies in the future on Bonaventure's relation to twentieth century thinkers.

BONAVENTURE'S RELEVANCE

At first glance, it may seem woefully anachronistic to examine Bonaventure in relation to twentieth century thought. For he lived in an age separated from ours by seven centuries, an age whose life-style, modes of thought, and challenges seem very foreign to our own. In contrast with the stable, homogeneous, and religious world of the Middle Ages, we live in a secular environment, overwhelmed by change and bewildered by diversity. In the accelerating pace of change, we find ourselves numbed by future shock and confused by conflicting visions of the future: images of utopia and of cosmic catastrophe. Science and technology have conquered outer space at the very moment when we are exhausting the natural resources that support the future of technology and scientific research. On the religious scene, pluralism has supplanted a narrow orthodoxy, and ecumenism has expanded to the horizon of world religions.

Furthermore the major group which previously had drawn resources from the Middle Ages — namely, the Roman Catholic community — has to a large extent abandoned its medieval heritage. After Vatican II, many Catholics have thrown off medieval thought-patterns and are facing the modern world on its own terms. Even if they were interested in their past, Bonaventure seems too forgotten to be recalled. During the neo-scholastic revival, it was Thomas not Bonaventure who was in the fore; and within his own Franciscan tradition, Bonaventure was eclipsed by Duns Scotus. Therefore to see Bonaventure in relation to contemporary thought may seem like an irrelevant and even impossible task.

I believe that this task is neither impossible nor irrelevant. But in order to face this task squarely, we must begin by asking the question: How is Bonaventure related to contemporary thought? I do not wish to approach this question superficially, claiming that Bonaventure is "relevant" in a popular way; nor do I wish to impose medieval thought-patterns on the contemporary scene. On the contrary, I hold that one must penetrate through the distinctive medieval dimensions of Bonaventure's system to reach those universal issues that perdure beyond the particularity of historical epochs. Bonaventure represents one of the richest traditions in Western thought — a tradition that has flourished in different historical eras and in diverse geographic settings. It developed in the Byzantine East in the golden era of the Greek Fathers; it flourished in the Latin West from the early to the high Middle Ages; it flowered in the Renaissance and in the nineteenth century and it has emerged in a number of ways in the twentieth century. Bonaventure inherited this tradition from both Greek and Latin sources, and he exercised his genius in developing one of the most complex syntheses that this tradition has achieved. His success lay in the fact that he brought the depth of this tradition to bear on the challenges of his day, tapping its creative resources that are not limited to a particular time or place.

It is precisely this creative depth that is effective in meeting the challenges of a particular age. If we in the twentieth century are to meet the challenges of our day and of the future, then we must be in touch with all the resources of our past. It is crucial for us to know, in depth, the tradition Bonaventure represents; and it is especially beneficial to know that tradition in the rich synthetic form that Bonaventure has bequeathed to us. When he brought his tradition in contact with the issues of his day, he penetrated deeply into the mystery of reality. It is not surprising that he touched levels which are universal, which transcend the differences of historical periods and which are significant for us now in the twentieth century. It is on this level of creative depth that Bonaventure is relevant to the twentieth century. And it is through the coincidence of opposites that we can find our way into the universal issues and to the creative contributions that Bonaventure can offer to our times.

To relate Bonaventure to contemporary thought is complicated by both the richness and variety of twentieth century Christian theology. In scanning its development, one is struck by great polarities and intricate patterns of unity. After World War I and into the sixties, Christian theology was dominated by the figure of Karl Barth and by existentialist thought. In contrast with the liberal theology of the nineteenth century, this neo-orthodoxy focused on man's fallenness and on his radical need for salvation in Christ. Influenced by Heidegger, existentialist theologians, such as Rudolf Bultmann, analyzed man's subjectivity in its inauthenticity and in its authentic possibilities which could be realized through Christ. Paul Tillich combined the existentialist emphasis on subjectivity with a theology of culture. Karl Rahner based his theology on a notion of subjectivity drawn from existentialism and Transcendental Thomism.

During the sixties, a strong reaction set in to the supernaturalism of Barth and to the individualism of existentialism. The 'death of God' movement and secular theology proposed a 'religionless Christianity'. In a number of currents, the theological focus shifted from the individual to the collective and the cosmic. Interest developed in the thought of Teilhard de Chardin, which drew into a single theological perspective the entire physical universe and the totality of history. In the United States, Whiteheadian process theology gained increasing attention. Having been shaped by the scientific revolutions at the turn of the century, process thought took into account the entire universe and the temporal process as related to God. With roots in Hegel and Marx, the theology of hope, which developed in Germany, applied the eschatological consciousness of Biblical revelation to modern man in his social and political dimensions and in his hopes for the future. Closely associated with the theology of hope, liberation theology emphasized man's need to be freed from collective social, economic, and political oppression. Throughout the twentieth century interest in ecumenism has grown, both within Christianity and in relation to other religions. Christian theologians have attempted to expand their horizons to encompass the rich variety of man's religious experience and to develop a theology of the interrelation of religions.

Amid this complexity we can discern a number of themes that have resonance with Bonaventure's thought. The notion of God as dynamic has been a dominant motif of twentieth century theology; it is found in the Trinitarian theology of Rahner and Tillich and in the theology of hope. The same theme — with emphasis on God's involvement in the world — is developed in Whiteheadian process theology and in Teilhard's evolutionary vision, where it is expressed through the latter's doctrine of the cosmic Christ. In Tillich and Rahner the presence of God is analyzed in human subjectivity; in a number of these theologians God's presence within the structures of the world and the dynamics of history becomes the basis of a theology of culture and a theology of history. In the case of the ecumenical theologians, God's presence in human experience and in the varieties of cultural forms provides the basis of a theology of ecumenism, formulated through the doctrines of the Trinity and Christ.

We see here a configuration of themes that coincides with the main outlines of Bonaventure's thought: the dynamic doctrine of God expressed in Trinitarian terms; the intimate relation of God and the world — within human subjectivity, in the structure of the universe, in the forms of culture and in the dynamics of history; the mystery of Christ the center, as the expression of God's presence in the world and as the unifying center of all dimensions of the cosmos. In the course of this chapter, we will see how these central themes draw Bonaventure into dialogue with contemporary thinkers; and in the following chapter we will see how Bonaventurian themes provide a resource for ecumenism. Our path or bridge between Bonaventure and the twentieth century will be the coincidence of opposites. Just as the coincidence of opposites led us into the depth of Bonaventure's vision, so it can lead us into the depth of the universal issues, where Bonaventure's thought transcends its medieval particularity and has direct bearing on the problems of the twentieth century. The coincidence of opposites will not only be our gateway into these problems but will provide the very solution which Bonaventure can offer as his distinctive contribution to the Great Dialogue.

In the course of this study, I will deal with three areas of Bonaventure's thought, seen through three types of the coincidence of opposites: (1) the Trinity, where self-sufficiency coincides with dynamism; (2) God and the world, where the infinite coincides with the finite; and (3) the Christocentric universe, where unity coincides with diversity. Our exploration will presuppose our previous exposition of Bonaventure's thought and our analysis of its various types of coincidence of opposites. With this as a background, we will recall the essential points as these touch universal issues and relate Bonaventure to twentieth century problematics.

THE DYNAMIC TRINITY

As we have seen, Bonaventure's doctrine of the Trinity is the foundation of his entire vision; along with the Christocentric pole, it provides the architectonic design of his system. In his theology, the Trinity is seen primarily as the mystery of the divine fecundity, with the Father as the fecund source of the Trinitarian processions. Thus Bonaventure can apply to the Father the principles of fecund primordiality and the self-diffusion of the good. According to the principle of fecund primordiality — derived from the *Liber de causis* — the Father is primary and hence the fecund source of the divine processions. According to the principle of the self-diffusion of the good — derived from the Pseudo-Dionysius — the Father is the source of the absolute self-diffusion of the good in the Trinitarian processions.[1] This Trinitarian self-diffusion involves a dynamic coincidence of opposites, in which the Father's fecundity expresses itself in a movement into the Son and a return in the unity of the Spirit. Thus the Son is the *medium* of the Trinitarian dynamism or, as Bonaventure calls him, the *persona media* of the Trinity. This dynamic coincidence of opposites involves another; namely, the coincidence of unity and plurality. Since the Father's fecundity emanates in the Son and the Spirit, the dynamic Trinity necessarily involves a coincidence of unity and diversity on the level of the divinity itself.[2]

Although Bonaventure's doctrine of God involves a number of types of coincidence of opposites, I will focus here on one: namely, the coincidence of self-sufficiency and self-communication. It is true that Bonaventure emphasizes the dynamic aspect of God, but not to the neglect of God's self-sufficiency. In fact, he achieves one of the most impressive integrations of these two aspects of the divinity. As Arthur Lovejoy has pointed out in his book *The Great Chain of Being*, there has been a tension throughout the history of Western thought between two images of God: God as self-sufficient absolute and God as self-communicating fecundity.[3]

As self-sufficient, God is the timeless absolute, the unmoved mover, distant from the world and radically unlike the world. On the other hand, as self-communicating, God is outgoing, related, involved, sharing his perfections with the world. These two images seem incompatible and according to some are ultimately irreconcilable. Often in the history of thought, the image of God as self-sufficient has won out, producing a view of God as static and unrelated, a view which has been severely criticized in the twentieth century by Alfred North Whitehead and Charles Hartshorne.[4] In contrast, the image of God as self-communicating has produced a finite God, dependent on the world for the activation of his fecundity.

This, then, is the dilemma facing theologians: If they ignore the divine fecundity, they produce an image of God as distant and unrelated — an image far removed from the Biblical God, who reveals himself as involved in the world and history even to the point of redeeming mankind through the Incarnation and Crucifixion. On the other hand, if theologians ignore the divine self-sufficiency, they run the risk of reducing God's transcendence to the limits of the world. How resolve this dilemma? Bonaventure faced the problem squarely, reconciling these two images of God through the coincidence of opposites. In the person of the Father in the Trinity, the two images coincide: As unbegotten, the Father is the root of the self-sufficiency in the Godhead, for he proceeds from no one. At the same time he is the fountain and source of the divine processions. Bonaventure not only sees these two images coexisting in the Father, but he sees them present by way of a coincidence of mutually affirming complementarity. This means that one implies and demands the other. For Bonaventure, to be unbegotten implies that the Father begets the Son; and to beget the Son implies that the Father is unbegotten. Thus by affirming one, we simultaneously affirm the other. According to Bonaventure's conception, then, we can say: *Because* the Father is absolutely self-sufficient, he is absolutely self-communicating.[5]

What are the implications of this? It means that the image of

God as dynamic, processive, self-communicating is not swallowed up by the image of God as self-sufficient. It enables Bonaventure to develop one of the richest doctrines of God as dynamic in the history of theology, a doctrine that has much to say to the process philosophers and theologians of modern times who have taken such pains to affirm the image of God as dynamic. I believe that the most significant contribution of Bonaventure to modern thought is his position that God is absolutely dynamic in his inner life and hence does not have to depend on the world to manifest himself.[6] Bonaventure claims that God is absolutely good; but the good is self-diffusive. Therefore God must be self-diffusive in an absolute way. This absolute self-diffusion of the good can be realized only in the Trinitarian processions: in the Father's generation of the Son and in their spiration of the Holy Spirit. If God had to depend on the world in order to diffuse his goodness, he would never be able to communicate himself adequately, for as Bonaventure says: "the diffusion that occurred in time in the creation of the world is no more than a pivot or point in comparison with the immense sweep of the eternal goodness."[7]

The metaphysical implications of this position are profound and far-reaching. Bonaventure has placed the ultimate dimension of God's transcendence precisely in his self-diffusing fecundity. This is indeed paradoxical, for the divine fecundity has led thinkers to see God immanent in the world, even to the point of being dependent on the world for the actualization of his fecundity. For Bonaventure God transcends the world in two ways: by his infinity in contrast with the world's finitude; secondly, by not being dependent on the world for the activation of his fecundity. What does this mean metaphysically? It frees God from the world and the world from God. For God does not need the world to activate his absolute fecundity, and the world does not have to sustain the overpowering self-diffusion of God.

Throughout the history of thought, the notion of divine fecundity has produced two problems: on the one hand, it has relativized God by placing his boundless fecundity on the Procrustean bed of the world; on the other hand, it has absolutized the world, at least in some respects. For example, philosophers have claimed that the principle of divine fecundity demands that all possibles be actualized within space and time and that this world is necessarily the best possible world. Bonaventure was acutely aware of the problems of the divine fecundity and developed a doctrine of divine transcendence based on fecundity. Yet Bonaventure's position in the history of this problem has not been adequately recognized, as is illustrated by the fact that in his survey of the problem in *The Great Chain of Being,* Lovejoy makes no mention of Bonaventure nor does he take into account the logic of Bonaventure's solution.[8]

In modern times, the problem of the divine fecundity has been acutely felt in Hegel's philosophy, where we find one of the most powerful statements of God as dynamic in the history of thought.[9] On this issue, it is important for Bonaventure to enter into dialogue with Hegel, not only because the latter's doctrine is classic, but because it reveals in striking terms the underlying problematic behind the twentieth century's probing of the mystery of God as dynamic. The problematic has been underscored by religious thinkers who have criticized Hegel because he seems to make the world necessary for the self-manifestation of God. To counter Hegel, some would merely affirm God's transcendence through his infinity, claiming that Hegel's system is inadequate because it collapses into pantheism. Such a critique touches only half of the problem for it fails to take into account the metaphysics of the divine fecundity. The dynamics of the divine fecundity must not be ignored but must be confronted directly. If it is allowed to remain dormant, it will inevitably surface, at times naively and destructively, without the clarification of critical reflection. At this point Bonaventure could enter the debate, for he confronted the logic of fecundity directly. He affirmed the divine fecundity not only relatively, but absolutely. At the same time, he wanted to allow the world to share this fecundity without having to bear the impossible burden of the fullness of divine fecundity. There is reason to think that Bonaventure could make a significant contribution in a dialogue with Hegel and his critics. Bonaventure might lead critics to re-examine Hegel's texts to see if, in fact, Hegel held a doctrine of God equivalent to Bonaventure's; or if not, at least he might provide an alternative to Hegel's dynamic God which would allow critics to accept other elements of Hegel's system.

WHITEHEAD AND PROCESS

Alfred North Whitehead also makes God dependent on the world in a way that goes counter to classical metaphysics and Christian theology.[10] He criticizes the fusion of the notion of God as unmoved mover and eminently real:

> The notion of God as the 'unmoved mover' is derived from Aristotle, at least so far as Western thought is concerned. The notion of God as 'eminently real' is a favourite doctrine of Christian theology. The combination of the two into the doctrine of an aboriginal, eminently real, transcendent creator, at whose fiat the world came into being, and whose imposed will it obeys, is the fallacy which has infused tragedy into the histories of Christianity and of Mahometanism.[11]

This he feels is a distortion of the Christian message for "there is, however, in the Galilean origin of Christianity yet another suggestion . . . It dwells upon the tender elements in the world, which slowly and in quietness operate by love."[12] As a metaphysical grounding of this alternative image of God, Whitehead develops his doctrine of the primordial and consequent nature of God, through which God is intimately involved in the creative process of the world, without destroying the autonomous creativity of each element in the process.[13] God's primordial nature provides the ground of possibilities for each of the "actual entities" — the microcosmic units that make up the temporal process, in the Whiteheadian scheme.[14] Each actual entity incorporates into itself an inheritance from the past and in its freedom produces its own novel realization in what Whitehead calls its "concrescence" before it perishes in the process. Its novel concrescence, however, provides data for the realization of future actual entities. Although God and the past contribute to the concrescence of an actual entity, they do not determine it. Rather each actual entity remains autonomously self-affirming in its becoming in the temporal process. In this way, the becoming of the actual entity is the realization of novelty. From one point of view Whitehead can say, "Apart from God, there could be no relevant novelty."[15] But from another point of view, novelty is realized by the actual entity itself in the process. Even with God as the ground of the process, the actual entity retains its autonomous self-creativity. Thus the temporal process can be looked upon as a collaborative enterprise involving God and the world.

The primordial nature of God is complemented by his consequent nature. As Whitehead says, "He is the beginning and the end."[16] As he was the beginning of the process in his primordial nature, so he is the completion of the process in his consequent nature. And in his consequent nature God himself is completed and enriched by the temporal process. Although his primordial nature is unchanged and complete, his consequent nature is in a state of becoming as a result of the temporal process. Since this pole is consequent upon the creative advance of the world, it is termed God's "consequent" nature. Actual entities do not perdure within the process; they last momentarily and perish. God draws up, or objectifies, these novel concrescences into his consequent nature, thus preserving everlastingly the values realized in the process. This everlasting existence is called "objective immortality." By drawing these values into himself, God is enriched in his consequent nature. Since in his primordial nature, God is deficient in actuality, he needs the temporal process for his fulfillment. But this enrichment is not aimed exclusively at God's own satisfaction; rather, he makes these values available again for the temporal process. Whitehead speaks of this as God's love for the world, saying: "What is done in the world is transformed into a reality in heaven, and the reality in heaven passes back into the world. By reason of this reciprocal relation, the love in the world passes into the love in heaven, and floods back again into the world. In this sense, God is the great companion — the fellow-sufferer who understands."[17]

Thus God is intimately involved in the temporal process, which Whitehead calls "the creative advance into novelty."[18] However, since God is not eminently real for Whitehead, he does not possess creativity in an absolute way. Rather both God and the world are caught in creativity, which in some sense transcends both and which Whitehead assigns to the category of the ultimate in his system.[19] For Whitehead God is dynamic, not because he actualizes in himself the absolute expression of creativity, but as ground of the temporal process and as intimately involved in the temporal flow, which enriches his consequent nature as he in turn causes his love to flow back into the process.

Bonaventure's system bears certain resemblances to Whitehead's but with crucial differences. As for Whitehead, creativity is paramount for Bonaventure, but Bonaventure affirms absolute creativity of God, whereas Whitehead affirms it as relative. It must be noted here that Bonaventure does not affirm this absolute creativity through God's relation to the world, but within God's inner Trinitarian life. Furthermore, Bonaventure's image of God is not produced by the formula that Whitehead criticizes: namely by the fusion of the unmoved mover and the eminently real. Rather Bonaventure combines the opposites of self-sufficiency (unmoved mover) and self-communication (creativity). He considers both of these opposites as eminently real in the classical metaphysical and theological sense: namely, that God contains all perfections pertaining to these poles, in an absolute way, in a mode unlike that of creatures.

Like Whitehead's God, Bonaventure's God is dipolar, but completely within his inner life and not in relation to the world. Of course, for Bonaventure God is intimately related to the world because he is absolutely creative and related within his inner Trinitarian life, but not in a way that would make him dependent on the world. In an approach that is reminiscent of Bonaventure,

Whitehead states six antonomies or coincidences of opposites in the final chapter of *Process and Reality*. They all deal with the relation of God and the world in the paradoxical mode expressed as follows: "It is as true to say that God creates the World, as that the World creates God." Whitehead immediately continues: "God and the World are the contrasted opposites in terms of which Creativity achieves its supreme task of transforming disjointed multiplicity, with its diversities in opposition, into concrescent unity, with its diversities in contrast."[20]

Like Whitehead, Bonaventure sees a coincidence of opposites between God and the world, but not precisely that of Whitehead; for Bonaventure sees a coincidence of opposites within the inner life of God which Whitehead does not affirm. In terms of Whitehead's system, Bonaventure's God is dipolar within his primordial nature, for he has a self-sufficient and a self-communicating pole. And unlike Whitehead, Bonaventure places pre-eminent creativity in the self-communicating pole of the divinity, on the level equivalent to the primordial nature of Whitehead's system. The coincidence of opposites within the divinity is the basis for the world's sharing in creativity. For Bonaventure the world shares in a creativity derived from the Trinity, not as for Whitehead in a category that transcends both God and the world. For Bonaventure the world shares in this creativity through the principle of participation. It must be remembered that for Bonaventure, the world participates not merely in being — in the self-sufficient pole of the divinity — but also in the divine creativity — in the self-communicating pole. In this way, Bonaventure's system allows him to make a stronger affirmation of the creativity of the temporal process than Whitehead's system does for it allows him to affirm the participation of the process in the pre-eminent creativity of the Trinitarian processions.

Although creativity within the universe cannot match the infinite creativity of the Father as *fontalis plenitudo,* nevertheless all of the creativity in the universe is a positive sharing in this absolute eternal creative act. The whole world, then, shares in the primordial creativity of the generation of the Son from the Father. In taking this perspective, we imply that there are two lines to Bonaventure's exemplarism: (1) one line moving from the world to the Son, from the embodied forms to their archetypes to the *Ratio Aeterna*; (2) another line moving from the world to the Father, from creativity in the world to the Trinity as dynamic process — a process in which the Word or *Ratio Aeterna* is being eternally generated as an eternally novel expression of the Father. In Bonaventure's vision, then, the entire universe is a vestige of the Trinity, meaning that it not only reflects the power, wisdom, and goodness of the Trinity, but shares in the Trinity's dynamic process. In addition to being a vestige of the Trinity, man is an image and thus shares more fully in the divine creativity. Man the maker, the artisan, the creator approaches more closely the divine archetype of all art and making.

Echoing Augustine, Bonaventure describes the Son as the *Ars Patris* (the Art of the Father).[21] Thus the Trinitarian God is seen as the Maker and Artist *par excellence*. It is this image of God that stands behind Bonaventure's *De reductione artium ad theologiam*.[22] All mankind, all creativity in the universe can be traced back to the Art of the Father; for all creativity shares in this primordial creativity. Drawing his data from the everyday world of the Middle Ages, Bonaventure lists the seven mechanical arts given by Hugh of St. Victor in his *Didascalicon*: weaving, armor-making, agriculture, hunting, navigation, medicine, and drama.[23] Every craftsman, artisan, or maker — as well as every philosopher when he forms and expresses his thought in ideas and words — shares in the Art of the Father, in the creativity of the generation of the Son. As the title of the work suggests, Bonaventure employs the classical medieval *reductio*, which unlike its modern counterpart does not mean a devaluation, but rather a leading back or retracing of a concrete object or activity to its ground in the divinity. When the artisan makes a product, then, he shares in the Trinitarian creativity.

Thus for Bonaventure the artisan is not merely copying archetypal forms in the divine mind; he is creating something radically new — not apart from, but along with the divine *fontalis plenitudo*. In one line of exemplarity, the artisan's creative idea moves back to its ideal model in the divine mind. But in another line of exemplarity, the artisan shares in the primordial fecundity of the Father. With the Father the artisan shares not only in the creation of the external object, but in the generation of the archetypes in the Son. Thus in a most profound sense the artisan shares in a novelty that transcends his own isolated activity; for his creative act participates in the eternal novelty of the divine generation.

Not only the artisan, as image of the Trinity, but also the entire universe as vestige shares in this dynamism; thus the world of matter as well as human creativity shares in the Trinitarian process:

> But the seminal reasons [*rationes seminales*] cannot exist in matter without the generation and production of form; neither can intellectual reasons [*rationes intellectuales*] exist in the soul without the generation of a word in the mind. Therefore ideal reasons [*rationes ideales*] cannot exist in God without the generation of the Word from the Father in proper proportion. This is a mark of dignity, and if it is appropriate to the creature, how much more so can it be inferred about the Creator. It was on account of this that Augustine said that the Son of God is the "art of the Father."[24]

Notice the medieval *reductio,* with the Franciscan emphasis on the movement from the lowest to the highest, from the dynamism of matter to the dynamism of the Father. With his exemplaristic logic Bonaventure observes that if dynamism is appropriate to the creature, how much more so to the Creator. Bonaventure's thoroughgoing exemplarism is in harmony with Whitehead's statement that "in the first place, God is not to be treated as an exception to all metaphysical principles, invoked to save their collapse. He is their chief exemplification."[25] However, when Bonaventure strives to discover in God the chief exemplification of creativity, he penetrates beyond God's external creative activity and enters into the inner life of the Trinity to discover unsurpassable creativity in the Trinitarian processions.

To place the ultimate source of creativity in the Trinity allows Bonaventure to maintain simultaneously several opposites. Man can share in the primordial work of creation, but at the same time remain dependent upon God. In Bonaventure's vision he can make the extreme Aristotelian-Thomistic affirmation of dependence, and at the same time the extreme Platonic-Augustinian exemplaristic affirmation of sharing in the divinity. Thus in man, the microcosm, the opposites join. Man is supremely creative, for he shares the supreme creativity of the *fontalis plenitudo*; at the same time he is supremely dependent, for ultimately he is not the *fontalis plenitudo* but only shares in its fullness in a limited way. Thus in man's creative activity many lines of opposites converge: transcendence and immanence, eternity and time, form and novelty.

Is there something in Bonaventure's system comparable to Whitehead's consequent nature of God, whereby God is enriched by the process? Although Bonaventure did not formulate the issue this way, I believe it is possible to do so. Creativity has two modes of manifestation — eternally within the divinity and externally within temporal creation. On the divine level within the Trinity, creativity is complete, with no limitations; it does not have, and cannot have, an absolute external manifestation within creation. Thus on the creaturely level it is open to a variety of possibilities. In God's external manifestation, then, we can discern a unique realization of God's perfection: namely, its external manifestation amid a variety of possibilities. Something new is added to the perfection of the world through the creativity actualized in time; and since the world manifests unique aspects of God, then we can say that God is enriched in his external manifestations both by his initial act of creation and by the creativity actualized within space and time by his creatures.

Of course, seen in this perspective, God's enrichment is not the same as in Whitehead's system. In Bonaventure God is saved from contingency by the fact that his creativity is eternally actualized in an absolute degree within the Trinity. Granted this, we can establish a coincidence of opposites between God and the world along the lines of Whitehead's antonomies, but without the implications of God's dependence on the world. Thus for Bonaventure, it is as true to say that the world creates God (in his external manifestations) as that God creates the world. By activating their creativity through participation, creatures bring to realization novel expressions of the ultimate, unbounded divine creativity at the heart of the Trinitarian life. Hence God is not the unmoved mover, aloof and detached, but self-communicating goodness, intent upon sharing his creativity with creatures and upon their realization of his creativity for their own and for his enrichment.

This, then, is Bonaventure's response to the problem of the divine fecundity. Through a coincidence of opposites within the divinity, he offers a solution to the problem surveyed in Lovejoy's *The Great Chain of Being* and which persists to this day in Western thought. It is a matter of historical significance that Bonaventure addressed himself to this problem in the thirteenth century. But it is a matter of philosophical and theological significance that he reached a solution that has much to contribute to the Great Dialogue in our time. By requiring that God be absolutely fecund, Bonaventure faced the problem squarely. By situating this absolute fecundity in the Trinity through the coincidence of opposites, he freed God from dependence on the world and the world from having to bear the impossible burden of expressing the fullness of the divine fecundity. Bonaventure's God is indeed transcendent, but not by being unrelated to the world; he is transcendent precisely because he is self-diffusive. Since his fecundity, and hence his relatedness, are actualized absolutely and eternally within the Trinity, there is a basis for his full involvement in the world. Bonaventure's God, then, is at least as dynamic and as manifesting as Hegel's God, and as involved in the creativity of the temporal process as Whitehead's God. But Bonaventure's God is freed from the ambiguities that would make him dependent on the world and enmeshed in the process. Liberated from dependence on the world, Bonaventure's God can be absolutely dynamic in his inner life; yet he does not remain wrapped up in himself, in splendid divine isolation. Quite the contrary, his transcendent dynamism is precisely the source of his further diffusion in creation. Without being overwhelmed by that dynamism, creatures share in the absolute divine creativity through participation in the eternal novelty of the generation of the Son by the Father.

GOD AND THE WORLD

Through the coincidence of opposites Bonaventure was able to offer a profound solution to the problem of the divine fecundity: by placing absolute self-communication on the level of the divine self-sufficiency. Through another type of the coincidence of opposites — that of the infinite and the finite — he can offer a solution to another vexing problem: God's relation to the world. As Lovejoy has pointed out, those traditions that affirm God as self-sufficient absolute produce an otherworldly perspective, separating God from the world and emphasizing the dissimilarity between God and the world.[26] This image of the distant God goes counter to the sense of God's presence in the world conveyed in Biblical revelation, especially in the mystery of Christ. It is understandable, then, that the immanence of God has been emphasized by such twentieth century thinkers as Whitehead, Hartshorne, Teilhard de Chardin, Tillich, and Rahner.

It should come as no surprise to discover that Bonaventure has something to contribute to this discussion. For he was the heir and interpreter of Francis of Assisi, who expressed the greatest sense of the immanence of God in the history of Christianity. In fact, for Western culture as a whole Francis has become the symbol of the religious sense of the divine immanence. Bonaventure shared Francis' vision, seeing the presence of God throughout creation — in the lowliest of creatures and across the vast panorama of the universe. Creatures are like a mirror reflecting God, a path leading to God, a statue depicting God, a stained glass window which reflects the richness of God's fecundity. Bonaventure gave a philosophical and theological foundation to this Franciscan vision — through his doctrine of exemplarism in the Word, in whom the infinite and the finite coincide. In the twentieth century discussion over the immanence of God, it would be beneficial to listen to the chief spokesman of Francis of Assisi; for Bonaventure's theological interpretation matches in depth the intensity of Francis' religious experience.

Paradoxically, in Bonaventure's thought the very principle that accounts for God's transcendence is the root of his immanence. Bonaventure had founded God's transcendence in his fecundity, which is so great that it cannot be exhausted within the world. However, when God expresses himself in creation, he does so out of the ultimate mystery of Trinitarian fecundity. When the Father generates the Son, he generates in the Son the archetypes of all he can make. As Bonaventure says: "The Father generated one similar to himself, namely the Word, co-eternal with himself; and he expressed his own likeness and as a consequence expressed all the things that he could make."[27] Thus the Father's fecundity which expresses itself in the Word also produces in the Word the *rationes aeternae* of all that can be made. These eternal reasons within the Son are the ontological ground of each individual creature. Thus Bonaventure can say that things have a threefold existence: They exist in the Eternal Art (in the Son), they exist also in matter, and they exist within the mind.[28] The most important dimension of their existence is in the Eternal Art, within the Son as Image and Word of the Father. Thus creation has an eternal existence within the interior life of the Trinity; for creation, as grounded in the eternal reasons is co-eternal with the generation of the Son from the Father. There exists, then, an eternal and very intimate relationship between God and the world.[29]

Because all creatures have an eternal existence within the Son, creation *ad extra* is intimately related to God. When God freely creates *ad extra*, the world now has existence not only in the

Eternal Art, but also in space and time. But this space-time existence does not rupture the relation between God and the world.
Rather the world is intimately related to God because of its existence in the Son, through the eternal reasons which are the
ontological ground of creatures. The relation between creatures
and God is so intimate that Bonaventure can say: "I will see myself better in God than in my very self."[30] Through their exemplaristic grounding in the Word, all creatures reflect God and
lead man to God. With great precision, Bonaventure divides creatures into various levels of representing God: shadow, vestige,
image, and similitude.[31]

Although creatures reflect God, they are not swallowed up in
God as drops of water in the ocean; rather in reflecting God,
their own individuality is intensified. While being intimately
related to God, they remain radically themselves. Bonaventure
holds that within the Word there are archetypes of each individual thing, not merely universal ideas. This is Bonaventure's
way of affirming the Franciscan sense of the importance of individuality and the value of uniqueness. St. Francis had this sense
to a heightened degree, and it was expressed later by Duns Scotus
in his doctrine of *haecceitas,* or thisness, that property by which
a thing is an individual. Although Scotus expressed this Franciscan sense of individuality by transforming an Aristotelian mode
of thought, Bonaventure expressed the same sense through Platonic exemplarism.[32]

In the coincidence of opposites between God and creatures, the
opposites are maintained and intensified by their coincidence.
For Bonaventure all the types of the coincidence of opposites —
whether in the Trinity or in the world — are opposites of mutually affirming complementarity. That means that there is real
opposition: both poles remain intact and are not absorbed in
the other. God is not absorbed in the world, nor the world in
God. But it means also that these opposites actually coincide, that
they are internally related and not merely juxtaposed externally.

The opposites interpenetrate and by this interpenetration intensify their uniqueness.

God and the World in Process Thought

The coincidence of God and the world is a major theme in contemporary thought. Whitehead, Hartshorne, and the process theologians criticize the classical theological tradition for separating God and the world to such an extent that the God of Christian theology hardly seems to be the same as the God of Biblical revelation.[33] It is here that Bonaventure has something pointed to say to process thinkers, for he represents an ancient and long-lived tradition in Christian theology that affirms an intimate relation between God and the world. In dealing with the history of thought, Hartshorne and the process school in general describe two forms of metaphysics: classical and neo-classical.[34] The latter refers to the metaphysics of Whitehead, expressed chiefly in his book *Process and Reality*. Within classical metaphysics, the chief target criticized by process thinkers is classical theism, which affirms a doctrine of God's transcendence above the temporal process in such a way that he is not intimately involved in the world. In assigning absolute perfection to God, classical theism radically separates God and the world. In discussion and debate, it is usually Aristotelian-Thomism that bears the banner of classical theism, and the discussion often focuses on the Aristotelian category of relation. In the Aristotelian analysis of relation, the world is said to be related to God, but God is not related to the world. In contrast, by denying that God is absolutely immutable, neo-classical theism can affirm an intimate involvement of God in the world. However, by polarizing Aristotelian-Thomism and Whitehead, neo-classical theists often have given the impression that all classical theists prior to Whitehead made a radical separation between God and the world.

There has been an ongoing argument as to whether the neo-classical assessment of Thomism is accurate.[35] Is the Thomist God as unrelated to the world as the neo-classical theists claim?

Added to this is another question: Has neo-classical theism accurately read the history of thought? Has all classical theism emphasized the distance between God and the world? If we examine Bonaventure's tradition in the light of the pluralism of the Middle Ages, then the answer to that question must be in the negative. Bonaventure's tradition is both ancient and long-lived; it flowed from the Greek Fathers and was a major current in both the twelfth and thirteenth century West. It affirms an intimate relationship between God and the world based on the Trinitarian nature of creation and on the Son as Image of the Father and as the divine mediating principle between the Father and the world, while remaining consubstantial with the Father. I wish to make it clear that Bonaventure's tradition is by no means identical with neo-classical theism. The way in which God is related to the world in both positions is significantly different. Bonaventure affirms a stronger position of God's transcendence than is affirmed by neo-classical theists. However, this does not mean that Bonaventure stands at the opposite end of the spectrum, in the Aristotelian camp. Quite the contrary. Bonaventure and his tradition stand at a midpoint between the two, affirming with equal vigor the immanence and the transcendence of God. Perhaps a reexamination on a broad basis of the various traditions of the Middle Ages might bring about a reinterpretation of the history of thought on the part of neo-classical theists.

As we have seen, Bonaventure's way of relating God and the world is through exemplarism, which in turn is based on expressionism. When the Father generates the Son, expressing his perfect Image and Word, he produces in the Son the archetypes of all he can make. Creation outside the Trinity is an external expression of these archetypes or "eternal reasons," which have their primary existence within the Word. Thus creation as a whole and all creatures in their radical individuality manifest the Son and reflect back to the Son. This, however, is not a weak or tenuous reflection. Quite the contrary! For the deepest reality of each creature is its eternal grounding in the archetypes in the divine mind. Thus through the archetypes in the Word, Bonaventure establishes a most intimate relation between God and the world — a relation effecting a coincidence of opposites of the infinite and the finite mediated by the Son.

This doctrine of exemplarism is a Platonic heritage, which had been given a distinctly Christian interpretation by being situated within the mystery of the Trinity. It is interesting to note that Whitehead also incorporates a major strand of Platonism into his treatment of the relation of God and the world. Whitehead builds into his system "eternal objects," which are similar to the eternal forms and ideas of Plato, and like Augustine situates these eternal objects in God.[36] However, Whitehead conceives these eternal objects as pure potentialities for the specific determination of actual entities in the world. In contrast, Bonaventure conceives the "eternal reasons" (rationes aeternae) as eminently actual and not as merely pure potentialities for actualization in creation. They are eminently actual since they exist on the divine level and possess the eminent reality of God. It is true that they are also potentialities for actualization in creation, but prior to their actualization in space-time, they have a pre-eminent actualized reality in the Son. For just as the Son is pre-eminently actualized in being generated eternally by the Father, so the eternal reasons in the Son share in this actuality.

As in the case of creativity treated above, I believe the crucial difference between Bonaventure and Whitehead lies in whether or not God is eminently real and hence eminently actual, not only in his self-sufficient being but also in his inner creativity. For Whitehead, God is not eminently real in the classical sense and hence his relation to the world makes up for his deficient actuality. For Bonaventure, God is eminently real and has his inner creativity eternally actualized in the Trinitarian processions. It is precisely this inner creativity that establishes a pre-eminent relation between God and the world — through the eternal reasons in the Word.

Although Bonaventure's doctrine of exemplarism establishes

an intimate relation between God and the world, it seems to threaten creativity and novelty in the world. The problem again is over the eminent reality of the eternal reasons. In Whitehead's system, since the eternal objects lack eminent reality, they can be brought to actualization by the temporal process in creative novelty. On the other hand, Bonaventure's eternal reasons, possessing eminent reality and actuality, seem to lock man in a cyclic process that strips him of creativity. Although he can use his creative powers to arrive at new forms, what he discovers and produces is merely a reflection of an eternal idea that is pre-existent and eminently real in the mind of God. Although man is in a process, the process is cyclic and the goal is recollection, not the creation of novelty. For all of his apparent creativity, man is merely caught in an eternal return, where he is rediscovering a blueprint that was eternally sketched in God's mind.

If, however, Bonaventure's exemplarism is situated within his Trinitarian theology, the value of creativity is not negated but affirmed in a pre-eminent way. As indicated above, there are two lines of exemplarism in Bonaventure: one moving from the world to the Son and the eternal reasons within the Son; another moving from the world to the Father, to that eternal creativity from which the Trinitarian processions spring.[37] By following the line of exemplarism leading into the Trinity, Bonaventure breaks out of the circle of the eternal return. The pre-eminent actuality of the eternal reasons is balanced by the pre-eminent, actualized creativity of the Father. If the world participates in the mystery of the dynamic Trinity, then it shares in the unbounded creativity and the eternal novelty of the generation of the Son. This, I believe, is a stronger creativity and novelty than one finds in Whitehead's system, although it clearly involves a different metaphysical understanding of both creativity and novelty.

To return to Whitehead's position on God's relation to the world, we see that God is involved in the world in a number of ways. He is the locus of the eternal objects which are the potentialities for the actualization of actual entities; he is the principle of limitation for actual entities and the source of their subjective aim. After an actual entity achieves its novel actualization of creativity, God draws up into his consequent nature its objective realization, making it available to the ongoing process. Thus God has several levels of relatedness to the world. In Whitehead's system, the world has to achieve what the Trinity achieves for Bonaventure. In Bonaventure's system, God is eminently real, possessing pre-eminently actualized creativity and relatedness within the Trinity. For Whitehead God depends on the world for the actualization of his creativity; thus his relation to the world is bound up with his need to achieve actualization. In Bonaventure, God is eminently creative independently of the world; but because of the eminent reality of the eternal reasons, he is most intimately involved in the world. In Bonaventure's system, the eminent reality of the eternal reasons functions in a way similar to Whitehead's eternal objects and the consequent nature of God, establishing the relation between God and the world.

Unlike Whitehead, Bonaventure affirms God's immanence without threatening his transcendence. This is achieved through a more complex coincidence of opposites than one finds in Whitehead's system. For Bonaventure, creativity and relatedness must be actualized in God; this is a matter of necessity and not contingency, since it pertains to the divine nature itself and is not dependent on God's free choice. However, this necessary actualization of creativity and relatedness is realized not in creation but in the Trinity, through the coincidence of self-sufficiency and self-communication. This coincidence of opposites allows for the coincidence of necessity and contingency in creation. On the divine side there is absolute necessity since the divine fecundity must of necessity be eternally actualized in the Trinity. On the side of the world, there is complete contingency since the world is neither necessary nor adequate for God's self-diffusion. Yet necessity and contingency coincide in appropriateness (*convenentia*) since it is appropriate for God to express his inner fecundity *ad extra*. The Word, who is the necessary expression of the

Father, is the *medium* of the divine free self-diffusion in creatures, the locus of the eternal reasons which link God and creatures in most intimate relation through the preeminent reality
they derive from the Word. Through this complex orchestration
of opposites, Bonaventure gives speculative expression to the
mystery of God's fecundity and immanence which Francis experienced in such depth and simplicity.

TEILHARD AND BONAVENTURE

Teilhard's version of process thought is closer than the Whiteheadian version to Bonaventure's system. This is true not only
of the issue of God's relation to the world, but of the system as a
whole.[38] Teilhard's vision is explicitly Trinitarian, although this
aspect of his thought is not systematically developed. Except for
a few isolated passages, Teilhard merely assumes the classical Christian doctrine of God; he does not make the metaphysics of God's
relation to the world a central theme as Whitehead does. Unlike
Whitehead's God, Teilhard's is eminently real and Trinitarian.
Although Teilhard's doctrine of God is classical and hence does
not introduce contingency in God, it is clearly within the fecundity
tradition as identified by Lovejoy. Unlike Thomas Aquinas,
for example, Teilhard does not emphasize the radical dependence
of the world on God's self-sufficiency, although his notion of
Omega includes this notion. Rather Teilhard emphasizes the
divine involvement in the creative process of the world through
God's sharing his creative energy with the universe. This energy
is imparted to the evolutionary process by the cosmic Christ, present throughout the universe, drawing evolution to its culmination.[39] In many respects Teilhard's cosmic Christ is similar to
Bonaventure's doctrine of the Son as the *medium* of the divine
presence and of the return of creatures to the unity of the Father.
Both Bonaventure and Teilhard have a strong doctrine of Christocentricity, in contrast with the Whiteheadians, who are God-
centered. Just as for Bonaventure, the creative aspect of God and

his intimate involvement in the world are articulated in Teilhard's system through his doctrine of Christ.

Teilhard's religious sensibility is not unlike that of Francis
and Bonaventure. With the Franciscans, he shares a cosmic sense,
an awareness of the vast sweep of creation and of the presence of
God in all creatures. The divine immanence, which Bonaventure expressed through the exemplarism of the Word, Teilhard
expresses through his doctrine of the cosmic Christ. As Omega
of evolution, Christ is present in and energizing the entire cosmos,
from the least particle of matter to the convergent human community. In his work entitled "Christ in the World of Matter,"
Teilhard gives several images that lead one to an awareness of
Christ's presence in matter.[40] Teilhard describes a picture of
Christ that seems to expand and encompass the universe, a Host
whose whiteness penetrates to the center of all particles of matter.
He suggests that the world is a crystal lamp illumined from within
by the light of Christ. The image of the glowing crystal lamp
illustrates graphically a central term in Teilhard: "diaphany",
meaning from its Greek roots "to appear through." In Teilhard
this term refers to the appearing of God through matter, to the
shining of Christ through the cosmos. For those who can see,
Christ shines in a diaphany, through the cosmos and in matter.

The diaphany of Christ is no mere static self-revelation. Christ
is present in his power; he is dynamic and transforming. He imparts energy which brings matter to its fulfillment: ". . . under
the influence of this inner light which penetrated it, its fibres were
stretched to breaking-point and all the energies within them were
strained to the utmost."[41] In the minute particles within the
atom, Christ is present and his energy is driving matter to its
evolutionary goal in the process of Christogenesis: ". . . Christ
himself does not act as a dead or passive point of convergence, but
as a centre of radiation for the energies which lead the universe
back to God through his humanity."[42] The whole cosmic process
is seen as a working out of the Incarnation and an extension of
the Eucharist: the coming to be of Christ, the growth of Christ
in the universe.

Teilhard's Christocentric cosmic mysticism is linked with a specific cosmology, which is an integration of his scientific studies and his religious faith. Like Whitehead, Teilhard is concerned with a cosmology that includes both a creative advance and the divine immanence. Whereas Teilhard's cosmos is evolutionary, moving in progressive stages of development towards the goal which he calls Omega, Whitehead's is processive, but not progressive. Teilhard sees the entire universe in a process of evolution, moving from matter to spirit. This process goes through successive states: First, particles of matter unite to form more complex units until life appears on the earth. Within the biosphere, or sphere of living things, the process of complexification continues until man appears and with him the noosphere or sphere of mind. Evolution continues within the noosphere, with the development of consciousness and the complexification of the human community. The whole process moves towards greater interiorization, to greater consciousness, to greater union in love. This tendency is found from the atom to man — from the cluster of atoms in a molecule to the uniting of men in a world community. All of this is effected by the action of Omega, or Christ, at every point of the way — on the center of the atom and on the center of the human person — bringing each to a greater union that interiorizes, individualizes, and thus leads to new possibilities: to an ultimate hominization and Christification of the cosmos. Thus the process of evolution is seen as a Christogenesis, or a coming to be of Christ.[43]

It would be out of the question to compare Teilhard and Bonaventure point for point in their cosmological views. The thirteenth century lacked the scientific knowledge, the historical data, and the sense of process that are part of the twentieth century experience. Medieval man lived in a Ptolemaic universe, composed of concentric spheres which moved the planets and stars. The universe was hierarchically structured with the earth at the center, then the moon, then the planets and the sun, then the crystalline heaven, and finally the empyrean. The material universe was composed of four elements: earth, air, fire, and water. Animal species were created by God in the beginning and remained basically fixed. The same was true of man. There was change and development in history — as the Incarnation and redemption attested — but the full import of this was not consciously grasped. The Copernican revolution, the development of science, the emergence of history in the nineteenth century were all to contribute to the change from the medieval world view to that of the twentieth century.

Bonaventure's cosmology differs vastly from that of the twentieth century — and from Teilhard's in particular. And yet Bonaventure's thought has a dynamic quality that is not incompatible with the process and evolution in Teilhard. On the theological and philosophical level, Bonaventure's thought is dynamic — open to novelty and development. This dynamic quality comes to the fore at key points of his system and overflows the structure of his medieval universe.

One can see more than a morphological similarity between Bonaventure and Teilhard, for the Franciscan tradition played a significant role in shaping the development of science in Western culture. Interest in the material world was typical of the Franciscan spirit. It permeated both spirituality and intellectual inquiry. By their concern for observation and experimentation, the Franciscan thinkers of the Middle Ages were the forerunners of modern empirical science. It is not surprising, then, that out of the empirical scientific tradition, there should arise a man like Teilhard, who discovers in the material world the very diaphany of Christ that inspired the medieval Franciscans to explore the world of matter.

CHRIST THE CENTER

A dialogue between Bonaventure and Teilhard on cosmic Christocentricity would be very fruitful. Once again the coincidence of opposites provides the means of contact, this time through the coincidence of opposites at the center of the mandala. As we observed in the development of Bonaventure's thought, cosmic

Christocentricity emerged late and did not reach a self-reflective articulation. In Teilhard's case, cosmic Christocentricity was prominent even in his early period and was developed extensively throughout his life. Whereas Bonaventure linked Christ the center with exemplarism, Teilhard linked Christ the center with evolution. For Teilhard Christ is the center of evolution in the sense that the energies of the process are centered on Christ as Omega of evolution. We can find abundant evidence that in Teilhard's thought Christ functions as the center of a cosmic mandala. Like Bonaventure's works, Teilhard's abound in mandala symbols. In the *Itinerarium* the soul proceeds on a journey which is in a mandala design with Christ as the center; in *The Phenomenon of Man* Teilhard describes a cosmic journey which has a similar mandala pattern, also with Christ as the center.[44]

In the *Itinerarium,* Bonaventure describes the concrete stages in the soul's evolution to God: through the material world, sense knowledge, its natural faculties, as enlightened by grace, through knowledge of God as one and Triune, and finally in mystical ecstasy. The journey involves a process of interiorization from the outer to the inner to the above — to union with God. Love is the driving force: the journey begins in desire and ends in union.

If we shift the center of focus from the individual soul to the entire cosmic process, we can glimpse the outline of Teilhard's *Phenomenon of Man.* In Teilhard's view the entire cosmos is on a journey to God — in a process of divinization which Teilhard calls Christogenesis. This involves stages similar to Bonaventure's: the material world, sensitive life, man and his further development towards the Omega. The divinization takes place through interiorization, from the *without* to the *within* to the Omega. Love is the force that energizes the process, leading to progressive union with Christ Omega.

In each case, Christ the center of the mandala activates the journey of the soul and the evolution of the universe. In both systems, Christ functions as the coincidence of cosmological opposites: the creator and the creature, divinity and matter. But he also functions as the cosmic center in whom all the opposites of the universe are centered and coincide. Thus as center of the mandala, Christ brings together the unity and diversity of creation. Christ is also the dynamic center, drawing both the human soul and the universe through the stages of a journey into union with the Father. In Teilhard, the Christocentric cosmic mandala requires the evolutionary process which he derived from his scientific research. This is a controversial aspect of Teilhard's system and one not shared by Bonaventure's medieval cosmology. Thus although there are interesting parallels in the two systems, there are important differences. It would be illuminating to make a detailed study of the way in which Christ the center affects the very structure and dynamics of the universe in each system.

At this point Bonaventure can enter into a larger dialogue that involves not only theologians, but secular culture as well. This is the dialogue over the future, which deals with such questions as: What is the relation of God to time? Of Christ to time? What is the theological meaning of the future? What roles does eschatology play in the Christian vision? This issue has arisen sharply both from theology itself and from secular culture. Biblical research over the twentieth century has drawn into focus the centrality of salvation history and of eschatology in the Christian vision. In secular culture the forces of change have accelerated so rapidly in the last ten years that modern man is bewildered and numbed by "future shock." On the horizon he sees a pending ecological crisis and the threat of nuclear destruction; at the same time advances in science and technology augur a creative, utopia-like future.

These issues were explored in a conference held in 1971 in New York City, with such theologians as Pannenberg, Moltmann, Metz, Cobb, Ogden, Mooney, and Hefner. The theme of the conference was Hope and the Future of Man, and it drew together in dialogue three strands of contemporary theology seriously concerned with the future: American process theologians, Teilhardians, and theologians of hope.[45] The discussion centered on alternate models of the future: How did each group conceive the future, and what basis of hope did it discern? Underlying many of the points discussed lay the basic issues of Christocentricity: What relation, if any, does Christ have to the structure of the universe and to time? Does the mystery of Christ, as Teilhard holds, have a physical effect upon the universe and direct the forces of evolution towards a successful outcome? Or is the cosmological structure more God-centered, as the process theologians maintain, with the result that the future is less affected by the mystery of Christ? From another perspective, is the mystery of Christ to be situated in the realm of history and not nature, as some eschatological theologians hold, liberating man from oppression rather than activating a cosmic process of growth?

At this point of the dialogue Bonaventure would have much to contribute. As one of the major articulators of Christocentricity in the history of theology, Bonaventure can enter the contemporary dialogue to clarify issues and to contribute towards solutions even in the highly-accelerated time world of the twentieth century. From a historical point of view, it is important to have Bonaventure's position recognized in the present discussion. For he came at a time when both Christocentricity and eschatology reached a new level of consciousness in Western culture. Francis' Christocentricity and Joachite eschatological consciousness were not only present in Bonaventure, but were synthesized within his system. Once again the key to this synthesis was the coincidence of opposites. Like many of his medieval contemporaries, Bonaventure had a heightened future-awareness; he was oriented to the age-to-come. But this did not erase Christ from the center of history. Through his Trinitarian model of Christ the middle person *(persona media)* of the Trinity, he was able to anchor his eschatological consciousness in Christ as the center of history. And through his Franciscan sense of the divine presence in the universe, he was able to see Christ as the center of the universe. Thus Christ is simultaneously the center of the universe and the center of history. What does this mean for secular culture? For hope for the future? Does it lead inevitably to Teilhard's position: that matter evolves towards spirit and ultimately toward Omega? Does it mean that the temporal process will contribute to the spiritual eschaton and that on the temporal level the process will have a successful outcome? These are indeed crucial questions. Although Bonaventure may not be able to give final answers, he does offer a resource whose richness cannot wisely be ignored at the present critical moment.

TILLICH AND RAHNER

Bonaventure can also enter into dialogue with the systems of Paul Tillich and Karl Rahner. There is a striking similarity on the general structural level among the systems of these three thinkers. This can be accounted for by the fact that all three give different expressions to the same generic Christian Neo-Platonic tradition which we identified in our first chapter. Although Rahner has been influenced in many ways by Thomism, his Trinitarian theology is self-consciously derived from the Greek Fathers. As in Tillich's thought, the Trinity provides the chief structural design of his system. Tillich's system emerges out of the tradition of German romanticism, which gives its own expression — often problematically — to Trinitarian themes of the Christian Neo-Platonic tradition. An in-depth analysis of Tillich's thought will show that his treatment of man and the human situation reflects the Trinitarian vestige and image tradition which Bonaventure shares from common Augustinian roots.[46] Since Bonaventure is the major representative of the Christian Neo-Platonic tradition in the high Middle Ages, it would be most enlightening to draw him into dialogue with two twentieth-century representatives of the same tradition.

For our present purposes, however, we wish to establish the dialogue not on the general Trinitarian structural level but on the issue of man's knowledge of God in subjectivity.[47] This is a major theme in twentieth century theology and one of the most experiential ways of encountering the coincidence of opposites. For man grasps within the finite structures of human subjectivity the presence of God as the unconditional ground of Being (Tillich) and the 'Whither' of transcendence (Rahner). Thus human subjectivity is the locus of the coincidence of the finite and the infinite. This approach to God through subjectivity was explored in a classical fashion by Augustine and has become associated with the mainstream Augustinian tradition in Western culture. In the case of Rahner, Tillich, and Bonaventure, this approach through subjectivity is integrated into the larger Trinitarian design of their systems.

Tillich was aware of Bonaventure's position and made the claim that his own thought was in continuity with the Augustinian-Franciscan tradition. In his important essay "The Two Types of the Philosophy of Religion," he refers specifically to Bonaventure:

> The Franciscan school of 13th century scholasticism, represented by Alexander of Hales, Bonaventure, and Matthew of Aquasparta developed the Augustinian solution into a doctrine of the principles of theology, and maintained, in spite of some Aristotelian influences, the ontological type of philosophy of religion. Their whole emphasis was on the immediacy of the knowledge of God. According to Bonaventure, "God is most truly present to the very soul and immediately knowable"; He is knowable in Himself without media as the one which is common to all. For He is the principle of knowledge, the first truth, in the light of which everything else is known, as Matthew says.[48]

Tillich proceeds to develop his own position in continuity with Bonaventure and the early Franciscan tradition. He gives his formulation of the principle that underlies this approach: "Man is immediately aware of something unconditional which is the prius of the separation and the interaction of subject and object, theoretically as well as practically."[49] In the light of this principle Tillich develops his own doctrine of man's knowledge of God, of symbolic expressions of God, and of ontological certainty and the risk of faith. At this point it would be important to bring Bonaventure into dialogue with Tillich in order to clarify issues and to situate Tillich in the proper historical context. Tillich has been under attack by critics from two camps — the Barthian and the Neo-Thomist — who criticize him from the presuppositions of their own positions. In many instances Tillich's statements are misread, for they are viewed from an alien perspective and not in the light of the Augustinian-Franciscan tradition in which he himself intended them to be viewed. It would be an enormous contribution to Tillich scholarship if he could be situated within the Bonaventurian tradition. This is not to say that Tillich's thought is identical with Bonaventure's. In fact, some of the most penetrating criticisms of Tillich can be leveled precisely from within the Bonaventurian tradition. But a balanced evaluation of Tillich and his contribution to the twentieth century must await a full-scale investigation of the Bonaventurian tradition and its relevance to issues of the twentieth century.[50]

Like Tillich, Karl Rahner approaches God through human subjectivity. Whereas Tillich moves within the Augustinian-Franciscan tradition, Rahner takes his point of departure from the Transcendental Thomism of Joseph Maréchal.[51] Situating itself within the Kantian critique, this Transcendental Thomism turns to subjectivity, where it finds an approach to God in the dynamism of the spirit towards the Infinite. In man's search for knowledge, we discern within the horizon of consciousness an openness to God, whom Rahner calls the 'Whither' of transcendence:

> We may fittingly suppose that man in his knowing and willing is a being of absolute and unlimited transcendence. All his spiritual acts, no matter what their object, are founded on this transcendence, which is a reaching forward of knowledge and will. . . . It is also obvious that the most primordial, underivative knowledge of God, which is the basis of all other knowledge of God, is given in the experience of transcendence, in so far as it contains, implicitly and unobjectivated, but irrecusably and inevitably, the 'Whither' of transcendence, which we call God.[52]

Although formulated in the context of the Kantian critique, Transcendental Thomism has roots in the Augustinian tradition.

It would be illuminating to explore these Augustinian roots by drawing Bonaventure into dialogue with Transcendental Thomism, since he is the chief witness in the high Middle Ages of the Augustinian approach to God through subjectivity. As we have seen previously, he extensively explored the Augustinian position in key texts in the *Itinerarium,* in the disputed questions *De scientia Christi* and *De mysterio Trinitatis* and in the sermon *Christus unus omnium magister.*[53] Such a dialogue with Bonaventure would have several advantages: It could clarify the epistemological issues, helping to sort out the distinctive Aristotelian and Augustinian elements in Transcendental Thomism. It would help relate Rahner and Tillich, thus clarifying the development of twentieth century theology. And it could throw light on the Transcendental Thomist interpretation of Thomas and on the movement of thought in the thirteenth century.

It is generally accepted that there was a major shift of consciousness in the thirteenth century as a result of the influx of Aristotelian philosophy. The earlier Augustinian way of subjectivity was supplanted by the outer way of empiricism, with the point of departure taken from the sense world. Thomas' epistemology is clearly rooted in the sense world and proceeds through the Aristotelian doctrine of abstraction. How much of the Augustinian epistemology does Thomas retain? This is a complex question and one that has been raised by the work of the Transcendental Thomists in the twentieth century: Maréchal, Rahner, and Lonergan. Over the past fifty years all three men have engaged in major interpretations of texts of Thomas.[54] Remaining within Thomas' generic Aristotelian-empirical orientation, they nevertheless discovered a dimension of subjectivity which opens up to the religious sphere. I am inclined to believe that their interpretation of Thomas has the support of the historical context. If the awareness of subjectivity constituted so deep a current in medieval culture, as the evidence drawn from Bonaventure indicates, then there is reason to expect that a dimension of subjectivity could be retained even with a shift of consciousness.

Since Transcendental Thomists have taken their point of departure from the Kantian critique, they run the risk of "reading into" the texts of Thomas a notion of subjectivity that is modern. However, one could take a medieval point of departure — from the Augustinian-Bonaventurian tradition — and arrive at the Transcendental Thomist position. Such an approach would proceed from the Augustinian-Bonaventurian awareness of the reflection of God as absolute Truth and absolute Good within the human spirit. This coincidence of God and the spirit is dynamic, drawing man to absolute Truth in all finite truths and to absolute Good in all finite goods. Open to this transcendent horizon, then, the human spirit in its very quest for knowledge would be seen as involved in a dynamic process of self-transcending striving towards the Good. And, of course, for Bonaventure the Good could not existentially draw man's spirit towards it unless it were already present deep within him as a coincidence of opposites — though at first with a veiled and not yet recognized presence. This transcendent horizon of the spirit's drive towards being, both as true and as good, is the clearly recognizable ancestor of Transcendental Thomism's "dynamism of the spirit towards the Infinite" (Maréchal, Rahner) and the "unrestricted drive to know" (Lonergan).

The claim of the Transcendental Thomists to have discovered a subjective dimension in Thomas calls for a serious restudying of the role of subjectivity in the thirteenth century — against the background of the Augustinian-Bonaventurian tradition.[55] There is work to be done in clarifying the precise relation of the alleged subjective dimension in Thomas with the subjectivity traditions that preceded him. Such an enterprise would involve serious collaboration among intellectual historians, Transcendental Thomists and Augustinian-Bonaventurian subjectivists. Such an exploration could lead to a significant re-interpretation of subjectivity in the thirteenth century and a significant reassessment of the thought of Thomas in the light of the Bonaventurian tradition.

Although twentieth century man stands at a far remove from

Bonaventure's medieval world, he can find in the Franciscan's thought a rich resource for dealing with crucial issues of our time. It is true that Bonaventure's Ptolemaic universe has been transformed by successive scientific revolutions — from Copernicus to Newton, Darwin, and Einstein. Yet the basic questions of God's relation to the universe remain, whether these be posed in terms of the new physics, as in Whitehead, or in the evolutionary perspective of Teilhard. The religious eschatology of the Middle Ages has been recast into secular concerns by liberation theology. And the journey into subjectivity, which Augustine opened for medieval man, must now encompass territory charted by Freud and the existentialists. Yet in all these areas Bonaventure has something to contribute — not merely in a generic way as a major philosopher and theologian, but in the sense that his specific concerns touch the heart of contemporary issues. His doctrine of the dynamic God, of the processive universe and of the path through subjectivity all have a contemporary ring. And in each area the coincidence of opposites illumines both the depth of his vision and its point of contact with twentieth century concerns.

These same resources, which Bonaventure offers, can come to the aid of the twentieth century Christian as he attempts to relate in a new way to the diverse strands of the Christian tradition and to the religions of the world. Although Bonaventure lived in the enclosed Christian world of medieval Europe, his Franciscan cosmic sense and love of diversity can help modern man in dealing with the religious pluralism of our time. As we will see in the following chapter, Bonaventure has significant contributions to make both to Christian unity and to the dialogue of world religions.

CHAPTER IX

Bonaventure and Ecumenism

HIS is a unique moment in the history of religion. As our communication network encircles the earth, men are being drawn ever closer together — across the barriers of space, time, and culture. In this process of convergence, the religions of the world are meeting each other in a new way. Within Christianity the ecumenical atmosphere has spread over the last fifty years: first within Protestantism, then to Orthodoxy, and after Vatican II, in a striking fashion, to Catholicism. Now a more complex phenomenon is emerging on the horizon. The great religions of the world — of the East and the West — are coming together in a way unprecedented in the history of mankind. They are meeting in an atmosphere not of conquest, imperialism, or syncretism, but of mutual respect, responsive listening, and sharing. What will the future of ecumenism be? We cannot predict. But we can direct our efforts to make the most of the present moment. This is a time of opportunity and challenge. The theologian must have at his disposal the full resources of his tradition; he must be sensitive to the religious experience of other men; and he must have the imagination to develop new perspectives and new speculative structures in order to contact philosophies and theologies that seem radically alien to his own. In searching for a ground of unity among religions, he must respect the unique and absolute claims of each tradition.

In this age of ecumenism, Bonaventure can be a rich resource both for Christian unity and for establishing ecumenical relations between Christianity and the other religions of the world. It should not be surprising to discover in Bonaventure a resource

269

for ecumenism; for his person, his life, and his thought all reflect an irenic and ecumenical spirit, a respect for diversity, and a desire to achieve authentic unity. Throughout his life, in the turbulent mid-thirteenth century, he worked for peace and reconciliation. As Minister General and as cardinal at the Council of Lyons, he displayed an ability to reconcile opposites, bringing together disparate groups in a larger unity. This ability to reconcile opposites is seen also in his thought with its logic of the coincidence of opposites. In his theological synthesis, he integrated elements which many other thinkers have found incompatible: scholastic logic and mystical intuition, Aristotelian abstractionism and Platonic innatism, the Greek predilection for the universal and the Franciscan preoccupation with the individual.

In its subsequent history, Bonaventure's tradition has provided resources for ecumenism. For example, Nicholas of Cusa is similar to Bonaventure not only through the coincidence of opposites and the structure of his thought, but also in his ecumenical spirit and in his career as a cardinal in the service of the Church. Nicholas was heir to the same Christian Neo-Platonic tradition as Bonaventure and was directly influenced by Bonaventure's writings, perhaps in his development of the coincidence of opposites.[1] Just as Bonaventure worked for the union of the Greeks and the Latins at the Council of Lyons, so Nicholas worked for their reunion at the Council of Florence. Living in the expanding world of the early Renaissance, Nicholas extended his speculative theology farther into the area of ecumenism than Bonaventure did. In his *De pace fidei*, Nicholas developed a theory of ecumenism that encompassed Christians, Jews, and Muslims.[2] This same speculative tradition that produced such ecumenical spirits as Bonaventure and Nicholas can produce in our day a new flowering of ecumenical theology. In the expanding vision of the world, which has progressed from Bonaventure's closed Europe through the enlarged horizons of Nicholas' Renaissance to our own sense of a global community, this tradition can continue to be a major resource in developing a theory of global ecumenism through its logic of the coincidence of opposites and its ideal of diversity in unity.

THEOLOGY'S ECUMENICAL TASK

In the area of ecumenism, the contemporary theologian faces a threefold task: He must enlarge his theological horizons in order to become sensitive to the diverse strands of the Christian tradition; secondly, he must develop a speculative theological model that will encompass this diversity in an authentic unity; thirdly, he must discover new ways to relate Christianity to world religions. This threefold task must focus on the mystery of Christ, since paradoxically Christ is both the primary source of unity and the major obstacle to unity. For Christians Christ is the source of their identity, consequently the basis of any unity that exists or that might emerge. However, precisely because the mystery of Christ is so profound and multidimensional, it has produced diversity among Christians as well as unity. In the history of Christianity, different traditions have grounded their identity in diverse aspects of the mystery of Christ. Furthermore, the mystery of Christ is the ultimate root of the separation of Christianity from other religions. The more Christians become united among themselves by becoming conscious of their common identity in Christ, by that very fact they tend to separate themselves from other religions.

Because the mystery of Christ is the central resource and the central problem of ecumenism, I will focus on Bonaventure's Christology, seen from the standpoint of the coincidence of opposites. I will look upon his Christology from three points of view corresponding to the threefold task outlined above. I will view his Christology (1) as integrating some of the major strands of the Christian tradition; (2) as providing speculative tools that will help us develop a theology of Christian ecumenism; (3) as offering resources for the construction of a larger theology of ecumenism that will encompass Christianity and world religions. In each case the coincidence of opposites will be the key to unlock the ecumenical resources of Bonaventure's thought.

BONAVENTURE'S COMPREHENSIVE CHRISTOLOGY

Bonaventure's Christology is comprehensive, integrating major strands of the tradition's consciousness of the mystery of Christ. It comes at a pivotal moment in Christian history, at a time when the traditions of the Greek East and the Latin West were not yet radically broken apart. Yet the distinctly Western devotion to the humanity of Christ had already flowered within the early Franciscan movement, and the seeds of later Protestant Christologies were already sown. Granted Bonaventure's genius for integration, it is not surprising that he responded to this pivotal moment by producing one of the most comprehensive Christologies in Christian history. In the twentieth century, Catholics, Orthodox, and Protestants can look back to Bonaventure's Christology and find there distinctive aspects of their own consciousness of the mystery of Christ. Yet in Bonaventure they can see these distinctive aspects integrated into a unified whole, thus providing a basis for ecumenical union within the larger mystery of Christ.

The foundation of Bonaventure's Christology lies in his doctrine of the Logos, which is developed extensively and systematically throughout his writings.[3] This Logos Christology has three levels: in the Trinity, in creation, and in the soul's illumination and mystical union. Because the divinity is absolutely self-diffusive, the Father must generate the Son as his Image and Word. In generating the Son, the Father produces in the Son the archetypes of all that he can make. The Son is thus the Art of the Father, through whom all things are created and to whom they all reflect back as to their Exemplar. Finally, as Word and Truth, the Son illumines the minds of men when they know with certitude; and on the mystical level, he is the bridegroom of the soul, bringing the soul to union with the Father.

Bonaventure's Logos Christology reflects the distinctive Christology of the Greek Fathers, which is derived from the Alexandrian

school and which has formed the continuing tradition of the
Orthodox Church. The roots of Bonaventure's Logos Christology
actually go back to the Greek Fathers through the Pseudo-Dionysius and John Scotus Erigena. Another source, of course, is Augus-
tine, whose own Logos Christology has its roots in the common
Christian Neo-Platonism shared by him and the Greek Fathers.
On the level of the Trinity and creation, Bonaventure's Logos
Christology has striking similarities with that of Athanasius and
the Cappadocians. Although Bonaventure's illumination theory is
derived from Augustine, it has its counterpart in the Greek world.
On this point it would be fruitful to compare the treatise on
Christ as *Paidagogos* of Clement of Alexandria with Bonaventure's
Christus unus omnium magister. Bonaventure's Logos mysticism
clearly reflects Origen's classical commentary on the Canticle of
Canticles.[4]

Bonaventure's Christology, then, reflects the distinctive Logos
Christology of the first millenium of Christian theology, both in
the East and in the West. However, coming as it does at a pivotal
point in history, it also reflects the distinctive Christology of the
next millenium in the West, among both Catholics and Protestants; for Bonaventure integrates into his Logos Christology the
characteristic Western devotion to Christ's humanity, his passion
and death. Rooted in the West's sense of the particular and the
historical, this devotion to Christ's humanity was finding expression during the high Middle Ages in various sectors of life. It
reached a climax in Francis of Assisi, whose life-style was a radical
imitation of Christ's and whose stigmata embodied the two aspects
of this devotion: identification with the concrete particularities
of Christ's humanity and participation in his suffering and death.

Bonaventure expressed this devotion in both his speculative
and mystical theology. He laid the foundation in the speculative
theology of the Incarnation in his *Commentary on the Sentences*
and the *Breviloquium*; and he developed the distinctive Franciscan
themes in such treatises as the *Itinerarium*, the *Tree of Life*, and
the biographies of Francis.[5] His speculative soteriology focuses

on the passion and death of Christ, incorporating the satisfaction theory of Anselm, which expressed the medieval world's sense of the need for redemption from guilt and which remained the dominant theme in the Reformation and into the twentieth century in both Protestant and Catholic circles.[6] In keeping with the Western tradition, Bonaventure did not emphasize the resurrection as much as the Greeks did. However, his soteriology has more of an implicit resurrectional dimension than many other Western Christologies, since it is grounded on the theme of the reform (*reformatio*) of the image of God. Derived from Augustine, this theme in Bonaventure reflects the divinization motif of the Greek Fathers. For Bonaventure the redemption involves not merely a liberation from the guilt of sin, but a turning of the image to its Exemplar, the Word, which involves a transformation and divinization that participate in the mystery of the resurrection.[7]

Bonaventure's Christology is crowned by his doctrine of Christocentricity. In the first of the *Collationes in Hexaemeron,* he develops the theme of Christ the center of all the sciences: metaphysics, physics, mathematics, logic, ethics, politics, and theology.[8] Bonaventure describes Christ as the center of the Trinity, the *medium* between the divinity and creation, the illumination of men's minds, as the center of the cosmos and the redeemer who overcomes the forces of evil and transforms death into life and leads the soul back to unity with the Father. Thus Christ is the center of human existence, of the universe, and of salvation history. Bonaventure's Christocentricity has resonance in the East in the theology of Maximus the Confessor and in such diverse contemporary Western theologies as that of Barth, Bonhoeffer, and Teilhard de Chardin. In Bonaventure's Christocentricity all the lines of his thought converge and reach their climax, for he uses the notion of Christ the center to integrate into a unified whole all the different strands of his comprehensive Christology.

A Resource for Speculative Theology

Having described Bonaventure's comprehensive Christology,

I will now examine it as a resource for a speculative theology of ecumenism, first within Christianity and then in relation to world religions. In this section I will not limit myself to an exposition or interpretation of Bonaventure, but will draw material from him, attempt to complete his system and develop speculative possibilities that extend beyond the horizons of his thought.

As a basis for a speculative theology of ecumenism, we can draw from Bonaventure the notion of *the fullness of the mystery of Christ*. It is true that he did not develop this notion in the precise sense in which I am taking it, but it is suggested by the comprehensive nature of his Christology and is thoroughly compatible with his system. The full mystery of Christ would be seen as encompassing the many aspects integrated into Bonaventure's system, and leaving open the possibility of other aspects in addition to these. We would then see that the various Christian traditions have been sensitive to different aspects of the total mystery of Christ. Since each aspect is related to the total mystery as microcosm to macrocosm, then in grasping one aspect of these traditions, to some extent, we have grasped the whole. Hence Orthodox, Protestants, and Catholics can relate to those aspects that ground their identity, and through these participate in the full mystery of Christ. Through ecumenical convergence, they can come to a deeper sharing in aspects of the mystery that have been submerged in their own traditions, but cultivated in others.

What are the speculative roots of this conception in Bonaventure's system? Foundational in his system — and in the early Franciscan milieu — is the awareness of God's fecundity and of the expression of this fecundity in creation. This stands at the base of the Franciscan joy in creation, in diversity and in the value of each individual thing, no matter how apparently insignificant. Theologically, Bonaventure describes the Father as the *fontalis plenitudo,* whose fullness expresses itself in the generation of the Son and the spiration of the Spirit. This notion of *fontalitas* and *plenitudo,* Bonaventure applies to the Father and to the act of creation.[9] He also speaks of the fullness of Christ's wisdom, grace, and merit; and in the *Apologia pauperum* he uses the notion of Christ's fullness as a basis for the diversity of forms of the Christian life.[10] Just as the plenitude of the Eternal Word is expressed in the diversity of creatures, so the plenitude of the incarnate Word is mirrored in the different ways of Christian perfection. This clearly suggests an application to ecumenism, based on the principle that Christ is the fullness of the expression of the Father: the Father expresses himself in the Son and through the Son in creation. Furthermore, the divine fecundity achieves an unsurpassable expression in the Incarnation, since in Christ the eternal is expressed in time, the highest in the lowest, the beginning in the end.[11]

Here the notions of fullness and expression are linked with the logic of the coincidence of opposites and the concept of Christ the center. The norm for fullness is the expression by way of the union of opposites through perfect centering. This norm is realized in an unsurpassable way in Christ, in whom opposites are joined as in a universal center. Hence we can speak of the mystery of Christ expressing in an unsurpassable way the unsurpassable *fontalis plenitudo* of the Father. This means, then, that in its fullness the mystery of Christ touches all levels of the universe, all dimensions of human experience, and the entire sweep of history. In Christ, the greatest coincidence of opposites, all things are drawn together as to their center.

If we apply this complex model to the sphere of Christian ecumenism, we can say that all authentic Christian traditions are related to Christ as to their center and through Christocentricity are related to the fullness of the mystery of Christ. This establishes their identity as Christian and is the root of their unity. Because of the richness and complexity of the full mystery of Christ, these traditions have realized different aspects of the mystery: for example, Christ as Logos, as incarnate in history, in his passion or resurrection. This accounts, at least in part, for the diversity of traditions. In an ecumenical context, these traditions can discover their common center in Christ and recognize that their authentic diversity is a reflection of the larger mystery in which they all participate. By sharing their diversity, while rooted in a common center, each can enter more fully into the mystery of Christ and its progressive realization in history.

BONAVENTURE AND WORLD RELIGIONS

Having seen Bonaventure as a resource for Christian ecumenism, we move now to a larger horizon and ask the question: What can Bonaventure contribute to the dialogue of world religions? I believe that he provides special resources both from a historical and a contemporary perspective. He can help us understand the Christian tradition in its richness and at a decisive period in the shaping of Western culture. Because of his awareness of the depth and nuances of religious experience, he can make us sensitive to the dimension of religious experience in other traditions. Because of the complexity of his thought — his blending of philosophy, theology, and mysticism — he can provide resources for understanding other traditions and for formulating the uniqueness of the Christian claim. And he can offer speculative material for building bridges between Christianity and even the most diverse traditions.

From a historical perspective, Bonaventure and his time deserve special study in the light of the convergence of world religions. The thirteenth century witnessed an extraordinary confluence of major strands of Western religion and philosophy. Christianity, Judaism, and Islam were caught not only in tension among themselves, but in a common struggle with Greek philosophy and science. Bonaventure's thought represents one of the major attempts to deal with these tensions. Through Bonaventure and the struggles of his day, we can observe a major formative period in the history of world religions. A re-examination, then, of the thirteenth century in the light of the history of world religions would be enormously fruitful at the present time.

From another standpoint, Bonaventure's thought can be a speculative resource at the present time. His vision is distinctively

Christian; for he not only treats the mysteries of the Trinity and Christ extensively and systematically, but he makes them the central and architectonic elements of his synthesis. The result is a world view that is unmistakably Christian. Yet at the same time, his thought has a universal quality that opens to a broad ecumenism. It is this twofold aspect of Bonaventure's thought which I believe is its most valuable quality at the present time and which I would like to explore here. I will treat three areas, indicating how contemporary writers have used Bonaventure's thought either explicitly or implicitly in their approach to world religions. Each area involves a different type of the coincidence of opposites which we have previously studied: (1) the coincidence of God and the world in Bonaventure's broad notion of revelation, as employed by Robley Whitson; (2) the coincidence of opposites in Bonaventure's doctrine of the Trinity as a way into Buddhism and Hinduism, as suggested by the approach of Raymond Panikkar; and (3) the coincidence of opposites in Bonaventure's notion of Christ the center as a point of contact with the Tantric traditions of Hinduism and Buddhism and as a speculative resource for developing a Christian theology of world religions.

REVELATION AND EXPERIENCE

Our first area of study is Bonaventure's doctrine of revelation. It is precisely here that we find the basis of his broad ecumenism. Bonaventure grounds his doctrine of revelation in the Trinity itself: in the Father's self-diffusive expression of the Son. This Trinitarian expressionism is the basis for the doctrine of exemplarism, since in expressing himself in the Son, the Father produces in the Son all that he can make. Thus the Son is the exemplar of creation; as the Son expresses the Father, so the world expresses the Son. Consequently, theophany is fundamental to the structure of the universe; it is coextensive with creation and human experience and constitutes the deepest metaphysical and theological dimension of reality. Thus God is manifested throughout the cosmos, and in the multiple dimensions of human ex-

perience. Therefore through the coincidence of opposites Bonaventure can find the reflection of the Trinity in the material universe, in the human psyche, and in man's productive activity.[12]
It is this aspect of Bonaventure's vision that Robley Whitson has
taken up in his book *The Coming Convergence of World Religions.* In his chapter entitled "The Revelational in Religion," he
cites Bonaventure explicitly; in fact he takes Bonaventure as his
major source, both as a historical witness to a broad ecumenical
attitude within Christianity and as a resource for a contemporary
theologian to establish connections with the great traditions of
the world.[13]

One of the problems of linking Christianity with Oriental religions is the concept of revelation. Judaism, Christianity, and
Islam claim to have received a revelation from God which is embodied in their sacred books: the Bible and the Koran. On the
basis of this revelation they distinguish themselves from other
religions, and on this basis scholars of comparative religion have
distinguished between revelational and non-revelational religions.
By drawing from Bonaventure, Whitson re-examines this issue.
Although Bonaventure gives a special place to the book of Scripture, he does not isolate it from the book of creation or the book
of life. The book of Scripture is to be read in the larger context
of the theophanic universe. The entire universe and human experience are basically revelational; hence the book of Scripture
is organically related to the book of creation. Whitson cites texts
from Bonaventure's disputed questions *De mysterio Trinitatis,*
indicating the theophanic nature of the universe through the
metaphor of the book. Through the book of creation, the book
of Scripture, and the book of life, the Trinity is revealed:

> . . . the foundation of the whole Christian faith . . . has a triple
> testimony . . . considered from the standpoint of three books: the
> book of creation, the book of scripture and the book of life . . .
> The book of creation . . . first shown to our senses gives a twofold
> testimony . . . For every creature is either a vestige only, of God such
> as are corporeal natures, or also an image of God as are intellectual
> creatures.[14]

Although this double testimony of the book of creation was adequate for man in his state prior to sin, the book of creation has become obscured and the eye of man has been clouded by sin. So divine providence has given the testimony of a second book, the book of Scripture. In addition to the book of creation and the book of Scripture, Bonaventure calls attention to the testimony of the book of life:

> But since "not all obey the Gospel," and this truth [that is, the doctrine of the Trinity] is above reason, therefore Divine Wisdom provided an eternal testimony, which indeed is the book of life. Now this book of life through itself and in itself explicitly and expressly gives irresistible testimony . . . to those who with face unveiled see God in the homeland [that is, at the completion of man's journey of return to God], but on the way it gives testimony according to the influence of the light which the soul is capable of in the wayfarer's state . . . It enlightens in two ways, namely, through an innate light, and through an infused light . . .[15]

Whitson takes Bonaventure's notion of the book of life and applies it to human experience. For Whitson, the book of life refers not directly to the Son in the Trinity, but to human experience as it reflects God. Although this is a non-technical use of the Bonaventurian term, I believe that it is quite compatible with Bonaventure's vision; for it expresses the theophanic nature of human experience. In the light of an expanded notion of revelation derived from Bonaventure, Whitson examines the Buddha's enlightenment experience and texts from Confucianism and reads them as revelational. In this way he is able to see as revelational two religious traditions which are usually placed at the opposite pole from the revelational religions of Judaism, Christianity, and Islam. Whitson's use of Bonaventure suggests that the latter's thought can provide a large speculative framework for two positions current among Christian theologians: that non-Christians are saved not in spite of but through their religions; and that Christianity will not understand fully its own revelation until it sees it in the light of the religious experience of all men.

TRINITARIAN MODEL

While Whitson sees human experience as revelational, Raymond Panikkar believes that one must distinguish various forms of religious experience. Whereas Whitson draws from Bonaventure's doctrine of the coincidence of God and the world, Panikkar approaches the problem through a Trinitarian model of the coincidence of unity and diversity. In his book *The Trinity and the Religious Experience of Man,* he examines three types of religious experience which correspond to three aspects of the divinity.[16] Found throughout the world, these three types of religious experience can be understood in the light of the Christian doctrine of the Trinity. By using this Trinitarian approach to world religions, Panikkar is able to relate Christianity to Buddhism and Hinduism at points where these traditions differ most widely from Christianity.

Stated very briefly, Panikkar's position focuses on silence, speech, and unity. The deep religious experience of silence he relates to the Father in the Trinity and to the Buddhist experience of nirvana. Speech is related to the Son, for the Son is the expression, the Word and the Image of the Father. In this perspective, Judaism, Christianity, and Islam can be seen as religions of the word; for it is in and through the word that God communicates to man. While these religions reach their goal in and through the word of God, the Buddhist moves to the depth of silence by negating the way of the word, of thought, of logos. This is seen very graphically in the techniques of Zen Buddhism. While the Buddhist negates the word to achieve silence and the Christian moves through the Word to the Father, the advaitan Hindu experiences the unity of himself and the Absolute. This experience of undifferentiated unity is the third element in Panikkar's Trinitarian approach. This experience of unity or immanence Panikkar relates to the Spirit in the Trinity, for the Spirit is the union of the Father and the Son. Thus in Panikkar's perspective, Buddhism can be called the religion of the Father; Judaism, Christianity, and Islam the religion of the Son; and advaitan Hinduism the religion of the Spirit.

Panikkar's approach through the Trinity provides a model for dialogue which allows for pluralism while affirming unity. The Christian can relate to the Buddhist as one who has contacted the silence of the Father and to the advaitan Hindu as one who has experienced the mystery of the unifying Spirit. In this way, the Christian can respond positively to the other traditions without having to reduce them to his own; rather he can accept difference in unity according to a Trinitarian model.

In developing his approach, Panikkar situates himself in the Bonaventurian tradition, stating: "We would like here to approach the Trinitarian mystery in a more direct way following up the more dynamic thrust of the Greek patristic tradition and the Latin Bonaventurian scholastic."[17] Panikkar not only reflects the Bonaventurian tradition but extends it to a new level. In an article on Panikkar's position,[18] I have argued that his Trinitarian approach harmonizes with the classical vestige tradition and brings this tradition into the realm of universal religious experience. Following Augustine, Bonaventure saw the reflection of the Trinity in the material world and in the psyche. Christian theologians have also seen the reflection of the Trinity in the Old Testament and in the triads of Greek philosophy. It is not surprising, then, that a contemporary theologian like Panikkar — at a time when the religions of the world are converging — should find a reflection of the Trinity in the divergent strands of man's religious experience as these have developed in their highest forms. In order to grasp the significance of Panikkar's approach, I believe that one should situate it within the tradition of Trinitarian theology of which Bonaventure is one of the foremost spokesmen. Hence Bonaventure offers rich resources here, not only to support Panikkar's approach from the Christian tradition, but also to provide technical clarification for his distinctive mode of theological thinking.[19]

Panikkar's thought calls for a radical re-examination of the

Christian doctrine of the Trinity, since his ecumenical vestige doctrine includes elements that have not been formally thematized by the Christian tradition. For example, he describes the Father as silence rather than power. The question arises: Is Panikkar's position contrary to the Christian tradition? Or is the convergence of religions bringing to light a dimension of the Trinitarian mystery that has been latent in the past? Bonaventure's thought can be of great assistance here. In addition to his explicit vestige doctrine, Bonaventure has a systematic treatment of the Father. In both cases, the Father is conceived as power: In the power, wisdom, and goodness of creation, the Father is reflected in power; in the Trinity Bonaventure describes the Father as *fontalis plenitudo,* the fecund source of the generation of the Son. Is there in Bonaventure a hint of the silence of the Father? I believe there is. Bonaventure acknowledges that *innascibilitas* and *paternitas* (unbegottenness and paternity) both apply to the Father, and he claims that *innascibilitas* is the root of *paternitas.*[20] If we make explicit the logic of the coincidence of opposites which permeates Bonaventure's system and apply this logic to the Father, then we can see that the element of power in *paternitas* is balanced by silence; hence we can interpret *innascibilitas* as silence.[21]

This leads us to re-examine the seventh chapter of the *Itinerarium.* Does the seventh chapter express a type of apophatism in which all finite modes of thought are transcended in the mystical experience? Certainly this is the case. But does it also suggest a second level of apophatism, in which one enters into that aspect of the divinity which Panikkar describes as the silence of the Father? I believe that there is evidence for this interpretation, which I will only briefly summarize here.[22] Note that the seventh chapter comes immediately after Bonaventure's treatment of the Trinity, which focuses on the Father as the source of the self-diffusiveness of the good in the Trinitarian processions. In the light of the logic of the coincidence of opposites and the interpretation of *paternitas* and *innascibilitas* given above, it would not be an exaggeration to read Bonaventure's quotations from the

Pseudo-Dionysius, with their images of darkness and silence, as referring to the silence of the Father.[23] In view of this, Bonaventure's concluding statement is especially suggestive:

> Let us, then, die and enter into this darkness. Let us silence all our care, our desires and our imaginings. With Christ crucified, let us pass "out of this world to the Father," so that, when the Father is shown to us, we may say with Philip: "It is enough for us."[24]

CHRIST AND WORLD RELIGIONS

The Christian, then, can approach world religions, as Whitson does, through Bonaventure's notion of cosmic revelation; and with Panikkar he can establish rapport with diverse traditions in the light of the Trinity. But there still remains the problem of Christ. While revelation and the Trinity are modes of universalizing the Christian perspective, the doctrine of Christ particularizes and differentiates. Ultimately it is Christ who separates Christianity from other religions. This is undoubtedly the most complex problem facing the Christian in the dialogue of world religions. Both Whitson and Panikkar acknowledge this problem and explore it. Bonaventure offers assistance here in two ways. First, he is quintessentially Christian; for him Christ is the center of the universe, of history, of human existence, of revelation. His Christology is both universalized and particularized. He blends the universalizing Logos Christology of the Greek Fathers with the particularizing incarnational Christology of the West. Hence, one can turn to Bonaventure for a richly articulated doctrine of Christ which is distinctively Christian to the core.

Paradoxically it is Bonaventure's notion of Christ the center that can open new ecumenical possibilities for Christology. If the notion of Christ the center is examined in the context of Mircea Eliade's research into primitive religions, of Carl Jung's research into the human psyche, and Giuseppe Tucci's research into the mandala in Hinduism and Buddhism, then we may be able to view incarnational Christology in a more ecumenical perspective.[25] In Chapter Six on the mandala, we have used this research in order to throw light on Bonaventure's notion of Christ the center.[26] In our present context we can see how Bonaventure's particularist Christology can be universalized in the light of this research, through the extensive presence of the symbol of the center in the history of religions. According to Eliade, the category of the center is widespread in primitive belief and ritual; according to Jung, the center can symbolize the Self, which is the root, organizing principle, and religious core of the psyche. Accepting the general lines of Jung's position, Tucci explores the meaning of the center in the use of the mandala in Oriental religions. The mandala design — with a circle or square and prominent center — is used in the Tantric traditions of Hinduism and Buddhism for meditation. The fact that the category of the center is found throughout the world and throughout history indicates a basis for ecumenism, even through incarnational Christology. Many complex problems remain. How is Christ related to the center of the Buddhist and Hindu mandalas and to the archetype of the Self as studied by Jung? If this is a fruitful area of investigation — as several fields of research have suggested — then among Christian theologians Bonaventure has much to offer since, as I have argued, the mandala structure is basic to his thought, with its coincidence of opposites and Christ as its center.

The notion of the center can be universalized by being found throughout the world and throughout the religious history of mankind. But there is another way in which it can be universalized: by providing a speculative framework for the Christian to relate to world religions. In this perspective, Christ in his particularity is seen as the cosmic center in whom a wide diversity is centered as in a coincidence of opposites. The diversity does not have to be reduced to a unity, as it would be in a universal Logos Christology. And it does not have to be maintained at the expense of unity, as it would be in a sheer particularist Christology. Rather diversity can be maintained precisely in its distinctiveness, but at the same time it can be related to the unity of the particularist center.

In order to establish the pattern of diversity, I will take my point of departure from the book by R. C. Zaehner, *Christianity and Other Religions*.[27] Here Zaehner proposes the thesis that Christianity integrates opposites which remain separated in other world religions. For example, Islam affirms the divine transcendence to the exclusion of immanence; and certain Hindu traditions affirm immanence to the exclusion of transcendence. However, in its doctrine of Christ, Christianity affirms the union of the transcendent and the immanent. Zaehner examines other religions and interprets them according to this model of polarities.

We can apply Bonaventure's Christological model to this description of the polarities in man's religious experience. For Bonaventure, Christ is the coincidence of opposites uniting the polarities of immanence and transcendence, and he is also the universal center. The entire spatio-temporal cosmos is centered on Christ and all men are related to him as the cosmic center. Thus the very particularist element in Christianity is universalized, not by being present in a universal way in all things and all people, but by being the cosmic center to which all is related. Thus for the fullness of the mystery of Christ we must look to the entire cosmos. Only in the diversity of the religions of the world is the fullness of the mystery of Christ revealed. Can we, then, call all men anonymous Christians? In a certain sense, yes; but this might be misleading. For they are related to Christ, the cosmic center, precisely by their differences, that is, by their cultivation of one of the poles of opposites that are united in Christ. In their case, it is only in the fullness of the mystery of Christ that their relation to Christ the cosmic center is discernible.

If one views the mystery of Christ through Bonaventure's perspective and sees Christ as the universal cosmic center, then he can see the rich diversity of religious traditions centered ultimately on Christ, but not necessarily immediately connected to him through a direct historical line. I must state here that this is intended as a Christian's theology of ecumenism and would not be an appropriate perspective for, say, a Buddhist's theology of ecumenism. In this Christian perspective, one can maintain his absolute claim about the particularity and uniqueness of Christ and yet, through Christ the center, encompass the diversity of man's religious experience.

We see, then, that in three major areas Bonaventure's thought is a rich resource for advancing the dialogue of world religions: in the doctrine of revelation, of the Trinity, and Christology. In each area, the coincidence of opposites operates in a different way, providing a rich complex of models of unity and diversity. The encounter between Bonaventure and world religions can have reciprocal advantages; for it can enhance our understanding of Bonaventure by enlarging our horizons, by forcing us to go deeper into his thought and by leading us to make explicit what was only implicit. This deeper understanding of Bonaventure can, in turn, shed new light on the Christian tradition not only in its past and present, but also in its future possibilities. As mankind moves forward toward the convergence of world religions, the journey can be clarified in many ways by the *itinerarium* which Bonaventure provides.

Our own journey into Bonaventure's thought has led us deeply into his vision. Guided by the coincidence of opposites, we have explored the major structural elements of his system: the Trinity, God's presence in creation, Christ the center. Drawn into the Bonaventurian universe through the coincidence of opposites, we can marvel at its richness, its complexity, and its fullness. In this vision we find ourselves not stranded in the Middle Ages but thrust into the heart of the problems of today and tomorrow. Having penetrated deeply into the mystery of man and God, Bonaventure is alive to the crucial issues of the twentieth century. Because he makes available the height, the length, the breadth, and the depth of the Christian religious experience, he can lead us towards Christian unity and draw us into the dialogue of world religions. Bonaventure has been true to his origins — to the spirit of Francis. He has grasped Francis' sense of the richness of God, of God's nearness to the world, of the importance of each creature,

and of the centrality of Christ. By being true to his origins, Bonaventure has become relevant to our day, and I venture to predict,
he will be relevant to the future as well.

NOTES

CHAPTER I

[1] Concerning the year of Bonaventure's birth, cf. below, p. 31.

[2] *S. Bonaventurae opera omnia*, edita studio et cura pp. Collegii a S. Bonaventura (Florentina, ad Claras Aquas, Quaracchi: 1882-1902), X volumina. Unless otherwise indicated, all references to Bonaventure's works will be to this critical edition, with the volume references given in parentheses. Cf. *Itin*. (V, 295-313); *Hexaem*. (V, 329-449).

[3] *Comm. Eccl.* (VI, 3-103); *Comm. Jn.* (VI, 239-530); *Comm. Lc.* (VII, 1-604); *Comm. Sp.* (VI, 107-233); *I, II, III, IV Sent.* (I-IV); *M. Trin.* (V, 45-115); *Sc. Chr.* (V, 3-43); *Perf. ev.* (V, 117-198); *Brevil.* (V, 201-291).

[4] Cf. n. 2, above. For a recent re-evaluation of the critical edition, cf. Ignatius Brady, "The *Opera Omnia* of Saint Bonaventure Revisited," in *Proceedings of the American Catholic Philosophical Association*, 48 (1974), 295-304.

[5] Cf. Étienne Gilson's treatment of this issue in his *The Philosophy of St. Bonaventure*, trans. Dom Illtyd Trethowan and Frank J. Sheed (Paterson, N.J.: St. Anthony Guild Press, 1965), pp. 3, 451, n. 7; cf. also Brady, *op cit.*, 296-297; cf. Leo XIII's approval of the scholia as showing the harmony of doctrine between Thomas and Bonaventure in his letter of Dec. 13, 1885 to the Franciscan Minister General published in Vol. III of the Quaracchi edition (III, i-ii).

[6] Étienne Gilson, *La philosophie de Saint Bonaventure* (Paris: Vrin, 1924); for English translation, cf. n. 5, above.

[7] *Ibid.*, p. 472; English translation by Frank J. Sheed, *op. cit.*, p. 448.

[8] My chief articles dealing with the *coincidentia oppositorum* in Bonaventure's thought are the following: "La 'Coincidentia Oppositorum' dans la théologie de Bonaventure," in *Actes du Colloque Saint Bonaventure, 9-12 septembre 1968, Orsay*, in *Études franciscaines*, 18 (Supplément annuel, 1968), 15-31; English version printed in *The Cord*, 20 (1970), 260-269, 307-314; "The Coincidence of Opposites in the Christology of Saint Bonaventure," *Franciscan Studies*, 28 (1968), 27-45; "Mandala Symbolism in the Theology of Bonaventure," *University of Toronto Quarterly*, 40 (1971), 185-201; "Bonaventure and Contemporary Thought," *The Cord*, 25 (1975), 68-78; the contents of these articles have been incorporated into the present book.

[9] Jacques Guy Bougerol, *Introduction to the Works of Bonaventure*, trans. José de Vinck (Paterson, N.J.: St. Anthony Guild Press, 1964); in addition to the references in n. 34 to Chapter Two, p. 294, below, cf. especially "St. Bonaventure et saint Bernard," *Antonianum*, 46 (1971), 3-79; "S. Bonaventure et Guillaume de Saint-Thierry," *Antonianum*, 46 (1971), 298-321; "S. Bonaventure et saint Anselme," *Antonianum*, 47 (1972), 333-361.

[10] Ignatius Brady, *op. cit.*; cf. also "The Writings of Saint Bonaventure Regarding the Franciscan Order," in *Atti del Congresso Internationale per il VII Centenario di San Bonaventura da Bagnoregio, Roma, 19-26 settembre 1974*, Vol. I, ed. A. Pompei (Roma: Pontificia Facolta Teologica "San Bonaventura," 1976), 89-112.

[11] Joseph Ratzinger, *The Theology of History in St. Bonaventure*, trans. Zachary Hayes (Chicago: Franciscan Herald Press, 1971).

¹² John Quinn, *The Historical Constitution of St. Bonaventure's Philosophy* (Toronto: Pontifical Institute of Medieval Studies, 1973).

¹³ *Hexaem.*, I, n. 12-17 (V, 331-332).

¹⁴ Zachary Hayes, "Christology and Metaphysics in the Thought of Saint Bonaventure," paper delivered at the University of Chicago, November 20, 1974. For other works of Hayes, cf. *The General Doctrine of Creation in the Thirteenth Century with Special Emphasis on Matthew of Aquasparta* (Munich: Schöningh, 1964); *What Manner of Man? Sermons on Christ by St. Bonaventure*, translation with introduction and commentary (Chicago: Franciscan Herald Press, 1974); "Toward a Philosophy of Education in the Spirit of St. Bonaventure" and "Revelation in Christ," in *Proceedings of the Seventh Centenary Celebration of the Death of Saint Bonaventure* (St. Bonaventure, N.Y.: St. Bonaventure University, 1975), pp. 9-27, 29-43.

¹⁵ *Itin.*, c. 6, n. 2 (V, 310-311); *Hexaem.*, I (V, 329-335).

¹⁶ *Itin.*, c. 6, n. 2 (V, 310-311); cf. below, pp. 101-107.

¹⁷ Cf. Bonaventure's treatment of knowledge of God's existence and the Trinity in *M. Trin.*, q. 1, a. 1-2 (V, 45-58).

¹⁸ Cf. Thomas Aquinas, *Summa theologiae*, I, q. 1.

¹⁹ Paul Tillich, *Systematic Theology*, Vol. I (Chicago: The University of Chicago Press, 1951), 59-66; Pierre Teilhard de Chardin, *The Phenomenon of Man* (New York: Harper and Row, 1965), esp. pp. 291-299.

²⁰ Cf. Anselm, *Epistola de incarnatione Verbi*, c. 4; *Monologion*, prol.; *Cur Deus Homo*, praef.; Richard of St. Victor, *De Trinitate*, I, c. 3-5. On the method of seeking *rationes necessariae* in Richard of St. Victor, cf. my article, "A Theology of Interpersonal Relations," *Thought*, 45 (1970), 61-65. On this method in Bonaventure, cf. Alejandro de Villalmonte, "El argumento de razones necesarios en San Buenaventura," *Estudios franciscanos*, 53 (1952), 5-44.

²¹ Cf. *The Great Conversation: The Substance of a Liberal Education*. Vol. I of *Great Books of the Western World*, ed. by Robert Maynard Hutchins (Chicago: Encyclopaedia Britannica, 1952); cf. also Mortimer J. Alder, "Preface" to *The Great Ideas: A Syntopicon of Great Books of the Western World*, Vol. II of *Great Books of the Western World*, xi-xxxi.

²² Cf. below, pp. 238-255.

²³ Mircea Eliade, *Patterns in Comparative Religion*, trans. Rosemary Sheed (New York: Sheed and Ward, 1958), pp. 240 ff., 417-23; cf. also Eliade, *Mephistopheles and the Androgyne*, trans. John Cohen (New York: Sheed and Ward, 1965), pp. 108-24; cf. also Erich Neumann, *The Origins and History of Consciousness*, trans. R.F.C. Hull (New York: Pantheon, 1954), pp. 8-10.

²⁴ Eliade, *Patterns in Comparative Religion*, pp. 417-23.

²⁵ Arthur Waley, *The Way and Its Power: A Study of the Tao Te Ching and Its Place in Chinese Thought* (London: Allen and Unwin, 1934).

²⁶ Hermann Diels, *Die Fragmente der Vorsokratiker*, 3 vols., ed. W. Kranz (Berlin: Weidmann, 1960-61); cf. John Burnet, *Early Greek Philosophy* (London: Adam and Black, 1930).

²⁷ Heraclitus, Fr. 67.

²⁸ Nicholas of Cusa, *De docta ignorantiā*, in *Nicolai de Cusa opera omnia* ed. Ernst Hoffmann and Raymond Klibansky (Leipzig: Meiner, 1932). Ernst Hoffmann makes the following observation: "Nicholas himself regarded this principle as his most important discovery, and he was convinced that this principle would enable him have a fresh look at the history of philosophy and to reform funda-

mentally the philosophy of his own time." Ernst Hoffman, in introduction to *Über den Beryll* (Leipzig: Meiner, 1938), p. 1. Cf. also Joseph Stallmach, "Zusammenfall der Gegensätze: Das Prinzip der Dialektik bei Nikolaus von Kues," *Mitteilungen und Forschungsbeiträge der Cusanus-Gesellschaft*, I (Mainz, 1961), 55 ff.

[29] G. W. F. Hegel, *The Phenomenology of Mind*, trans. J. B. Baille (London: Allen and Unwin, 1931); *Science of Logic*, trans. W. H. Johnston and L. G. Struthers (2nd ed.: London: Allen and Unwin, 1951). Cf. Karl Marx in *The Marx-Engels Reader*, ed. Robert C. Tucker (New York: W. W. Norton, 1972).

[30] Cf. Jolande Jacobi, *The Psychology of C. G. Jung*, trans. Ralph Manheim (New Haven: Yale University Press, 1951), pp. 12 ff., pp. 186-87. Cf. Jung's extensive study of the union of opposites in Alchemy: C. G. Jung, *Mysterium Coniunctionis*, Vol. XIV of the *Collected Works of C. G. Jung*, trans. R.F.C. Hull (New York: Pantheon, 1963).

[31] Thomas Altizer, "The Sacred and the Profane: A Dialectical Understanding of Christianity," in *Radical Theology and the Death of God*, by Thomas Altizer and William Hamilton (New York: Bobbs-Merrill, 1966), pp. 140-55. Cf. also Altizer, *Mircea Eliade and the Dialectic of the Sacred* (Philadelphia: Westminster, 1963).

[32] *Itin.*, c. 6, n. 5 (V, 311); English translation from *Works of Saint Bonaventure*, Vol. II *Saint Bonaventure's 'Itinerarium Mentis in Deum'*, trans. Philotheus Boehner (Saint Bonaventure, N.Y.: The Franciscan Institute, 1956), p. 93; Throughout, translations of the *Itinerarium* will be taken from this translation by Boehner, with slight changes in capitalization and punctuation. Unless otherwise noted, the other English translations will be my own.

[33] *Itin.*, c. 6, n. 7 (V, 213); Boehner, 95; Apoc. 1:8, 5:1; Ezk. 2:9.

[34] Eliade, *Patterns in Comparative Religion*, p. 29.

[35] In approaching this question through the concept of model, we are following a trend in various fields at the present time, e.g., the physical and social sciences and theology. Cf. Max Black, *Models and Metaphysics* (Ithaca, N.Y.: Cornell University Press, 1962); B. H. Kazemier and D. Vuysje (ed.), *The Concept and the Role of the Model in Mathematics and Natural and Social Sciences* (Dordrecht, The Netherlands: Reidel, 1961); Ian Ramsey, *Models and Mystery* (London: Oxford University Press, 1964); cf. also my article, "Models and the Future of Theology," *Continuum*, 7 (1969), 78-92.

[36] In accepting Eliade's general observations, I do not wish to imply that I will study Bonaventure according to Eliade's specific interpretation of the coincidence of opposites. There is reason to think that Bonaventure sees more of an interpenetration of opposites than is reflected at least in much of Eliade's study. Cf. Roberts Avens, "Mircea Eliade's Conception of the Polarity 'Sacred-Profane' in Archaic Religions and in Christianity," unpublished doctoral dissertation (Fordham University, 1971).

[37] Cf. Śankara's commentary in *The Vedānta-Sūtras, with the Commentary by Śankarācārya*, trans. George Thibaut, Vol. XXXIV and XXXVIII of *Sacred Books of the East*, ed. Max Müller (London: Oxford University Press, 1904).

[38] Cf. Parmenides in G. S. Kirk and J. E. Raven, *The Presocratic Philosophers: A Critical History with a Selection of Texts* (Cambridge: Cambridge University Press, 1960), pp. 263-285.

[39] Cf. Leucippus and Democritus, *ibid.*, pp. 400-426.

[40] Cf. the Gnostic and Manichaean texts in Robert Haardt, *Gnosis: Character and Testimony*, translated into English by J. F. Hendry (Leiden: Brill, 1971).

[41] Cf. Arthur J. Arberry, *The Koran Interpreted* (New York: Macmillan, 1955).

[42] Jean Calvin, *Institutes of the Christian Religion,* ed. John T. McNeill, trans. Ford Lewis Battles, Vol. XX and XXI of *The Library of Christian Classics* (Philadelphia: Westminster, 1960). Søren Kierkegaard, *Philosophical Fragments,* trans. David F. Swenson (Princeton: Princeton University Press, 1936); *Fear and Trembling,* trans. Walter Lourie (Princeton: Princeton University Press, 1941); *The Concept of Dread,* trans. Walter Lourie (Princeton: Princeton University Press, 1944). Karl Barth, *The Epistle to the Romans,* trans. Edwyn C. Hoskyns (London: Oxford University Press, 1953).

[43] Cf. n. 25, above.

[44] Martin Buber, *I and Thou,* trans. Ronald Gregor Smith (New York: Charles Scribner's Sons, 1937).

[45] Teilhard de Chardin, *op. cit.,* pp. 260-268.

[46] Thomas Aquinas, *Summa theologiae,* I, q. 1; II-II, q. 1-16.

[47] Cf. Martin Luther, *Lectures on Galatians,* trans. Jaroslav Pelican and Richard Jungkuntz, Vol. XXVI and XXVII of *Luther's Works,* edited by Jaroslav Pelican and Walter A. Hansen (St. Louis: Concordia, 1963-1964).

Chapter II

[1] On the history of Bagnoregio, cf. Francisco Macchioni, *Storia di Bagnoregio dai tempi antichi al 1503* (Viterbo: Agnesotti, 1956), cf. also Francesco Petrangeli Papini, *Civita di Bagnoregio* (Viterbo: Agnesotti, 1970) and *Bagnoregio: cronologia storica* (Viterbo: Agnesotti, 1972); on Bonaventure in relation to Bagnoregio, cf. Francesco Petrangeli Papini, *S. Bonaventura da Bagnoregio* (Vitebo: Agnesotti, 1962), esp. pp. 17-65; on the geological structure of Bagnoregio and its environs, cf. Giulio Schmiedt, "Visione aerea del territorio di Bagnoregio dalla antichita ai tempi di S. Bonaventura," *Doctor Seraphicus: Bolletino d'Informazioni del Centro di Studi Bonaventuriani, Bagnoregio,* 16 (1969), 41-63.

[2] Cf. Francesco Petrangeli Papini, "Un evento e una data fatali per Civita; il disastroso terremoto del 1695; il trasferimento della Cattedrale e dell'Episcopio a Rota; inizio dell'agonia di Civita," *Doctor Seraphicus: Bolletino d'Informazioni del Centro di Studi Bonaventuriani, Bagnoregio,* 16 (1969), 31-39.

[3] The medieval Cathedral of S. Donato, situated in what is called the Civita, was built no later than the eighth century and renovated and enlarged in the eleventh century and again modified in 1511: cf. Papini, *Civita di Bagnoregio,* p. 78. On Bonaventure's home, cf. *ibid.,* p. 151, number 24; also Papini, *S. Bonaventura di Bagnoregio,* p. 36, number 24; and p. 44.

[4] For photographs of this striking view, cf. Macchioni, *op. cit.,* front cover; and Papini, *S. Bonaventura di Bagnoregio,* p. 19; *Civita di Bagnoregio,* pp. 7, 29.

[5] Cf. below, pp. 172-197.

[6] Giuseppe Abate, "Per la storia e la cronologia di S. Bonaventura, O. Min.," *Miscellanea francescana,* 49 (1949), 534-568; 50 (1950), 97-130; for dating Bonaventure's works and the major events of his life, I am indebted to the recent research of Jacques Guy Bougerol, John Quinn, and Ignatius Brady: cf. the chronology in *S. Bonaventura 1274-1974,* ed. Jacques Guy Bougerol, Vol. II (Grottaferrata: Collegio S. Bonaventura, 1973), 11-16; John F. Quinn, "Chronology of St. Bonaventure (1217-1257)," *Franciscan Studies,* 32 (1972), 168-186; Ignatius Brady, "Bonaventure,

St." in *New Catholic Encyclopaedia*, Vol. II (New York: McGraw-Hill, 1967), 658-664.

[7] Cf. Brady, *op. cit.*, 658; cf. *De vita seraphici Doctoris*, in the Quaracchi critical edition, c. 1, n. 3 (X, 40).

[8] *Leg. maj.* prol., n. 3 (VIII, 505).

[9] *Leg. min.*, De transitu mortis, 8 (VIII, 579).

[10] Cf. Mariano di Firenze, in Zeffirino Lazzeri (ed.) "Una piccola vita inedita di S. Bonaventura," *Studi Francescani*, 1 (1914), 120.

[11] Cf. Jacques-Guy Bougerol, *Saint Bonaventure: un maître de sagesse* (Paris: Éditions franciscaines, 1966), pp. 8-11.

[12] The Brief of October 14, 1482, of Sixtus IV to the Franciscan Convent at Bagnoregio stated that Bonaventure "in dicta domo educatus exstitit"; cf. *Bull. Franc.* N.S., vol. III (1471-1484), Quaracchi, 1949, 838.

[13] Cf. Bougerol, *Saint-Bonaventure: un maître de sagesse*, pp. 11-30; Quinn, *op. cit.*, 186; Brady, *op. cit.*, 658.

[14] On the history of the Franciscan establishment at Paris, cf. Christian Eugène, "Saint Bonaventure et le grand couvent des cordeliers de Paris," in *Actes du Colloque Saint Bonaventure, 9-12 septembre 1968, Orsay*, in *Études franciscaines*, 18 (Supplément annuel, 1968), 167-182.

[15] *Ibid.*, 173; Bougerol, *Saint Bonaventure: un maître de sagesse*, p. 27.

[16] *II Sent.*, prael. prooem. (II, 2).

[17] Sixtus IV, in his bull of canonization of Bonaventure, printed in the Quaracchi critical edition, n. 6 (I, xl); for sources of the remark of Alexander, cf. the chronicles attributed to Bernard of Bessa, Bonaventure's secretary, in *Analecta franciscana*, III, 699; also *Chronica XXIV generalium, ibid.*, 324.

[18] *Ep. de tr. quaes.*, n. 13 (VIII, 336).

[19] Cf. Bougerol, *Saint Bonaventure: un maître de sagesse*, pp. 31-59; Quinn, *op. cit.*, 186; Brady, *op. cit.*, 658.

[20] Cf. Bougerol, *Saint Bonaventure: un maître de sagesse*, pp. 61-71; cf. chronology in *S. Bonaventura 1274-1974*, II, 11; Quinn, *op. cit.*, 181-198; Brady, *op. cit.*, 658.

[21] On this controversy, cf. Decima Douie, *The Conflict between the Seculars and the Mendicants at the University of Paris in the 13th Century* (London: Blackfriars, 1954); "St. Bonaventure's Part in the Conflict between Seculars and Mendicants at Paris," in *S. Bonaventura 1274-1974*, II, 585-612.

[22] Cf. Salimbene, *Cronica fratris Salimbene de Adam ordinis minorum*, in *Monumenta Germaniae historica: Scriptorum*, Vol. XXXII, ed. O. Holder-Egger (Hanoverae et Lipsiae: Impensis Bibliopolii Hahniani, 1905-1913), 309-310; cf. Quinn, *op. cit.*, 174-176.

[23] Cf. J. R. H. Moorman, *A History of the Franciscan Order: From its Origins to the Year 1517* (Oxford: Clarendon, 1968), pp. 105-204; Rosalind Brooke, *Early Franciscan Government: Elias to Bonaventure* (Cambridge: Cambridge University Press, 1959).

[24] On Joachim and his influence, cf. Margorie Reeves, *The Influence of Prophecy in the Later Middle Ages: A Study of Joachimism* (Oxford: Clarendon, 1969), pp. 3-228.

[25] Cf. Salimbene, *op. cit.*, 309-310.

[26] Cf. Angelo of Clareno, *Historia septem tribulationum ordinis minorum*, tribulatio 4, ed. Franz Ehrle, in *Archiv für Litteratur und Kirchen-Geschichte*, Vol. II (Berlin: Weidmannsche Buchhandlung, 1886), 271-287. On Angelo's account of the trial, cf. E. Randolph Daniel, "St. Bonaventure: Defender of Franciscan

Eschatology," in *S. Bonaventure 1274-1974*, ed. Jacques Guy Bougerol, Vol. IV (Grottaferrata: Collegio S. Bonaventura, 1974), 797-799.

²⁷ Cf. Moorman, *op. cit.*, pp. 140-154; Brooke, *op. cit.*, pp. 270-285.

²⁸ *Itin.* (V, 295-313); cf. below, pp. 75-95.

²⁹ *Leg. maj.* (VIII, 504-565); *Leg. min.* (VIII, 565-579); cf. *Archivum franciscanum historicum*, 7 (1914), 678.

³⁰ Cf. Fernand Van Steenbergen, *Aristotle in the West*, trans. Leonard Johnston (Louvain: Neuwelaerts, 1955); *The Philosophical Movement in the Thirteenth Century* (Edinburgh: Nelson, 1955). For a survey of scholarship on Bonaventure's relation to this Aristotelianism, cf. John Quinn, *The Historical Constitution of St. Bonaventure's Philosophy* (Toronto: Pontifical Institute of Medieval Studies, 1973), pp. 17-100.

³¹ On Bonaventure's work in relation to the Council of Lyons, cf. Bougerol, *Saint Bonaventure: un maître de sagesse*, pp. 117-130; cf. also the paper of Bougerol, "Le rôle de saint Bonaventure au Concile de Lyon 1274," delivered at the international conference entitled "1274 Année charnière, mutations et continuités," held at Lyons and Paris, September 30-October 5, 1974, to be published in the proceedings. Cf. Antonio Franchi, *Il Concilo II di Lione (1274) secundo la Ordinatio Concilii Generalis Lugdunensis* (Roma: Edizioni francescane, 1965).

³² *Chronica XXIV generalium*, in *Analecta franciscana*, III, 356; cf. the report of Bonaventure's death and funeral in the *ordinatio* of the Council, printed in Franchi, *op. cit.*, p. 95.

³³ Cf. the bulls of Sixtus IV and Sixtus V, printed in the Quaracchi critical edition (I, xxxix-lii).

³⁴ On the sources of Bonaventure's thought, cf. the recent research of Jacques Guy Bougerol, "S. Bonaventure et le Pseudo-Denys l'Aréopagite," in *Actes du Colloque Saint Bonaventure, 9-12 septembre 1968, Orsay*, in *Études franciscaines*, 18 (Supplément annuel, 1968), 33-123; "Saint Bonaventure et la hiérarchie dionysienne," *Archives d'histoire doctrinale et littéraire du moyen âge*, 44 (1969), 131-167; "Dossier pour l'étude des rapports entre saint Bonaventure et Aristote," *Archives d'histoire doctrinale et littéraire du moyen âge*, 49 (1974), 135-222; cf. the reference in n. 9 to Chapter One, p. 289, above.

³⁵ *Itin.*, c. 3 (V, 303-306); cf. Augustine, *De Trinitate*, VIII-XV.

³⁶ *Itin.*, c. 1, n. 9-15 (V, 298-299); cf. Augustine, *Contra Faustum*, XX, 7; *De vera religione*, VII, 13; *De Trinitate*, VI, 10, 12.

³⁷ *Itin.*, c. 1, n. 14 (V, 299).

³⁸ *Hexaem.*, XII, n. 14 (V, 386).

³⁹ *Loc. cit.*

⁴⁰ *Itin.*, c. 1, n. 15 (V, 299); Boehner, 49.

⁴¹ *I Sent.*, d. 2-34 (I, 46-596); *M. Trin.* (V, 45-115); *Sc. Chr.* (V, 3-43); *Brevil.*, p. I, c. 2-6; p. II, c. 12 (V, 210-215; 230).

⁴² On Bonaventure's Trinitarian theology, cf. Théodore de Régnon, *Études de théologie positive sur la Sainte Trinité*, vol. II: *Théories scholastiques* (Paris: Retaux, 1892), 435-568; A. Stohr, *Die Trinitätslehre des Hl. Bonaventura* (Münster in Westfalen: Aschendorff, 1923); J.-M. Bissen, *L'exemplarisme divin selon Bonaventure* (Paris: Vrin, 1929); Titus Szabó, *De. SS. Trinitate in creaturis refulgente doctrina S. Bonaventurae* (Rome: Herder, 1955); Luc Mathieu, "La Trinité créatrice d'après Saint Bonaventure," unpublished doctoral dissertation (Faculté de théologie de l'Institut Catholique de Paris, 1960); Winthir Rauch, *Das Buch Gottes: Eine systematische Untersuchung des Buchbegriffes bei Bonaventura* (München:

Max Hueber, 1961); Alexander Gerken, *Theologie des Wortes: Das Verhältnis von Schöpfung und Inkarnation bei Bonaventura* (Düsseldorf: Patmos, 1963); Olegario González, *Misterio trinitario y existencia humana* (Madrid: Ediciones Rialp, 1965).

[43] *I Sent.*, d. 2, a. un., q. 2 (I, 53-54).

[44] Richard of St. Victor, *De Trinitate;* Pseudo-Dionysius, *De caelesti hierarch.*, c. 4, n. 1; *De div. nom.*, c. 4, n. 1, ff.

[45] *I Sent.*, d. 2, a. un., q. 2 (I, 53).

[46] *I Sent.*, d. 27, p. 1, a. un., q. 2 (I, 468-474); cf. *I Sent.*, d. 11, a. un., q. 2 (I, 214-216).

[47] *I Sent.*, d. 27, p. 1, a. un., q. 2, ad 3 (I, 471); the source is not Aristotle but the *Liber de causis.*

[48] Cf. de Régnon, *op. cit.*, Vol. I, 335-365; Gregory Nazianzen, *Oratio II,* 38; Basil, *Homilia XXIV, Contra Sabellianos et Arium et Anomoeos,* 4; Pseudo-Dionysius, *De div. nom.*, c. 2, n. 7.

[49] *M. Trin.*, q. 8 (V, 112-115); *Brevil.*, p. I, cc. 2-3 (V, 210-212).

[50] *Itin.*, c. 6, n. 2 (V, 310-311).

[51] *Hexaem.*, XI, 11-25 (V, 381-384).

[52] Cf. below, pp. 101-130, 229-267.

[53] *I Sent.*, d. 43, a. un., q. 3 (I, 773).

[54] *M. Trin.*, q. 4, a. 2, ad 4-9 (V, 86-87).

[55] *Itin.*, c. 6, n. 2 (V, 310-311); Boehner, 55.

[56] *Hexaem.*, I, 17 (V, 332).

[57] *I Sent.*, d. 6-7, 9, 12-13, 27, 31 (I, 123-146, 176-192, 218-241, 464-494, 529-552).

[58] *M. Trin.*, q. 4, a. 2, ad 8 (V, 87).

[59] *I Sent.*, d. 27, p. 2, a. un., q. 2 (I, 484-487); d. 35-36 (I, 597-632); *Sc. Chr.* (V, 3-43).

[60] *M. Trin.*, q. 8, ad 7 (V, 115).

[61] *I Sent.*, d. 3, a. un., q. 2, ad 4 (I, 72-74).

[62] *Hexaem.*, I, 12-17 (V, 331-332).

[63] *M. Trin.*, q. 8, ad 7 (V, 115).

[64] *Hexaem.*, I, 12-17 (V, 331-332); *Red. art.*, 24 (V, 325). On Bonaventure's Christology, cf. references in n. 42, above; also W. Dettloff, " 'Christus tenens medium in omnibus': Sinn und Funktion der Theologie bei Bonaventura," *Wissenschaft und Weisheit,* 20 (1957), 28-42, 120-140; Bernardo Aperribay, "Christología mistica de San Buenaventura," *Obras de San Buenaventura,* vol. II (Madrid: Biblioteca de autores cristianos, 1957), 3-90; Nicolaus Simonelli, *Doctrina christocentrica Seraphici Doctoris S. Bonaventurae* (Iesi: Scuola Tipografica Francescana, 1958).

[65] *III Sent.*, d. 1-22 (III, 6-466); *Brevil.*, p. IV (V, 241-252); *Sc. Chr.*, q. 5-7 (V, 27-43).

[66] Col. 1:15-20.

[67] *Itin.*, prol. (V, 295-296).

[68] *Ibid.*, n. 3 (V, 295).

[69] *Ibid.*, c. 6, n. 7 (V, 312); Boehner, 95; Apoc. 1:8, 5:1; Ez. 2:9; cf. c. 7 (V, 312-313).

[70] Cf. below, pp. 63-64, 219-222, 258-262.

[71] *Lign. vit.* (VIII, 68-87).

[72] *Hexaem.*, I (V, 329-335).

[73] *Hexaem.*, I, n. 13, 24 (V, 331, 333).

[74] *Itin.*, c. 1, n. 14 (V, 299).

[75] Joseph Ratzinger, *The Theology of History in St. Bonaventure,* trans. Zachary Hayes (Chicago: Franciscan Herald Press, 1971), p. 110.

[70] For a study of Bonaventure, Aristotle and the Joachites, cf. Ratzinger, *op. cit.*, cf. also Bernard McGinn, "The Abbot and the Doctors: Scholastic Reactions to the Radical Eschatology of Joachim of Fiore," *Church History*, 40 (1971), 41-45; E. Randolph Daniel, *op. cit.*

CHAPTER III

[1] *Itin.*, c. 5-7 (V, 308-313); *Hexaem.*, I (V, 329-335).

[2] On the subject of microcosm and macrocosm, cf. James McEvoy, "Microcosm and Macrocosm in the Writings of St. Bonaventure," in *S. Bonaventura 1274-1974*, ed. Jacques Guy Bougerol et al., Vol. II (Grottaferrata: Collegio S. Bonaventura, 1973), 309-343.

[3] *Itin.*, prol., n. 2-3 (V, 295-296).

[4] Cf. the position of Philotheus Boehner in *Works of Saint Bonaventure*, Vol. II: *Saint Bonaventure's Itinerarium Mentis in Deum* (Saint Bonaventure, N.Y.: The Franciscan Institute, 1956), 19.

[5] *Itin.*, prol. n 2 (V, 295); Boehner, 31.

[6] *Loc. cit.*; Boehner uses the form "Mount Alverno," but for consistency with my text, I have altered this to the more common Italian designation "La Verna".

[7] *Itin.*, prol. n. 1 (V, 295); Boehner, 31; Ps. 119; 7; 121:6.

[8] *Ibid.*, n. 2 (V, 295); Boehner, 31.

[9] *Loc. cit.*

[10] *Le Considerazioni sulle stimmate*, con. 1; English translation by Raphael Brown, *The Little Flowers of St. Francis* (Garden City, N.Y.: Image Books, 1958), p. 173.

[11] *Leg. maj.* XIII, n. 3 (VIII, 542-543); cf. also *Leg. min.* (VIII, 575). Cf. Is. 6:2.

[12] *Itin.*, prol., n. 2 (V, 295); Boehner, 31.

[13] Cf. below, pp. 175-183.

[14] *Itin.*, prol. n. 2 (V, 295); Boehner, 31.

[15] *Ibid.*, n. 3 (V, 295); Boehner, 33.

[16] Cf. Boehner, *op. cit.*, 105.

[17] *Itin.*, c. 1, n. 8 (V, 298).

[18] *Ibid.*, n. 2, 9 (V, 297-298); Bonaventure refers to Christ as a ladder in *Itin.*, c. 1, n. 3; c. 4, n. 2; c. 7, n. 1 (V, 297, 306, 312).

[19] *Itin.*, c. 3, n. 1; c. 5, n. 1 (V, 303-308).

[20] *Itin.*, c. 1, n. 9 (V, 298); the reference here is to the material world, but the term *speculatio* is used in all headings of Chapters One through Six, thus referring to our consideration of the soul and of God himself. Cf. *Itin.*, c. 2, n. 1, 7, 13; c. 3, n. 5; c. 4, n. 7 (V, 299-301, 303, 305, 307-308).

[21] Cf. above, pp. 46-48.

[22] Cf. above, pp. 59-66.

[23] *Itin.*, prol. n. 3 (V, 295); Boehner, 33; II Cor. 12:2; Gal. 2:20.

[24] *Ibid.*, (V, 296); Boehner, 33; cf. Jn. 10:1, 9; Apoc. 22:14.

[25] *Ibid.*, c. 1, n. 9 (V, 298); Boehner, 45.

[26] Cf. *Itin.*, c. 2, n. 11-12; *I Sent.*, d. 3, a. un., q. 2, ad 4 (I, 72-74); *Brevil.*, p. II, c. 12 (V, 230).

[27] *Itin.*, c. 1, n. 11-12 (V, 298).

[28] *Ibid.*, n. 13 (V, 299); Boehner, 47.

[29] *Ibid.*, n. 14, (V, 299); Boehner, 47.

[30] *Loc. cit.*

[31] *Ibid.*, c. 2, n. 2 (V, 300); Boehner, 51.

[32] *Ibid.*, n. 7 (V, 301); Boehner, 55-56.

[33] *Ibid.*, n. 11 (V, 302); Boehner, 61; for the sources in Augustine of Bonaventure's thought on numbers, cf. *De vera religione*, c. 40-44, n. 74-82; *De musica*, VI.

[34] *Itin.*, c. 3, n. 1 (V, 303); Boehner, 63; cf. Augustine, *De Trinitate*, VIII-XV.

[35] *Itin.*, c. 3, n. 4 (V, 305); Boehner, 69.

[36] *Ibid.*, n. 5 (V, 305); Boehner, 69.

[37] *Ibid.*, c. 4, n. 2 (V, 306); Boehner, 73.

[38] *Ibid.*, n. 3 (V, 306); Boehner, 73.

[39] *Ibid.*, n. 5 (V, 307); Boehner 77; Apoc. 1:8, 21:6, 22:13.

[40] For an extensive study of the temple and other symbols in the *Itinerarium*, cf. Sister Lillian Turney, "The Symbolism of the Temple in St. Bonaventure's *Itinerarium Mentis in Deum*," unpublished doctoral dissertation (Fordham University, 1968); cf. also the reference to her paper in n. 2 to Chapter Six, below, p. 303.

[41] Ex. 25-28. Following closely the description of Exodus, Bonaventure uses the term *tabernaculum* or tent. Yet for the fullness of the word, it is more accurate to refer to it as the temple; for the tent developed into the temple, and it was under the form of temple that the symbolism later progressed. Also the Exodus account incorporates many elements from the later temple. Roland de Vaux writes: "It is only too obvious that much of this description [of the tabernacle in Exodus] is merely an idealization: the desert sanctuary is conceived as a collapsible temple, exactly half as big as the temple of Jerusalem, which served as the model for this reconstruction." *Ancient Israel: Its Life and Institutions,* trans. John McHugh, (New York: McGraw-Hill, 1961), p. 296. Cf. Frank M. Cross, Jr., "The Tabernacle," *Biblical Archeologist*, 10, (1947), 45-68.

[42] Cf. Yves Congar, *The Mystery of the Temple,* trans. Reginald F. Trevett (Westminster, Md.: Newman Press, 1962).

[43] Bonaventure's treatment of these images is in many respects similar to that of Richard of St. Victor in the *Benjamin major.* Richard uses the symbol of Mt. Sinai, where Moses received God's revelation, and the symbol of the temple. He sees them related as opposites, yet united since the top of the mountain and the innermost part of the temple symbolize the same aspect of the human soul. Cf. *Benjamin major*, IV, 23 (*PL* 196, 167A).

[44] *Itin.*, c. 3, n. 1 (V, 303).

[45] Cf. Boehner's explication of this symbolism, *op. cit.*, p. 120. *Itinerarium*, c. 3, n. 1 (V, 303); c. 5, n. 1 (V, 308); c. 6, n. 4 (V, 311).

[46] *Itin.*, c. 5, n. 1 (V, 308); Boehner, 81.

[47] In the *Benjamin major* the Cherubim also symbolize the fifth and sixth kinds of contemplation according to the scheme of Richard of St. Victor. Cf. *Benjamin major*, I, 11 (*PL* 196, 77A).

[48] *Itin.*, c. 5, n. 2 (V, 308); Boehner, 81; Ex. 3:14.

[49] *Loc. cit.*; cf. John Damascene, *De fide orthodoxa*, I, 9.

[50] *Itin.*, c. 5 (V, 308); Boehner, 81.

[51] Anselm, *Proslogion*, c. 2-4.

[52] *Itin.*, c. 5, n. 3 (V, 308-309).

[53] *Ibid.*, n. 4 (V, 309); Boehner, 83.

[54] *Ibid.*, n. 5 (V, 309).

[55] *Ibid.*, n. 7 (V, 309); Boehner, 85.

[56] *Loc. cit.*; Apoc. 1:8, 21:6, 22:13.

[57] *Loc. cit.*

[58] *Ibid.*, n. 8 (V, 310).

[59] *Loc. cit.*; Boehner, 87. Bonaventure is quoting Alanus de Insulis, *Theologicae regulae*, 7 (*PL* 210, 627 A-C).

[60] *Itin.*, c. 5, n. 2 (V, 308); Boehner, 87.

[61] Lk. 18:19.

[62] *Itin.*, c. 5, n. 8 (V, 310); cf. Dionysius, *De divinis nominibus*, c. 3, n. 1; c. 4, n. 1.

[63] Anselm, *Proslogion*, c. 2-5.

[64] Dionysius, *De caelesti hierarchia*, 4.

[65] Bonaventure uses the interpersonal vision of Richard of St. Victor, *De Trinitate*, III, c. 2 ff., and his concepts of the *dilectus* and *condilectus* in deriving the processions from the self-diffusive good.

[66] *I Sent.*, d. 27, p. 1, a. un., q. 2, ad 3 (I, 471).

[67] *Itin.*, c. 6, n. 2 (V, 311); Boehner, 91.

[68] *Ibid.*, n. 3 (V, 311).

[69] *Ibid.*, n. 4 (V, 311).

[70] *Ibid.*, n. 5 (V, 311).

[71] *Loc. cit.*; Boehner, 93.

[72] *Lot. cit.*

[73] *Loc. cit.*

[74] *Ibid.*, n. 6 (V, 311-312); Boehner, 93, 95.

[75] *Ibid.*, n. 7 (V, 312).

[76] *Loc. cit.*; Boehner, 95; Apoc. 1:8, 5:1; Ezk. 2:9.

[77] *Ibid.*, c. 7, n. 2 (V, 312); on passage as a coincidence of opposites, cf. Mircea Eliade, *Patterns in Comparative Religion*, trans. Rosemary Sheed (New York: Sheed and Ward, 1958), pp. 427-428.

[78] *Itin.*, c. 7, n. 2 (V, 312); Lk. 23:43.

[79] *Ibid.*, n. 5 (V, 313); Dionysius, *De mystica theologia*, I, 1.

[80] *Ibid.*, n. 6 (V, 313); Boehner, 101; Jn. 13:1; 14:8.

[81] Cf. below, pp. 101-114.

[82] Cf. below, pp. 118-126.

[83] *Itin.*, c. 5, n. 8 (V, 310); Boehner, 87.

CHAPTER IV

---

[1] Cf. above, pp. 49-67.

[2] Augustine, *De Trinitate*, V-VIII; cf. Harry Wolfson, *The Philosophy of the Church Fathers*, Vol. I (Cambridge: Harvard University, 1964), 350-359. On the differences between the Eastern and Western approaches to the Trinity, cf. Théodore de Régnon, *Études de théologie positive sur la Sainte Trinité*, 4 vols. (Paris: Retaux, 1892-1898).

[3] Cf. de Régnon, *op. cit.*, Vol. II: *Théories scolastiques*; Paul Vanier, *Théologie Trinitaire chez S. Thomas d'Aquin* (Montreal: Institut d'Études Medievales, 1953).

Vanier has pointed out a Dionysian influence in the *De potentia* and an Augustinian influence in the *Summa theologiae*. I have taken the latter as characteristic of Thomas since it is later in his career and has been recognized as the classical locus of his Trinitarian theology and hence a source of great subsequent influence.

⁴ *Hexaem.*, VI, n. 2-6 (V, 360-361); cf. below, pp. 217-220.

⁵ Arthur O. Lovejoy, *The Great Chain of Being* (Cambridge: Harvard University Press, 1936), passim.

⁶ *I Sent.*, d. 2, a. un., q. 2 (I, 53).

⁷ *Loc. cit.*

⁸ *Loc. cit.*

⁹ *I Sent.*, d. 27, p. 1, a. un., q. 2 (I, 468-474).

¹⁰ *Ibid.*, ad 3 (I, 471). Most modern scholars attribute the *Liber de causis* either to Alfarabi, who died in Bagdad in 950 A.D., or to David the Jew, who lived in Toledo in the second half of the twelfth century. On the authorship of the *Liber de causis*, cf. H. D. Saffrey, *Sancti Thomae de Aquino super librum de causis exposito* (Fribourg: Société philosophique, 1954), pp. xxi-xxv; and L. Sweeney, "Research Difficulties in the *Liber de Causis*," *The Modern Schoolman*, 36 (1959), 108-115.

¹¹ *I Sent.*, d. 27, p. 1, a. un., q. 2, ad 3 (I, 471).

¹² Cf. above, pp. 18-24.

¹³ Cf. n. 5, above.

¹⁴ *M. Trin.*, q. 8 (V, 112-115); *Brevil.*, p. I, c. 2-3 (V, 210-212).

¹⁵ *Itin.*, c. 6, n. 2 (V, 310); Boehner, 89.

¹⁶ *Loc. cit.*

¹⁷ *Loc. cit.*

¹⁸ Cf. below, pp. 238-262.

¹⁹ *Itin.*, c. 6, n. 2 (V, 310); Boehner, 89.

²⁰ *Hexaem.*, XI, n. 11 (V, 381-382); Jn. 16:15.

²¹ *Ibid.*, (V, 382).

²² *Ibid.*, n. 12 (V, 382); Richard of St. Victor, *De Trinitate*, III, c. 2.

²³ Cf. Alfred North Whitehead, *Process and Reality* (New York: Macmillan, 1929), pp. 519-533; Charles Hartshorne, *The Divine Relativity* (New Haven: Yale University Press, 1948). On this issue, cf. below, pp. 239-255.

²⁴ *Itin.*, c. 7, n. 1 (V, 312); Boehner, 97.

²⁵ *Ibid.*, n. 5 (V, 313); Dionysius, *De mystica theologia*, I, 1.

²⁶ *Itin.*, c. 7, n. 6 (V, 313); Boehner, 101; Jn. 13:1; 14, 8.

²⁷ Cf. below, pp. 281-284.

²⁸ *Hexaem.*, I (V, 329-335).

²⁹ *I Sent.*, d. 2-34 (I, 46-596); *M. Trin.* (V, 45-115); *Brevil.* p. I, c. 2-6 (V, 210-215); *Itin.*, c. 6 (V, 310-312); *Hexaem.*, I, n. 12-17 (V, 331-332).

³⁰ *Hexaem.*, I, n. 14 (V, 331-332); cf. below, pp. 138-139.

³¹ *Itin.*, c. 6, n. 2 (V, 310-311); *I Sent.*, d. 2, a. un., q. 3-4 (I, 54-58).

³² *Itin.*, c. 6, n. 3 (V, 311).

³³ *I Sent.*, d. 2, a. un., q. 2 (I, 53); cf. Richard of St. Victor, *De Trinitate*, III.

³⁴ *Loc. cit.*

³⁵ *Hexaem.*, I, n. 16 (V, 332).

³⁶ *I Sent.*, d. 3, p. 1, a. un., q. 2, ad 4 (I, 72-74); *Brevil.*, P. II, c. 12 (V, 230); *Itin.*, c. 1-4 (V, 296-308); *Hexaem.*, XII (V, 384-387).

³⁷ *I Sent.*, d. 6-7, 9, 12-13, 27, 31, 35-36 (I, 123-146, 176-192, 218, 241, 464-494, 529-552, 597-632); *Sc. Chr.* (V, 3-43); *Hexaem.*, I, n. 12-17 (V, 331-332).

[38] *Hexaem.,* XII, n. 3 (V, 385).

[39] *Brevil., p.* I, c. 8, n. 7 (V, 217); on the difference between Bonaventure and Thomas on this point, cf. Titus Szabó, *De SS. Trinitate in creaturis refulgente doctrina S. Bonaventurae* (Rome: Herder, 1955), pp. 31-43.

[40] *Haexaem.,* XII, n. 9 (V, 386).

[41] *Sc. Chr.,* q. 2, obj. 9 (V, 8).

[42] Augustine, *Soliloquia,* II, c. 5, n. 8.

[43] Anselm, *Dialogus de veritate,* c. 11.

[44] *Sc. Chr.,* q. 2, ad 9 (V, 10).

[45] Cf. Celano, *Vita prima,* c. 21, 28-29; *Vita secunda,* c. 18, 124-130; Bonaventure, *Leg. maj.,* c. 6-11 (VIII, 519-535); *Speculum perfectionis,* c. 116, 118; *Fioretti,* c. 22.

[46] On Bonaventure's epistemology, cf. *Sc. Chr.,* q. 4 (V, 17-27); *Chr. un. omn. mag.* (V, 567-574); *M. Trin.,* q. 1, a. 1 (V, 45-51); *Itin.,* c. 1-4 (V, 296-308); *Red. art.* (V, 319-325); *Hexaem.,* I, n. 13; XIII (V, 331, 384-387).

[47] *Hexaem.,* XII, n. 8 (V, 385).

[48] *M. Trin.,* q 1, a. 1 (V, 45-51); *Itin.,* c. 3 (V, 303-306); *Sc. Chr.,* q. 4 (V, 17-27).

[49] *M. Trin.,* q. 1, a. 1-2 (V, 45-58).

[50] Thomas, *Summa theologiae,* I, q. 2, a. 3.

[51] *M. Trin.,* q. 1, a. 1, concl. (V, 49).

[52] *Ibid.,* q. 1, a. 1, n. 1-29 (V, 45-48).

[53] *Ibid.* (V, 45).

[54] *Ibid.,* n. 1-10 (V, 45-46); John Damascene, *De fide orthodoxa,* I, c. 3; Hugh of St. Victor, *De sacram.* I, p. 3, c. 1; Boethius, *De consol.,* III, prosa 2; Augustine, *De Trinitate,* VIII-XV; Aristotle, *Poster.,* II, c. 18; *Metaph.,* I, c. 1; Augustine, *De civitate Dei,* XIX, c. 11-13.

[55] *Itin.,* c. 3, n. 1 (V, 303); Boehner, 63.

[56] *Loc. cit.*

[57] *Ibid.,* n. 2 (V, 303).

[58] *Ibid.* (V, 304); Boehner, 65; the quotation within the text is from Augustine, *De Trinitate,* XIV, 8, 11.

[59] *Itin.,* c. 3, n. 3 (V, 304).

[60] *Ibid.,* n. 4 (V, 305); Boehner, 69.

[61] *Sc. Chr.,* q. 4, concl. (V, 22).

[62] *Ibid.* (V, 23-24).

[63] *Ibid.* (V, 24).

[64] On justice in the souls of evil men, cf. *Sc. Chr.,* q. 4, fund. 23 and concl. (V, 19, 23); on charity, cf. *I Sent.,* d. 17, p. 1, a. un., q. 4, concl. (I, 301-302); on fear and love of God, cf. *II Sent.,* d. 39, a. 1, q. 2, concl. (II, 904).

[65] *Sc. Chr.,* q. 4, concl. (V, 23).

[66] *Ibid.* (V, 23-24).

[67] *II Sent.,* d. 39, a. 1, q. 2 concl. (II, 904).

[68] Cf. *Itin.,* c. 3, n. 2 (V, 303).

[69] *Itin.,* c. 4, n. 2 (V, 306).

[70] *Ibid.,* c. 5, n. 4 (V, 309).

[71] *Ibid.,* c. 1, n. 7 (V, 297-298).

[72] *II Sent.,* prooem. (II, 3-6).

[73] *Hexaem.,* I, n. 26 (V, 333).

[74] *II Sent.,* prooem. (II, 3-6).

[75] Quaracchi editors in *II Sent.,* prooem. (II, 6, note).

[76] *II Sent.,* prooem. (II, 4).

[77] *Loc. cit.*; cf. Anselm, *Dialogus de veritate,* c. 11.
[78] *II Sent.,* prooem. (II, 4).
[79] *Loc. cit.*
[80] *Loc. cit.*
[81] *Ibid.* (II, 5).
[82] *Loc. cit.*
[83] *Ibid.* (II, 6).

CHAPTER V

[1] *Hexaem.,* I; for our analysis of this *collatio,* we will use the text which appears in Vol. V, 329-335, of the Quaracchi edition, 1891, but will cite the parallel passages in the other version of the *collatio,* edited by Delorme: *S. Bonaventurae Collationes in Hexaemeron et bonaventuriana quaedam selecta,* ed. F. Delorme (Quaracchi: Collegium S. Bonaventurae, 1934).

[2] *Itin.,* c. 5-7 (V, 308-313); cf. above, pp. 91-93.
[3] *Itin.,* prol., n. 2-4 (V, 295-296).
[4] *Ibid.,* c. 4, n. 5 (V, 307); Boehner, 77; Apoc. 1:8, 21:6, 22:13.
[5] Cf. above, pp. 84-93.
[6] *Itin.,* c. 5, n. 7 (V, 309).
[7] *Ibid.,* c. 6, n. 3 (V, 311).
[8] *Ibid.,* n. 5-6 (V, 311-312).
[9] *Ibid.,* n. 7 (V, 312); Boehner, 95; Apoc. 1:8, 21:6, 22:13.
[10] *Ibid.,* c. 7, n. 1 (V, 312).
[11] *Hexaem.,* I, n. 11 (V, 331); Delorme, p. 5.
[12] On the meaning of *medium* in Bonaventure, cf. Alexander Gerken's survey in *Lexique Saint Bonaventure,* ed. Jacques-Guy Bougerol (Paris: Éditions franciscaines, 1969), pp. 97-98. Although Bonaventure distinguished between *medium* and *mediator* in his early writings, this distinction does not have an important place in his later works. Cf. Bonaventure, *III Sent.,* d. 19, a. 2, q. 2 (III, 409-411); cf. Gerken in *Lexique Saint Bonaventure,* p. 97.
[13] Cf. above, pp. 18-22.
[14] Cf. below, pp. 222-227.
[15] *Hexaem.,* I, n. 14 (V, 331-332); Delorme, p. 6; cf. above pp. 110-112.
[16] Cf. above, pp. 98-114.
[17] *Hexaem.,* I, n. 13 (V, 331); Delorme, p. 7.
[18] *Ibid.*
[19] Mircea Eliade, *Patterns in Comparative Religion,* trans. Rosemary Sheed (New York: Sheed and Ward, 1958), p. 29; cf. above, pp. 16-17.
[20] *Hexaem.,* I, n. 13 (V, 331); Delorme, p. 7.
[21] Jn. 16:28; *Hexaem.,* I, 17 (V, 332); Delorme, p. 7.
[22] *Hexaem.,* I, 17 (V, 332); Delorme, p. 7.
[23] *Ibid.,* n. 13 (V, 331); Delorme, p. 6; Augustine, *In epist. Ioannis,* tr. 3, n. 13.
[24] *Sc. Chr.,* q. 4 (V, 17-32); *Chr. un. omn. mag.* (V, 567-574); cf. above, pp. 118-126.
[25] *Ch. un. omn. mag.,* n. 9 (V, 569).
[26] Cf. *III Sent.,* d. 2, a. 1, q. 2, concl. (III, 40).

[27] *Red. art.* n. 20 (V, 324).

[28] *Hexaem.,* I, n. 18-20 (V, 332-333); Delorme, pp. 7-10.

[29] Cf. Phil. 2:5-12.

[30] *Hexaem.,* I, n. 21-22 (V, 333); Delorme, p. 10.

[31] *Ibid.,* n. 24 (V, 333); Delorme, p. 11.

[32] *Ibid.,* n. 25-30; Delorme, pp. 12-15.

[33] *Ibid.,* n. 28 (V, 334); Delorme, pp. 14-15.

[34] *Ibid.,* n. 31-33 (V, 334-335); Delorme, pp. 15-17.

[35] *Ibid.,* n. 34-36 (V, 335); Delorme, pp. 17-18.

[36] *Ibid.,* n. 37-38 (V, 335); Delorme, p. 18.

[37] Cf. below, pp. 172-197.

[38] Mircea Eliade, *The Sacred and the Profane,* trans. Willard R. Trask (New York: Harcourt, Brace, 1959), pp. 36-37.

[39] *III Sent.,* d. 1-17 (III, 6-377); *Brevil.,* p. IV, c. 1-7 (V, 241-248).

[40] *Brevil.,* p. IV, c. 2, n. 2 (V, 242); English translation by José de Vinck, *The Works of Bonaventure,* Vol. II: *The Breviloquium* (Paterson, N.J.: St. Anthony Guild Press, 1963), 147.

[41] *III Sent.,* d. 2, a. 1, q. 2, concl. (III, 40).

[42] *Loc. cit.;* cf. Augustine, *De spiritu et anima,* c. 18; Gregory the Great, *Moralia,* VI, c. 16, n. 20; *In evangelia homilia,* II, 29, n. 2.

[43] On the Scotist doctrine of the primacy of Christ in creation, cf. John Duns Scotus, *Rep. Par.,* lib. 3, d. 7, q. 4; *Op. Ox.,* lib. 3, d. 7, q. 3, dub. 1; Dominic Unger, "Franciscan Christology: Absolute and Universal Primacy of Christ," in *Franciscan Studies,* 23 (1942), 428-475.

[44] *Red. art.,* n. 20 (V, 324); English translation by Sister Emma Thérèse Healy, *Works of Saint Bonaventure,* Vol. I: *Saint Bonaventure's De Reductione Artium ad Theologiam* (St. Bonaventure, N.Y.: Franciscan Institute, 1955), 37-38.

[45] *Itin.,* c. 4, n. 5 (V, 307); Boehner, 77; Apoc. 1:8, 21:6, 22:13.

[46] *Brevil.,* p. IV, c. 1, n. 4 (V, 242); de Vinck, 146.

[47] Anselm, *Cur Deus Homo;* cf. Bonaventure, *III Sent.,* d. 20 (III, 416-434); *Brevil.,* p. IV, c. 9 (V, 249-250); for Bonaventure's reservation to Anselm's theory, cf. *III Sent.,* d. 20, q. 6 (III, 430-432).

[48] *III Sent.,* d. 18-22 (III, 377-466); *Brevil.,* p. IV, c. 8-10 (V, 248-252).

[49] *Brevil.,* p. IV, c. 9, n. 4 (V, 250); de Vinck, 171-172.

[50] *Ibid.,* c. 10, n. 3 (V, 251); de Vinck, 175; cf. *Hexaem.,* I, n. 21-22 (V, 333); Delorme, p. 10.

[51] *Hexaem.,* I, n. 21-30 (V, 333-334); Delorme, pp. 10-15.

[52] Cf. above, pp. 144-146.

[53] *Hexaem.,* I, n. 22 (V, 333); Delorme, p. 10.

[54] *Ibid.,* n. 24 (V, 333); Delorme, p. 11.

[55] *Ibid.,* n. 28 (V, 334); Delorme, p. 14.

[56] *Ibid.,* Delorme, p. 15.

[57] *Ibid.,* n. 30 (V, 334); Delorme, p. 15.

[58] *Loc. cit.*

[59] Cf. *Itin.,* esp. c. 4-7 (V, 306-313); *Lign. vit.* (VIII, 68-86); *Tripl. via* (VIII, 3-18); *Solil.* (VIII, 28-67).

[60] *Itin.,* c. 7, n. 6 (V, 313); Jn. 13:1, 14:8; Boehner, 101.

CHAPTER VI

---

[1] Emile Mâle, *Notre Dame de Chartres* (Paris: Paul Hartmann, 1948), pp. 9-10.

[2] For a study of Bonaventure's symbolism in the *Itinerarium*, cf. Sister Lillian Turney, "The Symbolism of the Temple in St. Bonaventure's *Itinerarium Mentis in Deum*," unpublished doctoral dissertation (Fordham University, 1968); cf. also by the same author, "The Symbolism of the Temple in Bonaventure's *Itinerarium*," paper delivered at the Congresso Internazionale Bonaventuriano, Rome, September 19-26, 1974, to be published in the conference proceedings.

[3] Étienne Gilson, *The Philosophy of St. Bonaventure*, trans. Dom. Illtyd Trethowan and Frank J. Sheed (Paterson, N.J.: St. Anthony Guild Press, 1965), p. 186.

[4] *Hexaem.*, I, n. 17 (V, 332); Delorme, p. 7.

[5] Cf. above, pp. 51-59, 98-118.

[6] *I Sent.*, d. 27, p. 1, a. un., q. 2, ad 3 (I, 470-472).

[7] *Loc. cit.*; cf. above, pp. 101-104.

[8] *Itin.*, c. 6, n. 2 (V, 310); Boehner, 89.

[9] *Loc. cit.*

[10] *Hexaem.*, I, n. 16 (V, 332); Delorme, p. 7.

[11] *Hexaem.*, XII, n. 14 (V, 386); Delorme, p. 144.

[12] *Itin.*, c. 1-4 (V, 296-308); *I Sent.*, d. 3, p. 1 (I, 66-80).

[13] *Ibid.*, c. 1, n. 13-14 (V, 298-299).

[14] Mircea Eliade, *Patterns in Comparative Religion*, trans. Rosemary Sheed (New York: Sheed and Ward, 1958), pp. 216-238; 367-387; *The Sacred and the Profane*, trans. Williard Trask (New York: Harcourt, Brace, 1959), pp. 21-65; *Images and Symbols*, trans. Philip Mairet (New York: Sheed and Ward, 1961), pp. 21-56.

[15] C. G. Jung, *Psychology and Alchemy*; Vol. XII *The Collected Works of C. G. Jung*, trans. R. F. C. Hull (New York: Pantheon Books, 1953).

[16] Cf. above, pp. 49-67.

[17] Jung, *op. cit.*, pp. 91-213; Eliade, *Images and Symbols*, pp. 51-56; *Yoga, Immortality and Freedom*, trans. Williard Trask (New York: Pantheon Books, 1958), pp. 219 ff; Giuseppe Tucci, *The Theory and Practice of the Mandala*, trans. Alan Houghton Brodrick (London: Rider, 1967).

[18] *Hexaem.*, I (V, 329-335); Delorme, pp. 1-19.

[19] *Itin.*, prol., n. 2-5; c. 1, n. 1-8 (V, 295-298).

[20] *Ibid.*, c. 3-6 (V, 303-312).

[21] *Itin.*, c. 5, n. 8 (V, 310); Boehner, 87. Alanus de Insulis, *Theologicae regulae*, 7 (PL, 210, 627 A-C). Cf. also *I Sent.*, d. 37, p. 1, a. 1, q. 1, ad 3 (I, 639); *M. Trin.*, q. 5, a. 1, ad 7-8 (V, 91); *Serm. 4, Vig. nat. Dom.* (IX, 94).

[22] *Brevil.*, p. VI, c. 3, n. 1 (V, 267).

[23] *M. Trin.*, q. 8, ad 7 (V, 115); cf. also *Brevil.*, p. V, c. 1, n. 6 (V, 253); *Red. art.*, n. 7 (V, 322).

[24] *M. Trin.*, q. 8, ad 7 (V, 115).

[25] *Hexaem.*, I, n. 11-38 (V, 331-335); Delorme, pp. 5-18.

[26] *Ibid.*, n. 12-14 (V, 331-332); Delorme, pp. 5-6.

[27] *Ibid.*, n. 12-17 (V, 331-332); Delorme, pp. 5-7.

[28] *Ibid.*, n. 18-20 (V, 332-333); Delorme, pp. 7-10.

[29] *Ibid.*, n. 21-38 (V, 333-335); Delorme, pp. 10-18.

[30] *Ibid.*, n. 24 (V, 333); Delorme, p. 11.

[31] *Loc. cit.*

[32] On the setting of the *Itinerarium* and Francis' vision, cf. above, pp. 71-77.

[33] *Itin.,* prol. n. 2 (V, 295).

[34] *Ibid.,* n. 3 (V, 295); Boehner, 33.

[35] Cf. above, pp. 85-86.

[36] Ex. 25-26.

[37] *Itin.,* c. 3, n. 1 (V, 303); Boehner, 63.

[38] *Ibid.,* c. 6, n. 7 (V, 312); Boehner, 95; Apoc. 1:8, 21:6, 22:13.

[39] Eliade, *Images and Symbols,* p. 52.

[40] Jung, *op. cit.,* p. 91.

[41] Tucci, *op. cit.,* p. viii.

[42] *Ibid.,* p. vii.

[43] Jung, *op. cit.,* p. 94.

[44] *Ibid.,* p. 41.

[45] Jolande Jacobi, *The Psychology of C. G. Jung,* trans. Ralph Manheim (New Haven: Yale University Press, 1964), p. 132.

[46] *Ibid.,* pp. 131-132.

[47] Eliade, *Images and Symbols,* pp. 27-56; *The Sacred and the Profane,* pp. 20-65.

[48] Eliade, *The Sacred and the Profane,* p. 37

[49] *Hexaem.,* I, n. 22 (V, 333); Delorme, p. 10.

[50] For numerous reproductions of the Seraph in art throughout the centuries, see Vittorino Facchinetti, *Le stimmate di S. Francesco d'Assisi nel vii centenario del grande miracolo (1224-1924)* (Milan: Casa Editrice S. Lega Eucaristica, 1924).

[51] *Leg. maj.,* XIII, n. 3 (VIII, 542-543); for Bonaventure's full description of the vision, cf. above, pp. 76-77; cf. also *Leg. min.* (VIII, 575). Cf. Is. 6:2.

[52] Jung, *op. cit.,* p. 184, n. 122.

[53] *Itin,* prol., n. 2 (V, 295); Boehner, 31.

[54] Cf. references in n. 14 above.

[55] *Lign. vit.* (VIII, 68-86).

[56] *Ibid.,* prol., n. 3 (VIII, 68-69); English translation by José de Vinck, *The Works of Bonaventure,* Vol. I: *Mystical Opuscula* (Paterson, N.J.: St. Anthony Guild Press, 1960), 98.

[57] On the history of *The Tree of Life* in art and for reproduction of artists' conceptions of the image, cf. *S. Bonaventure 1274-1974,* ed. Jacques-Guy Bougerol, Vol. I: *Il Dottore Serafico nelle raffigurazioni degli artisti,* introduction by P. Gerlach, text by Francesco Petrangeli Papini (Grottaferrata: Collegio S. Bonaventura, 1972), 6-9, 30-43; plates 1-9, 83.

[58] Cf. above, n. 52.

[59] C. G. Jung, *Psychology and Alchemy,* pp. 142, 209; cf. Jolande Jacobi, *op. cit.,* pp. 46-47, n. 2.

[60] *I Sent.,* prooem. (I, 1-14).

[61] *Ibid.* (I, 2).

[62] *Ibid.,* q. 1, concl. (I, 7).

[63] *Ibid.*

[64] *Brevil.,* prol. (V, 201-208).

[65] *Ibid.* (V, 201); English translation by José de Vinck, *The Works of Bonaventure,* Vol. II: *The Breviloquium* (Paterson, N.J.: St. Anthony Guild Press, 1963), 3.

[66] *Ibid.,* n. 1 (V, 203); de Vinck, 6; cf. Ez. 1:15 ff.

[67] *Ibid.,* n. 6 (V, 208); de Vinck, 21.

[68] *Ibid.* (V, 202); de Vinck, 4.

[69] Cf. below, pp. 217-220.

[70] Cf. especially Bonaventure's criticism of Aristotle in *Hexaem.,* VI, n. 1-5 (V, 360-361); Delorme, pp. 90-92.

[71] Cf. the interpretation of this image by Alanus de Insulis in *Theologicae regulae,* 7 (*PL* 210, 627 A-C).

[72] Joseph Ratzinger, *The Theology of History in St. Bonaventure,* trans. Zachary Hayes (Chicago: Franciscan Herald Press, 1971), p. 110.

[73] *Ibid.,* p. 141; the internal quotation is from Thomas, *II Sent.,* d. 1, q. 1, a. 5, arg. 7; cf. also arg. 5-6.

[74] Ratzinger, *op. cit.,* p. 141.

[75] Tucci, *op. cit.,* pp. 108-133.

[76] *Itin.,* prol. n. 2 (V, 295).

[77] *Loc. cit.*

[78] *Loc. cit.*

[79] *Ibid.,* n. 3 (V, 295).

[80] *Loc. cit.*

[81] Cf. Ratzinger, *op. cit.,* pp. 2-4.

CHAPTER VII

[1] Cf. above, pp. 18-22.

[2] Cf. Étienne Gilson, *The Philosophy of St. Bonaventure,* trans. Dom Illtyd Trethowan and Frank J. Sheed (Paterson, N.J.: St. Anthony Guild Press, 1965), where the difference between Thomas and Bonaventure is affirmed and Bonaventure's thought is explored for its own merit.

[3] Cf. Thomas's use of this method throughout the *Summa theologiae;* on his formal statement of method cf. *ibid.,* I, 1.

[4] Cf. Thomas Aquinas, *Summa theologiae,* I, 1, 1 and 32, 1.

[5] Cf. Thomas's treatment of the Trinity in the *Summa theologiae,* I, 27-43.

[6] *Ibid.*

[7] *Ibid.*

[8] Cf. the references in n. 20 to Chapter One.

[9] Cf. Thomas Aquinas, *Summa theologiae,* I, 32, 1; Théodore de Régnon, *Études de théologie positive sur la Sainte Trinité,* Vol. II: *Théories scolastiques* (Paris: Retaux, 1892), 22-48; 52-53; John Bligh, "Richard of St. Victor's *De Trinitate*: Augustinian or Abelardian?" *Heythrop Journal,* 1 (1960), 118-139.

[10] Cf. the observations of Karl Rahner, "Remarks on the Dogmatic Treatise 'De Trinitate,'" in *Theological Investigations,* Vol. IV, trans. Kevin Smyth (Baltimore: Helicon Press, 1966), 77-87.

[11] This is true not only of neo-scholastic manuals but also of Transcendental Thomism; cf. the references in n. 51 and 52 to Chapter Eight.

[12] Augustine, *De Trinitate,* V-VII; cf. Harry Wolfson, *The Philosophy of the Church Fathers,* Vol. I (Cambridge: Harvard University Press, 1964), 350-359.

[13] Thomas Aquinas, *Summa theologiae,* I, 2-43.

[14] Théodore de Régnon, *Études de théologie positive sur la Sainte Trinité*, 4 vols. (Paris, Retaux, 1892-1898).

[15] *Hexaem.*, I-XXIII (V, 329-449).

[16] *Dec. praec.*, 1267 (V, 507-532); *De donis*, 1268 (V, 457-503); *Hexaem.*, 1273 (V, 329-449).

[17] *Hexaem.*, VI, 2-6 (V, 360-361).

[18] *Ibid.*, n. 2 (V, 360).

[19] *Ibid.*, n. 3-4 (V, 361).

[20] *Hexaem.*, I, 12-17 (V, 331-332).

[21] *Hexaem.*, VI, n. 4 (V, 361).

[22] Bonaventure, *II Sent.*, d. 1, p. 1, q. 2 (II, 19-25); *Dec. praec.*, II, n. 25 (V, 514); *De donis*, VIII, n. 16-17 (V, 497-498); *Hexaem.*, I, 16: VI, 4 (V, 332, 361); Thomas Aquinas, *Summa theologiae*, I, 46; *Summa contra gentiles*, II, 31-38; *De aeternite mundi contra murmurantes*.

[23] Cf. J. R. H. Moorman, *A History of the Franciscan Order: From Its Origins to the Year 1517* (Oxford: Clarendon, 1968), pp. 83-204; Rosalind Brooke, *Early Franciscan Government: Elias to Bonaventure* (Cambridge: Cambridge University Press, 1959).

[24] Cf. Marjorie Reeves, *The Influence of Prophecy in the Later Middle Ages: A Study in Joachimism* (Oxford: Clarendon, 1969), pp. 59-70.

[25] *Ibid.*, pp. 45-75; 175-190.

[26] Cf. *ibid.*, pp. 16-27; for a review of scholarship on Joachim, cf. Bernard McGinn, "The Abbot and the Doctors: Scholastic Reactions to the Radical Eschatology of Joachim of Fiore," *Church History*, 40 (1971), 30-47.

[27] Joseph Ratzinger, *The Theology of History in St. Bonaventure*, trans. Zachary Hayes (Chicago: Franciscan Herald Press, 1971); cf. also E. Randolph Daniel, "St. Bonaventure: Defender of Franciscan Eschatology," in *S. Bonaventura 1274-1974*, ed. Jacques Guy Bougerol, Vol. IV (Grottaferrata: Collegio S. Bonaventura, 1974), 797-799.

[28] For the writings of Nicholas of Cusa, cf. the critical texts in his *Opera Omnia* in the edition by the Heidelberg Academy (Leipzig-Hamburg: F. Meiner, 1932).

[29] Cf. Jacques-Guy Bougerol, "S. Bonaventure et le Pseudo-Denys l'Aréopagite," *Actes du Colloque Saint Bonaventure*, in *Études franciscaines*, 18 (Supplément annuel, 1968), 33-123; Francis N. Caminiti, "Nicholas of Cusa: *Docta Ignorantia*, a Philosophy of Infinity," unpublished doctoral dissertation (Fordham University, 1968), pp. 17-31.

[30] Bonaventure, on the term *docta ignorantia*, cf. *Brevil.*, p. V, c. 6, n. 8 (V, 260); on the coincidence of opposites, cf. *Itin.*, c. 5-7 (V, 308-313); *Hexaem.*, I (V, 329-335); cf. Caminiti, *op;. cit.*, pp. 23-26; also by Caminiti, "Nikolaus von Kues und Bonaventura," in proceedings of Das Cusanus-Jubiläum, published in *Mitteilungen und Forschungsbeiträge der Cusanus-Gesellschaft*, IV (Mainz, 1964), 129-144.

[31] Cf. above, pp. 18-22.

[32] Cf. Nicholas of Cusa, *De docta ignorantia*; cf. Caminiti, "Nicholas of Cusa: *Docta Ignorantia*, a Philosophy of Infinity"; Henry Bett, *Nicholas of Cusa* (London: Methusen, 1932), pp. 144-204; H. Lawrence Bond, "Nicholas of Cusa and the Reconstruction of Theology: the Centrality of Christology in the Coincidence of Opposites," in *Contemporary Reflections on the Medieval Christian Tradition: Essays in Honor of Ray C. Petry*, ed. George H. Scriver (Durham, N.C.: Duke University Press, 1974), pp. 81-94.

[33] Cf. Nicholas of Cusa, *De docta ignorantia*, I-II; cf. Bett, *op. cit.*, pp. 144-163.

[34] Nicholas of Cusa, *De docta ignorantia*, I.

[35] *Ibid.*, iii; English translation taken from *Unity and Reform: Selected Writings of Nicholas de Cusa*, ed. John Patrick Dolan (Notre Dame: University of Notre Dame Press, 1962), p. 65.

[36] Cf. Nicholas of Cusa, *De sapientia* and *De visione Dei*; cf. the treatment of the centrality of Christ in Bond, *op. cit.*

CHAPTER VIII

[1] On the principle of the fecundity of primordiality, cf. *I Sent.*, d. 2, a. un., q. 2 (I, 53-54); d. 27, q. 1, a. un., q. 2, ad 3 (I, 471). On the principle of the self-diffusion of the good, cf. *Itin.*, c. 6, n. 2 (V, 310-311); Dionysius, *De caelesti hierarchia*, 4.

[2] *Itin.*, 6, n. 2 (V, 311); cf. above, pp. 98-114.

[3] Arthur O. Lovejoy, *The Great Chain of Being* (New York: Harper and Brothers, 1960), *passim*.

[4] Alfred North Whitehead, *Process and Reality* (New York: Macmillan, 1929), pp. 519-533; Charles Hartshorne, *Man's Vision of God and the Logic of Theism* (Chicago: Willet, Clark, 1941*); The Divine Relativity* (New Haven: Yale University Press, 1948); (with William L. Reese) *Philosophers Speak of God* (Chicago: The University of Chicago Press, 1953).

[5] *I Sent.*, d. 27, p. 1, a. un., q. 2 (I, 468-474).

[6] *Itin.*, 6, n. 2 (V, 310-311); *Hexaem.*, XI, n. 11-12 (V, 381-382).

[7] *Itin.*, c. 6, n. 2 (V, 310); Boehner, 89.

[8] Lovejoy, *op. cit.*

[9] G. W. F. Hegel, *The Phenomenology of Mind*, trans. J. B. Baillie (London: Allen and Unwin, 1931); *Science of Logic*, trans. W. H. Johnston and L. G. Struthers (2nd ed.; London: Allen and Unwin, 1951). Cf. the religious issues as presented in Emil L. Fakenheim, *The Religious Dimension in Hegel's Thought* (Bloomington: Indiana University Press, 1967) and the interpretation and critique of Hegel in Frederick Copleston, *A History of Philosophy*, Vol. VII (Westminster, Md.: Newman Press, 1963), 189-201.

[10] Whitehead, *op. cit.*, pp. 519-533.

[11] *Ibid.*, p. 519.

[12] *Ibid.*, p. 205.

[13] *Ibid.*, pp. 521-533.

[14] *Ibid.*, pp. 27-30; 521-526.

[15] *Ibid.*, p. 248.

[16] *Ibid.*, p. 523.

[17] *Ibid.*, p. 532.

[18] *Ibid.*, pp. 196, 340, 529.

[19] *Ibid.*, pp. 30-32; 528-530.

[20] *Ibid.*, p. 528.

[21] *Red. art.*, n. 20 (V, 324); Augustine, *De Trinitate*, VI, c. 10, n. 11.

[22] *Red. art.* (V, 319-325).

[23] *Ibid.*, n. 2 (V, 319); Hugh of St. Victor, *Didascalicon*, II, c. 21.

[24] *Red. art.*, n. 20 (V, 324); Augustine, *De Trinitate*, VI, c. 10, n. 11.

[25] Whitehead, *op. cit.*, p. 521.

[26] Lovejoy, *op. cit.*, pp. 42-45.

[27] *Hexaem.*, I, n. 16 (V, 332).

[28] *Itin.*, c. 1, n. 3 (V, 297).

[29] Cf. above, pp. 114-118.

[30] *Hexaem.*, XII, n. 9 (V, 386).

[31] *I Sent.*, d. 3, p. 1, a. un., q. 2, ad 4 (I, 72-74); *Itin.*, c. 1-4 (V, 296-308).

[32] Cf. above, pp. 114-118; John Duns Scotus, *Rep. Par.*, 1. II, ch. 12, q. 6, n. 8 and n. 13; *In Metaph.*, 1. VII, q. 13, n. 9 and n. 26.

[33] Cf. n. 4, above, and Schubert M. Ogden, *The Reality of God and Other Essays* (New York: Harper and Row, 1966).

[34] *Ibid.*

[35] Cf. Anthony Kelly, "God: How Near a Relation?" *The Thomist*, 34 (1970), 191-229; "Trinity and Process: Relevance of the Basic Christian Confession of God," *Theological Studies*, 31 (1970), 393-414; William J. Hill, "Does the World Make a Difference to God?" *The Thomist*, 38 (1974), 146-164; W. Norris Clarke, "A New Look at the Immutability of God," in *God Knowable and Unknowable*, ed. Robert J. Roth (New York: Fordham University Press, 1973), pp. 43-72. Cf. also the writings of Walter E. Stokes listed in *Process Theology*, ed. Ewert H. Cousins (New York: Newman Press, 1971), pp. 361-362.

[36] Whitehead, *op. cit.*, pp. 69-70.

[37] Cf. above, pp. 242-243.

[38] Cf. Pierre Teilhard de Chardin, *Oeuvres de Pierre Teilhard de Chardin*, 11 vols. (Paris: Seuil, 1955-1973).

[39] On Teilhard's Christology, cf. Christopher F. Mooney, *Teilhard de Chardin and the Mystery of Christ* (New York: Harper and Row, 1966); George A. Maloney, *The Cosmic Christ: From Paul to Teilhard* (New York: Sheed and Ward, 1968); Robert Hale, *Christ and the Universe: Teilhard de Chardin and the Cosmos* (Chicago: Franciscan Herald Press, 1972).

[40] Pierre Teilhard de Chardin, *Hymn of the Universe*, trans. by Simon Bartholomew (New York: Harper and Row, 1965), pp. 41-50.

[41] *Ibid.*, p. 48.

[42] Pierre Teilhard de Chardin, *The Divine Milieu* (New York: Harper and Row, 1965), p. 123.

[43] Pierre Teilhard de Chardin, *The Phenomenon of Man* (New York: Harper and Row, 1965), pp. 291-310; *Science and Christ*, trans. by René Hague (New York: Harper and Row, 1965), pp. 53-66.

[44] Teilhard de Chardin, *The Phenomenon of Man*, cf. especially pp. 291-310.

[45] Cf. the proceedings of the conference published in *Hope and the Future of Man*, ed. Ewert H. Cousins (Philadelphia: Fortress Press, 1972).

[46] Cf. Karl Rahner, *The Trinity*, trans. by Joseph Donceel (New York: Herder and Herder, 1970); *Theological Investigations*, Vol. IV, trans. Kevin Smyth (Baltimore: Helicon Press, 1966), 36-73; 77-102, 221-252. Paul Tillich, *Systematic Theology*, 3 vols. (Chicago: The University of Chicago Press, 1951-1963).

[47] Cf. Karl Rahner, *Spirit in the World*, trans. by William Dych (New York: Herder and Herder, 1968); *Theological Investigations*, Vol. IV, 48-60; Paul Tillich, *Theology of Culture* (New York: Oxford University Press, 1959), pp. 10-29.

[48] Tillich, *Theology of Culture*, p. 13.

[49] *Ibid.*, p. 22.

⁵⁰ A basis for such a balanced evaluation has been laid by the work of John Dourley, *Paul Tillich and Bonaventure: An Evaluation of Tillich's Claim to Stand in the Augustinian-Franciscan Tradition* (Leiden: E. J. Brill, 1975); cf. also his article "God, Life and the Trinity in the Theologies of Paul Tillich and St. Bonaventure," in *S. Bonaventura 1274-1974*, ed. Jacques-Guy Bougerol, Vol. IV (Grottaferrata: Collegio S. Bonaventura, 1974), 271-282.

⁵¹ Joseph Maréchal, *Le point de départ de la métaphysique*: 5 vols. (1922-1947), especially, Cahier V: *Le Thomisme devant la philosophie critique* (Brussels: Éditions Universelles, 1949²).

⁵² Rahner, *Theological Investigations*, Vol. IV, 49-50.

⁵³ Cf. above, pp. 118-126.

⁵⁴ Maréchal, *op. cit.*; Rahner, *Spirit in the World*; Bernard Lonergan, *Verbum: Word and Idea in Aquinas* (London: Darton, Longman and Todd, 1968).

⁵⁵ Cf. the work of Camille Bérubé in *S. Bonaventura 1274-1974*, Vol. III, 161-200, "De la théologie de l'image à la philosophie de l'object de l'intelligence chez saint Bonaventure"; (with Servus Gieben) Vol. II, 627-654, "Guibert de Tournai et Robert Grosseteste sources inconnues de Saint Bonaventure, suivi de l'édition critique de trois chapitres du *Rudimentum Doctrinae* de Guibert de Tournai." Cf. also Bernard A. Nachbahr, "Pure Reason and Practical Reason: Some Themes in Transcendental Philosophy and in St. Bonaventure, *Ibid.*, Vol. III, 449-461.

CHAPTER IX

¹ Cf. above, pp. 222-223.

² Nicholas of Cusa, *De pace fidei cum epistola ad Joannem de Segovia*, ed. Raymond Klibansky and Hildebrand Bascour (Hamburg: Meiner, 1970).

³ I Sent., d. 6-7, 9, 12-13, 27, 31 (I, 123-146, 176-192, 218-241, 464-494, 529-552); Sc. Chr. (V, 3-43); Brevil., p. IV, c. 1 (V, 241-242); Itin., c. 4 (V, 306-308); Red. art. (V, 320-325); Ch. un. omn. mag. (V, 567-574); Hexaem., I, 12-17 (V, 331-332).

⁴ Clement of Alexandria, *Paidagogos*; Origen, *In Canticum canticorum*; Bonaventure, Ch. un. omn. mag. (V, 567-575); on Logos mysticism in the Origen tradition, cf. Itin., c. 4 (V, 306-308).

⁵ III Sent., d. 1-17 (III, 6-377); Brevil., p. IV (V, 241-252); Itin. (V, 296-313); Lign. vit. (VIII, 68-86); Leg. maj. (VIII, 504-565); Leg. min. (VIII, 565-579).

⁶ III Sent., d. 18-22 (III, 377-466); Brevil., p. IV, C. 8-10 (V, 248-252); Lign. vit., n. 17-32 (VIII, 75-80).

⁷ Itin., c. 3-4, 7 (V, 303-308, 312-313).

⁸ Hexaem., 1 (V, 329-335). Cf. above, pp. 135-146.

⁹ I Sent., d. 27, p. 1, a. un., q. 2 (I, 468-474); cf. I Sent., d. 11, a. un., q. 2 (I, 214-216); Brevil., p. I, c. 2-3 (V, 210-212); M. Trin., q. 8 (V, 112-115); cf. especially M. Trin., q. 8, ad 7 (V, 115). Cf. above, pp. 52-59, 101-118.

¹⁰ III Sent., d. 13-14 (III, 274-326); Brevil., p. IV, c. 5-7 (V, 245-248); Apol. paup. (V, 233-330).

¹¹ Itin., c. 6, n. 5-7 (V, 311-312).

¹² Hexaem., I, 12-17 (V, 331-332); M. Trin., q. 8 ad 7 (V, 115); Itin., c. 1-3 (V, 296-306); Red. art. (V, 319-325). Cf. above, pp. 56-59, 81-84, 242-244.

[13] Robley Whitson, *The Coming Convergence of World Religions* (New York: Newman Press, 1971), pp. 147-165.

[14] *M. Trin.*, q. 1, a. 2, concl. (V, 54); Whitson, *op. cit.*, p. 152.

[15] *Ibid.* (V, 55); Whitson, *op. cit.*, p. 153.

[16] Raymond Panikkar, *The Trinity and the Religious Experience of Man* (New York: Orbis Books, 1973); cf. the earlier versions of this work: *The Trinity and World Religions* (Madras: The Christian Literature Society, 1970) and "Towards an Ecumenical Theandric Spirituality," *Journal of Ecumenical Studies,* 5 (1968), 507-534.

[17] Panikkar, *The Trinity and the Religious Experience of Man*, p. 45.

[18] Ewert H. Cousins, "The Trinity and World Religions," *Journal of Ecumenical Studies,* 7 (1960), 476-498.

[19] *Ibid.*, 492-498.

[20] *I Sent.*, d. 27, p. 1, a. un., q. 2, ad 3 (I, 470-472).

[21] Cf. above, pp. 107-110.

[22] Cf. *ibid.*

[23] *Itin.*, c. 7, n. 5 (V, 313); Dionysius, *De mystica theologia*, I, 1.

[24] *Ibid.*, c. 7, n. 6 (V, 313); Boehner, p. 101; Jn. 13:1, 14:8.

[25] Mircea Eliade, *Patterns in Comparative Religion*, trans. Rosemary Sheed (New York: Sheed and Ward, 1958), pp. 367-387; C. G. Jung, *Psychology and Alchemy*, Vol. XII *The Collected Works*, trans. R. F. C. Hull (New York: Pantheon Books, 1953), pp. 91-213; Giuseppe Tucci, *The Theory and Practice of the Mandala*, trans. Alan Houghton Brodrick (London: Rider, 1961).

[26] Cf. above, pp. 172-197.

[27] R. C. Zaehner, *Christianity and Other Religions*, Vol. CXLVI of *The Twentieth Century Encyclopedia of Catholicism* (New York: Hawthorn, 1964).

INDEX

To Text And Notes

311